P9-BJX-951

Like a Song, Like a Dream

LIKE A SONG, LIKE A DREAM

A Soviet Girl's Quest for Freedom

Alla Rusinek

With an afterword by Ezra Rusinek

Charles Scribner's Sons New York

1 3 5 7 9 11 13 15 17 19 V/C 20 18 16 14 12 10 8 6 4 2

Printed in the United States of America
Library of Congress Catalog Card Number 72-1222
SBN 684-13019-X (cloth)

Acknowledgments

I would like to acknowledge the help of Jesse Z. Lurie who played such an important part in the writing of this book; of Norbert Slepyan, my editor for his continual guidance; and of my father-in-law, E. Rusinek, for his valuable contributions.

1

According to my papers, on the 28th of May 1949, I was born in Moscow.

My mother did not know the date of her birth, but she used to say that she remembered she had been born in winter. If I had not known my birthdate, I probably would have established it by means of a similar memory. When I was still small enough to be carried on my father's shoulders, I was taken to Red Square. I remember riding my father above an endless crowd of people, shouting, singing, laughing happily, carrying paper flowers and portraits. And far away on the brown marble of Lenin's mausoleum, there stood the man in the portraits, waving his right hand to the crowd. In his usual military uniform and thick moustache, Stalin could not be mistaken. So I could always say that I was happy enough to be born in time to see Stalin alive.

When we think about our childhood, it comes to us in episodes that have found their places deep in our memory. They quietly sleep there in nests until some train of thought disturbs them and they awake. And pictures, old family pictures, show you a child who lived her own life, but who can give you through memories we all share in common some of her impressions.

I was a plump child with an extraordinarily big, bald head and unbelievably large cheeks, as if I kept something in store for a rainy day. My mother and aunts later told me in secret that I was a very ugly child and that they didn't like to show me in public. It was no secret to me though. My older sister Myra, with her wonderful curly hair and beautiful face, was the "film star" in the family, and next to her I looked even more ugly.

Yet I did not entirely accept the world's verdict of me. I thought everybody was wicked, and I constantly bore a grudge against them. Why didn't they say anything about my big dark eyes? I liked my eyes and, since no one else did, I admired them myself.

When I was four years old, I dreamt that all our relations came to visit us. They were beautifully dressed and noisy. Gathering around my sister, they praised her with exclamations of delight. Everyone forgot about me, and I sat under the bed next to a night pot, a huge lump in my throat. One of my aunts noticed me and took me in her arms, smiling mockingly, as though understanding my feelings. The lump melted and I began to cry. I awoke from the dream with a feeling of wetness all around and under me. Mother looked at me with surprise and smiled knowingly.

That was a time of short silk dresses and small straw hats, and my father's ambition was to dress his daughters in silk and velvet. I still remember two of those dresses—my sister's, white with green flowers, and mine, dark brown with free designs in yellow. Mother never got rid of old clothes, and we could always find neatly tied in bundles our baby caps or mama's jacket, red with white spots, which she wore when she was pregnant. Much later, I would take that jacket with me to a new world.

My sister was eight and I was six when something strange happened. We were then going to the kindergarten. Mother and father were both working and had their own life of adult people which we knew nothing about. We couldn't follow their talks, but one day we just noticed that they had begun to shout at each other more often. The air in our room suddenly grew stuffy, the darkness more gloomy. And then everything changed. I remember mother running back and forth holding both of us by the hand.

There was a place in Moscow which used to be a symbol of our short happy childhood. It was a port on the Moscow River where father worked as an accountant on a ship. He often took us with him on journeys in summer, and we felt as though we were queens on that ship that looked so rich with its carved wooden staircases, mirrors, and carpets.

The port had a beautiful park with rows of bushes and trees and bright flowers. A huge stone woman, a happy and strong

Soviet woman with a small model of a ship in her hands, welcomed us at the entrance. Soviet working people liked to come to this park on Sundays to renew their feelings of richness and strength which had been weakened by exhausting work.

One day that summer of 1955—I was then six—mother took both of us there, but again it was all different. She was running angrily, deeply unhappy. Frightened, we tried to keep up with her. But father's ship had already left. It would come back in a month, but father would never return to our home, to our dark room with the big wardrobe that divided it into two parts, one for children and the other for parents. There was a young woman on his ship, who worked in the barber shop. She was much younger and prettier than my mother, and my father, who was handsome and sexy, didn't need anything else. He was fifty-four years old and his new—third—wife was twenty-four.

For many years I couldn't understand what mother and father had found in common with each other that had caused them to marry. The answer came to me much later when I myself understood that love is too wicked to give people an ability to really understand each other. "Love is so cruel that you can fall in love with a goat," a Russian proverb says. Neither of them was a goat, yet love played a cruel trick on them.

* * *

The year 1913 was one of prosperity for the great Russian Empire. The shops and marketplaces were full of goods. The country was rich. But poor people everywhere are always poor. If you don't have money, you can only stand aside and watch. Sometimes it's worthwhile to run away from poverty.

Abram, a house painter from Dvinsk, a small Latvian town, decided to move. "*Meshane makom, meshane mazel*"—"Change of place, change of luck," Jews say.

Poverty haunted this quiet, pious man and his family. He couldn't look into his wife's eyes. When he had proposed to her eight years before, he had brought her parents from Germany to Dvinsk to show them his house full of good furniture. Only then did they give consent to the marriage. After the wedding, when the parents left for Germany, the furniture also left. Abram had borrowed it from his neighbor. The young bride wept for three days, and Abram, trying to console her, promised to work hard and to buy her even better furniture.

Eight years passed and things got worse. They already had four children. One day Abram said to his wife, "Listen to me, Sheinele, a good man gave me a piece of good advice. It is easier to live in Russia. Life is cheaper there. There is a good town of Vologda there. Good Jews also live there and they are rich and they need painters."

Sheina shrugged her shoulders and they moved.

Abram moved to save his children from hunger, but he himself was doomed to die of starvation. Thirty years later, after Leningrad had been blockaded for a year by the Germans, he died. His son took his skeleton covered with skin to the place where thousands were being buried, and later could not even find the place.

Still, the children of Abram Glazman were not among the Jews of Dvinsk, Riga, Germany, and Holland—among tens of thousands of them—who were shot and burned in Rumbula, the forest near Riga. They were not there because "a good man gave a piece of good advice" to Abram Glazman: move.

"And Abram took his wife Sarah and they went forth to go into the land of Canaan, and into the land of Canaan they came," says the Bible. But. . . .

"Out of the frying pan into the fire," the Russian saying goes. Soon after coming to Vologda, Sheina died of consumption, slowly and quietly, without complaint. Abram stopped working and did nothing but pray. His four children—Moishe, Musja, Pesja, and Basja—had to earn their living and feed their pious father. One by one, their mother's beautiful German dresses disappeared into the bazaar. Together with them, the spirit of a proud and beautiful woman began to sift out of the house. The two oldest sisters, Musja and Pesja, went to the bazaar to sell *papirossen.** Musja, the eldest, with long figure and long face, adjusted to the new profession very quickly. Pesja, a short girl with a round figure and a mass of curly hair, stood near her

* Cigarettes.

quietly, looking down. She was the only one in the family to inherit Sheina's proud spirit and it prevented her from doing the low business of selling. In the evening they both went to the house of rich relatives to get their portion of two hot potatoes for dinner.

One day, when they were as usual selling their papirossen, a strict man in a military uniform came up to them and told them to leave the bazaar and never come back. It was the Great October Revolution of 1917, which shook the world and forbade Musja and Pesja to sell *papirossen* in the bazaar. All private business was forbidden—and praying also. Abram had to work. His children went to school.

Well, it was a good thing to study. Abram didn't have anything against it. Musja still did everything about the house. Moishe was also working. Two of the girls were carried away by their studies. Pesja couldn't tear herself from books, and whenever Musja asked her to help with the housework, Pesja began to cry. Pesja became very quiet and reserved. Nobody could understand her new world, nobody could enter it.

"But *kinderlach*," Abram would say, "today is Shabbat, you can't go to school. Our God blessed Shabbat, the seventh day. You are Jews and have to keep it. I forbid you to go to school today."

Next Saturday the children left the house as if to go for a walk. The books had already been hidden in the yard under the fence and covered with straw. Soon they were at school. It didn't take long after this incident for Moishe to become Michail; for Musja, Maria; Pesja, Polina; and Basja, Berta.

And it was so that one day Polina took a big basket, put in it her dress, a warm scarf, two sheets and some money, and left for the railway station on her way to the new world. She went to Moscow.

Father was gone and everything changed in our family. In fact, there was no family any more. I loved my father more than my mother, although he was very strict and I was often afraid of him. But sometimes he was very affectionate. I loved his smell and his unshaven cheeks when he used to take me on his lap in the evenings (many, many years later, when I touched unshaven cheeks which were not those of my father, I remembered him).

I knew that he was disappointed in me. He had only wanted a second baby in the hope of having a son, but I turned out to be a girl and he could not even look at me for some time. I knew this, but hoped by my strong attachment to win his love, and had nearly achieved it when he left.

I believed that he would come back some time. And he did. I was not yet seven then and Myra was eight. She had already finished the first year of school and was learning to play the violin. I didn't do anything but attend a kindergarten.

One day our kindergarten group went out for a walk. It was March and rather cold. I was dressed in very shabby shoes and an old coat which was tight on me. Everything had changed since father had gone.

We were walking in pairs when I noticed a man staring at me. He was very dark: his clothes, hair, sad eyes, and unshaven cheeks, all dark. His face seemed so familiar to me that I stopped. But it was several minutes before I realized that this was my father.

"Father!" I screamed and rushed to him crying. I embraced his legs and buried my face in his coat. He stood, stroking my head.

"You didn't recognize me, did you?" I cried and thought that his face had changed very much. Only later I learned that the right side of his face was paralyzed. Crying, but happy with his coming, I felt that I loved him more than ever. I think it was because I began to feel sorry for him, though without understanding why.

Father had come to Moscow to arrange his affairs and was leaving soon for Krasnodar, a small town near the Black Sea, where he lived with his young wife. He wanted to take both of us with him to spend spring and summer at the sea, but as Myra had to study I went alone without feeling much sorrow about leaving everything and everyone behind. I was with my father and very happy. When the summer was over, I flatly refused to go back. I don't remember the reaction of the two sides, but somehow I stayed.

I spent my first year at school with the other children of the town, typical village children who were often dull. I felt far ahead of them and none of them seemed to challenge me. I had come from "the capital." I was elected monitor of the class and was the teacher's favorite. That was when my vanity triumphed. I was brilliant and snobbish, generously helpful and strict with my classmates. They didn't object, but dully accepted me. Russian village people are often like that. Soon I completely forgot my life in the capital, adopted my classmates' village language, and became suntanned and skinny—in other words, provincial.

We lived in a big wooden house with a garden surrounded by a wooden fence. We had ducklings, chickens, and a dog. In the summer I spent most of the day in the yard. My father and his wife, Marina, whom I gradually began to call "mama," were at work or went together to the sea. I was left alone and walked around our garden or stood at the gate looking at the street. But I was not bored. It was hot and dusty in summer. Our street, deeply rutted from the carriage wheels and the horses' legs, was covered with thick layers of gray, warm dust. I buried my feet in it or drew lines with a wet finger on my dirty naked body. I could be happy alone for many hours, as I had so many things to think about. I thought and patiently waited for my father.

One day they didn't come back for a long time and I began to feel terribly hungry. There was nothing in the house that I could eat, so I wandered about the yard thinking about my hunger and suffering from it. Suddenly, while passing our dog, I noticed a dry slice of brown bread in the dust. My mouth began to water. I squatted and stared at it. It looked very good, but could I take bread from a dog? Of course, she wouldn't eat it. It was too dry. But it is just not good taste to take food from a dog. And then, the bread was dirty. But I could shake it well and the dust would come off. But could I take it if it was already lying in the dust near a dog?

I squatted and thought for a long time. At last I took the bread. When my father and Marina returned, I didn't say a word. I couldn't tell my father about my degradation. I loved him and wanted to be loved. In fact, I was jealous, but I didn't show it, realizing that Marina had more right to him than I had. So I loved him silently. Sometimes he asked me to scratch his back when it itched. I sat behind his pale back with its tiny freckles and thought it was not beautiful or manlike. And to ask a girl to scratch your back was also not in good taste. My fingers ached from the effort, but my father was rarely satisfied. Each time, I finished this ceremony exhausted and offended deep within me.

However, this didn't happen often and didn't make me love my father less—or be less proud of him. He was a big, important man, an accountant on a sovkhoz (Soviet collective farm). And he often told me that an accountant was more important than the director. I didn't doubt him and proudly told my classmates this and made them believe it.

* * *

My father came from a very well-to-do family of Ashkenazic Jews who had lived in Turkmenia, in the little Oriental town of Tchardjow. Oh, these eternally wandering Jews! How did they find their way there? Sephardic or Bokharan Jews living in Turkmenia came from the south. But what brought families of Eastern European Ashkenazic Jews to this distant and hot corner of the Russian Empire?

The family legend is that one of the great-grandfathers, Milchen by name, was drafted into the Czarist Army. According to the law of 1827 issued by Czar Nicholas I, Jewish boys of twelve were to be taken into the army for twenty-five years. This was one of the attempts of the Czars to convert Jews to Christianity by force. The first six years of this service were called "cantonment," and the soldiers were called "cantonists." My paternal great-grandfather was a cantonist.

The regiments of the Russian Army were based in Central Asia and, when the time of their service was over, the soldiers rarely went back to the places from which they were taken as little boys and where they were already forgotten. They preferred to remain in warm Turkmenia. With his name changed to Milkin (his Russian fellow soldiers couldn't pronounce Milchen), my great-grandfather, still true to the Jewish religion in his soul (as were most of these cantonists), settled in Tchardjow.

The next generation, my father's parents, were the owners of several hatshops and belonged to the upper middle class of the Jewish community in Turkmenia. Their four beautiful children, Rosa, Tsal, Esther, and Michael, enjoyed a happy and carefree childhood until. . . .

Again the Great October Socialist Revolution. . . . But who then cared about all these words. It was just a big disorder. No more shops, no hats, no family. Just as on a sinking ship everyone seizes his life preserver and the indifferent ocean carries each in a different direction, families were broken and dispersed.

And Tsalik, a handsome, heedless boy, suddenly found himself in the Red Army and in exile on a terrible island, Solovki, in the White Sea. He never meant to be bad and always thought only about women and an easy life. His parents had hoped to marry him into a well-to-do family and to give him half the business, to keep him within bounds.

Then everything was changed. In exile he married a Russian woman who couldn't bear him children. One day they found a baby girl crying on their porch and adopted her. With the passing years, she began to look more and more like Tsalik.

In the thirties they went to live in Moscow. Tsalik became an accountant. He loved to count money, dreaming that one day he would count his own capital. But then he was also artistic, loved music, and played the violin. He went through World War

II in the ranks of the millions of soldiers, was wounded, and came back like other millions, exhausted, penniless, ragged. Vague ambitions still lived in his tired mind and he was ready to begin again.

He worked as an accountant in a public dining room and there he met Polina. She was obviously unmarried, for she used to come there to have dinner every day. She was a vivid, busy woman far into her thirties. But there was something about her that attracted Tsalik. He began to talk to her. Polina was an important person. She worked as a Manager of the buildings of a whole district, and was very active in the Party. She enjoyed the respect and attention of all around her. Before the war she had been a teacher of history, but when the war broke out the Party had sent her to this job and she always accepted the place where the Party needed her. Dark-haired, with a mass of Jewish curls and green eyes, she was good-looking, but beginning to fade. She had never married. She was too busy.

There was something in this woman that Tsalik needed. Her strength, her activity, practical mind, contacts. He was definitely attracted to her; perhaps he even loved her. And her name was a touchstone. His mother had been Polina, his first wife had been Polina, and now this woman. . . .

Polina fell in love with the good-looking, sexy, ambitious, and definitely irresponsible man. She loved him with the love of an aging, busy woman; her whole being demanded him. She thought she could find a place for him in her hectic life and could even have children with him. At any rate, she wouldn't be lonely at night.

She brought him to her room and they began to live together. He never went back to his first family. His first wife did not give him a divorce, so he and Polina lived together unmarried. When their first daughter was born, they called her Miriam. Polina was against this symbol of nationalism, but he insisted. The choice of the second daughter's name then belonged to Polina and she called her a then popular Russian name—Alla.

The birth of the second child made the first wife surrender.

She divorced Tsalik and even came to his home to help with the babies, bringing with her their adopted first daughter.

On the 17th of June 1949, three weeks after the birth of their second daughter, Polina and Tsalik married; she was thirty-nine, he forty-eight. He felt young, and was filled with ambitious ideas. Of course, he had not thought of having two daughters, but he decided to make the best of it. "Polina," he used to say, "I could leave you, but I shall never leave my two daughters. They will be the happiest of children and I shall dress them in silk and velvet."

He left his job in the dining room and went to the north with a geological expedition because in the north the same professions received higher pay. He planned to stay there two years to make money, but within a year Polina had difficulty saving him from prison, for he was already in deep trouble for some illegal transaction.

When he came back home, she found in his pocket a letter from a Siberian woman who begged him to come back to her and their newborn daughter.

He was impossible, she thought. Such an old man! But she was mistaken. He was not old even in 1955 when, already fifty-four, he left her with two daughters and a pair of silk and velvet dresses for them.

A new daughter was soon born to him and his third wife. Only his tragic death stopped this hard and unhappy race after youth, women, and an easy life.

* * *

I had been living with my father and his wife for a year and a half when I began to notice some strange attention constantly being paid to me. My mother's sister came to our small town with presents for me and spent several fruitless hours with me, trying to get me to go back with her. I couldn't even understand her and thought the idea crazy.

After she left, father was constantly being called to some office or other and, by his sad and tired look, I understood that again it concerned me. Several times he knelt beside me and said,

"Maybe it would be better for you to go to your mother, dear. You will live in the capital. You will learn to play the piano." I was sure father himself didn't think this way, but wanted to give me a free choice. I appreciated this and hastened to assure him of my love and loyalty. He would stand up with a deep sigh, even sadder. Poor womanish heart! How could I understand then that if a man gives you a free choice, he already wants you to leave deep in his heart? Even when older, how often do we give credit to men for being gentlemen when they have already betrayed us.

Soon I myself was called to the mysterious place. It turned out to be a local court which was looking into the conditions of my life, my development, and the attitude toward me in the family. Mother was trying to get me back and had appealed to the Supreme Court which transferred the case to the local authorities. It proved to be a long and complicated process.

I made a very bad impression on the court. They wondered at the amount of hatred in the child's eyes and voice. I hated all of them and often didn't answer their questions, fearing traps. One thing I knew and said for sure: "I don't want to go back there." The judges tried to be kind and reassuring to me, an apparently downtrodden, underdeveloped child, but their kindness soon turned me to hysterics during the examination and I was left alone "lest a psychiatric trauma be caused to the child," so the documents read.

Yet the process continued and, like a loyal and silent dog, I used to wait for my father to come out of the court building. When he came out, I usually began to cry.

"Why are you crying, Alla?"

"I am sorry for you."

"Why? Nobody does me any harm, you silly girl. They are all polite and fair."

I didn't answer and continued to cry as we went slowly home, he holding me by the hand. I couldn't explain to him that I hated anybody humiliating him and this process was just that. I didn't want anyone asking him provocative questions. And I was sure that only I by my loyalty and love to him supported him at this difficult moment. But I kept these thoughts to myself, being afraid he would not understand and would treat me like a small child.

The verdict was reached. I learned about it only at the moment of its execution.

* * *

On a rainy day—or maybe it was a sunny day, but it seemed to me gray and threatening—I sat in the kitchen at a wooden table, looking at the plate before me. There was a feeling of alarm in me. I couldn't understand why I suddenly found myself alone in the house, while everybody went outside. To exorcise the fear which I could not explain, I swung my legs back and forth under the table, backward and forward, quicker, quicker, quicker. . . . Suddenly the door opened and my mother rushed into the room. She lifted me from the stool, crying, "My daughter!" and, carrying me under her arm, rushed back to the yard. I understood immediately that I was being taken away by force. I began screaming for help in a loud voice. My sister Myra followed behind us holding me by my feet. I bit my mother on her arm as hard as I could, but she didn't notice it until much later. Everybody was standing in the street—father, Marina, and, of course, the neighbors. All stood like statues, not moving and silent. A militiaman stood near my father. A truck was waiting in the street and in seconds I found myself pushed into it. Then, as if catching on at the last moment, everybody began to shout.

"My God, the child doesn't want to go to her mother," a woman in an apron with her arms crossed on her breast exclaimed.

"Alochka! We'll soon be together again!" father cried. The motor began to rattle, the truck shook and then moved forward, leaving everything and everybody behind. I sobbed and screamed for hours. "Papa will die without me!" I repeated hundreds of times, between sobs. I was sure he would not be able to live through our parting. I would not be able to help and comfort him. He would die of sorrow. I was so tortured at my helplessness that I couldn't stop crying. Finally, tired and exhausted, I fell asleep and awoke to find myself far away from my home and father.

Mother took us, reunited sisters, to the Black Sea where I enjoyed myself as much as I could, still hoping and thinking I would return to my father. Little by little, I began to appreciate the advantages of my new life, feeling clean and nourished, being taken care of and noticed by somebody.

When we returned to Moscow, I was carried away by the wonders of the life in the capital—a bathroom, a toilet in the flat, a telephone, and the whole big city seen out of the window. Mother immediately enrolled me in the musical school, which I left after two years of suffering. The two years in the village had passed not without their consequences. It was difficult for me to adapt. Yet in the elementary school I was an excellent pupil. After two short postcards, I stopped writing to my father and soon forgot him.

When he came to Moscow a year later, I hardly recognized him, avoided his eyes, and was terribly confused when he reminded me of my promise to come back to him. He held me by the elbows between his knees and I turned aside. I felt myself a traitor, but was powerless. I couldn't bear any more changes in my life. I wanted to be left alone and felt relieved when father left.

A year later in May of 1960, we learned that he had been killed by a drunken Georgian on the holiday of the 1st of May. We were excited and frightened for one day, but he had not been part of our lives and we didn't feel sorrow when he died. "A dog deserves a dog's death," mother commented and the incident seemed closed, at least for us.

But mother became more reserved and silent. She began to complain of inner sorrow and often cried, which we couldn't stand, for this was so strange for our strict, strong mother. She was afraid to stay at home alone and kept us from going to school. Often her scenes turned to hysterics. Finally, six months after the May accident, in December 1960, mother was taken to a mental clinic "in a deep manic-depressive state after a strong psychic trauma."

I couldn't understand all this and just tried to escape from my home life. My new life at school helped. I liked to study, enjoyed the feeling of belonging to a collective, to the Soviet people, to the country, to the world. When, about two years later, I heard about the assassination in the United States of President Kennedy, I was more upset about that than I had been about my own father's death.

I was concerned about the destiny of the world.

On my way to school, I like to push a little stone before me all the way from home to school. I find one somewhere near the entrance of our house and try to keep it with me. Then I have the feeling that I am not going alone but with a friend. I don't have to talk to him; on the contrary he helps me to think. Almost all of my classmates meet one another on the way to school and go together, but I don't have friends. And really it's better to go with a little stone in front of you. He doesn't speak and I don't have to listen to him. Whenever I meet my classmates by chance, I suffer because I don't understand what they are talking about. I listen to them silently or try to keep up a conversation which does not interest me. They talk about teachers, classmates, studies, and I like to think about something else. One day I asked my classmate whether she ever talks to herself. She did not understand and thought I was crazy. It is really better to walk with a little stone.

I never manage to get it to the school building. It is very difficult. Lessons begin at 8:30 and I leave my house at 8:20. I have only ten minutes and it is rather a long way. First I have to cross a very wide road heavy with traffic. I kick my stone very hard so that it will reach the opposite side and I run after it. Sometimes it strikes someone's feet and he looks at me as though I were mad. So I look back at him. What can I do? I don't say, "Sorry." It won't help. I *am* sorry, but I don't like saying useless words.

Then I have to pass through a big park. In the morning it is empty and I can walk freely with my companion. We pass a big fountain and enter a sidewalk with even rows of bushes. Here I always begin to think and, as I think very slowly, I begin to walk very slowly. At the end of the park, I suddenly realize I am late and I leave my companion and begin to run. In vain. I am always late. The pupils and the teachers on duty stand at the entrance and take my daybook to put a note in it. I promise, not them, but myself, not to be late anymore and to stop thinking on the way. But the same thing happens every day and I can't do anything with myself. I hate this word "can't" and myself for being so weak-willed.

It is no use trying to leave my home earlier. I am very sleepy in the morning and can hardly get my head off the pillow. Then I have to make something for my breakfast and wait until everyone finishes with the bathroom. We have two other families in our apartment, and everyone leaves at the same time. So we all run along the corridor half-dressed, hurrying to school or to work.

There are eleven people in our big three-room apartment. The largest room is occupied by the family of a Deputy Minister, the smallest by a shopcleaner and her two children. All the adults hate each other secretly, but we six children get on together fine.

I always forget to collect my books and notebooks the evening before and that takes time. Myra is also in a hurry. Her school is even farther and we irritate and bother each other. Mother leaves for her work. She is an economist in a housekeeping office. We all leave without saying good-by to each other as other families do. I don't think we like it at home.

Mother is always tired and Myra and I are irritable. Myra plays the piano and I can't do my homework, so we quarrel often. Mother doesn't pay any attention to us. She lies on the sofa, exhausted and sad. We don't ask her anything. We know that she is ill. And we don't help her very much because we don't like it at home. It is not good. I would rather think about something else.

I like my school very much. It is very interesting. I am already a sixth-year pupil and a member of a Pioneer organization.

I like to study, but more than that I like our social work at school. We have a lot of circles this year and I am a member of nearly all of them. I play in a drama circle and sing. I work in a geographical and botanical corner and I am a member of a group that makes the wall newspaper. Then this year we have a special task—to study the activities of the people's volunteer corps of our district during World War II and the general history of our district since the eighteenth century.

There is a beautiful eighteenth-century church in our district. It is the main object of my study. It is one of the few churches in Moscow still open to worshipers. These are all mainly old women. I hate standing there among the dreadful revivals of the past, but I have to do it because it is my task. I have found out that there are old inscriptions on the walls which I must find. I have already visited the church twice, but every time I fear to come up to the priest and ask him about them. I feel sick in that darkness among those bowing and mumbling people, candles, open coffins, and icon eyes looking straight at you wherever you move. Last time I suddenly saw a young woman with a boy standing quietly near the wall. They were both praying. My Pioneer conscience could not remain still. I decided to stare at them steadily. Maybe they would think I knew the boy and would report him to his school. He was probably a Pioneer and yet was doing such a terrible thing. I decided to make them leave the church through the shaming power of my stare.

The woman noticed my unwavering glance. She obviously became frightened and screened the boy as if protecting him from me. I felt uneasy and looked aside and hurriedly left the church.

All the way home I scolded myself for again being so weak-willed. I was not yet a Leninist Pioneer. But that frightened look of hers. . . .

I like to do social work because it gives me a feeling of being useful and it is interesting. Of course it takes a lot of time, but I don't hurry to go home after lessons. I don't like it at home.

I also don't like the first moment of entering the classroom.

It seems that everyone is staring at me and sees that something is not in order about me. Maybe it is my crumpled red necktie or my old disheveled dress with a shining big spot on my behind or on my elbows, or maybe there is a hole in my stockings. There shouldn't be, but I don't really remember. I never look into a mirror. I am afraid. Whenever I pass a big mirror in the lobby and happen to see myself, I think, how ugly I look. This terribly straight hair that is always in disorder and my bad complexion and thick brows. And the wrinkles in my stockings. I know all the other girls look prettier, but they must have grandmothers or perhaps even housemaids to help them in the morning. I can't do it for myself. No, that's not right. I can, but I have no time. I must try to be better. But their dresses are new and mine is very old and I can't do anything about it.

Poverty is not a vice and I never feel ashamed of it. It is just that I don't like that first moment of entering the classroom. I walk across the room quickly, trying to look as indifferent as possible, and take my seat, which I don't leave for the whole day. Then I begin to feel confident and even superior as I witness my classmates' failures in their studies.

During the breaks, the teachers usually don't allow us to stay in the classroom. We must walk in the hall, so all the pupils walk in couples in a big circle and the teachers on duty stand in the middle of it. This is law and order and I understand it, but I don't like it because I have no one to walk with me and I feel very awkward walking alone. Again there is that feeling of everybody staring at me. So I try to stay in the classroom if possible.

There are thirty-nine pupils in our class. Each desk has seats for two pupils, so there is one empty seat at one of the desks. This is my desk. I occupy it alone. On the first day I enter the classroom and take the desk I like, usually one of the first. All the others fight for the back seats and I don't like to do what everybody else does. Besides, I am not afraid of a teacher.

I enjoy being alone. This is my little world. If it were possible I would put a fence around it. I like to draw my world. It is a little wooden house with one window on a little hill. There is a winding path down to a river. There is no fence around my little house because it is surrounded by high mountains. I draw my world when I am bored by a lesson.

It isn't that I don't like my classmates. I do like them because I know that I must be kind to people. This is one of the main qualities that I want to achieve in my drive for self-perfection. But they seem to have something against me. I like to study and they all think that I value myself too highly. On the contrary, I feel I am full of shortcomings and try to work harder, but they don't seem to understand. They never elect me to the leading Pioneer posts, although every year I am so active. They all seem to think that I am snobbish, but I just don't want to show that I feel inferior because I am from a poor family and not the daughter of a diplomat or an army general, as some of them are.

But do I really feel that way? I know that in our country the poor have become the important people, so in fact I am better than they are. Our teachers say I am brilliant and something extraordinary as a person. I am assiduous, modest, and very responsible. The other day they learned that I washed the bedding at home and couldn't believe that we do it ourselves. Mother never gives it to the laundry. I like washing, but it does take a lot of time. When I am finished, I always call Myra to help me wring out the sheets and covers. We take it by the two ends and begin to twist it in different directions. We make a big sausage out of it. Last time Myra let it slip and it struck me on the head. It didn't hurt, but I was all wet and a little offended because it seemed like a slap in the face.

I like to make things clean. It is another part of my process of self-improvement. I must learn how to do everything. But frankly speaking I do not think poverty is such a nice thing, especially when mother takes free food from a public dining room and it turns out to be rotten stuff.

All my classmates seem to have something against me. Every year I feel it the first day I come to school. First, I sit alone when everyone else has his friend to sit with. Then they begin the registration and the teacher calls everybody one after another to her table to get the details about himself and his parents. The rest of us are supposed to do something else while this is going on, but we usually listen with fascination to the answers. It is interesting to know the background of everyone, beyond the walls of the school, what peculiarities and differences are behind the gray and brown uniforms, and the equality of the five-mark system of estimating our capacity. So we listen. "An army general." "A professor." "An actor." "A member of the USSR delegation to the United Nations." "An expert of a Department of the Foreign Ministry." "An international correspondent." And so on. My turn comes about in the middle. My name begins with "M." "Mother—an engineer of economics, father—dead, no father." It is all right, but I am already feeling ill because the beginning of my registration has been unpleasant. It bothers me every year and I cannot understand it.

First the teacher asks my name. "Milkina Alla Tsalevna." I always spell my father's name because no one can understand it. Then she asks my nationality and it begins. The whole class suddenly becomes very quiet. Some look at me steadily. Others avoid my eyes. I have to say this word. All the rest say, "Russian, Ukrainian." I have to say this word, which sounds so unpleasant. Why? There is really nothing wrong with its sound, "*Yev-rei-ka.*" But I never hear the word except when people are cursing somebody or I never see it unless it is written on the walls like an insult. Maybe it is just that people make it sound so unpleasant and there is really nothing wrong with the word. But I cannot solve the problem at the moment when I stand at the teacher's table and she looks at me impatiently. Every time I try to overcome my feelings, but each year the word comes out in a whisper: "Yev-rei-ka." It seems to me that all the faces of the pupils merge into one grinning mass. Having answered several other questions, I go to my seat, exhausted and upset.

Maybe all my problems have something to do with this. I heard one girl say that I was a typical Jew and an upstart and that Stalin hadn't killed enough of us. I didn't understand. I had never heard about Stalin having something to do with the Jews. I must find out about it. And I heard boys calling each other Jews when they were fighting. Why should this bother me? I live in the most progressive country in the world where there are many nationalities and all are brothers. Soon we shall all be simply Soviet citizens—national differences will remain with our parents. They are not important, I am sure, but there are some things I cannot understand.

A year ago my mother heard about this school and she was determined to enroll me in it. It is a special school where pupils study English and other subjects in English. My sister studies music and my mother wanted me to get some special education.

I didn't want to come. I dread all kinds of changes, especially when they involve competition. I am always afraid I will fail and it is very humiliating. But mother made me try and I passed all the examinations. But then I didn't find my name on the list. I had not been accepted. I called my mother at her job and told her about it. "It is all right, Mum," I tried to console her, "I am not upset, I can go to my old school." But she didn't listen to me. She already had something else on her mind. All the following week she was busy, visiting, telephoning. In the talks with her friends, she always said: "anti-Semites."

"Mum, what are anti-Semites?"

"Those who are against Jews."

"But why aren't they called anti-Jews?"

"I don't know. Maybe they think it sounds nicer. But it is all the same."

"And who are anti-Semites?"

"Those who didn't take you into the school."

"But why are they anti-Semites?"

"Leave me alone. I am tired. But don't be afraid. You shall study there. Children ought to be accepted when they have passed the examinations."

"You're right. But I don't like to push when someone doesn't want me. And I don't want you to beg."

"I am not begging yet. Right now I am demanding. And we have to do that. Otherwise we shall never achieve anything."

I became frightened. Mother talked as though we were surrounded by enemies. On the 1st of September, I didn't go to any school. Mother didn't surrender. Next day in the morning she took me by the hand and we went to the English school. In the lobby she met the Director, a tall, bony woman with a long, pale face. Instead of eyes, she had two gray little buttons, one pale pink button for her mouth, and you could see her nose only by looking at her from the side. All three buttons showed irritation at our appearance, but mother didn't even give her a chance to open her mouth.

"This is my daughter. I am hurrying to my job and she is staying here. She shall study here. And don't look so. . . . Soon you will be proud of having her at your school."

And she left. I felt a lump in my throat, but I was so frightened I couldn't even cry. The woman looked at me with disgust and told me to follow her. I followed and thought that I seemed to have been born to be humiliated at every step of my life.

I began to study and they soon acknowledged that mother was right. They talked about me at the parents' meeting as an example of diligence, excellent behavior, and loyalty. I liked being praised because it made me feel how good I could have been had I really worked hard. I begged my mother to go to one of these meetings and to listen, but she said: "It is not interesting. They always say the same things about you."

She never asked me about my studies. She was tired and sick.

* * *

I don't think they are anti-Semites. Maybe they were, but now they like me. And as far as Stalin is concerned, if he really did kill Jews, he is being condemned now.

When I first began to study, I liked him very much, even more than Lenin because he dressed in a military uniform, wore a moustache, and looked like my father. I used to fight with Myra about this. She said Lenin was a greater man. And I struck Lenin's portrait in our ABC book with my fist and she struck Stalin's. But then at school we were told that Stalin was not good and now nobody mentions him. But I understood how great Lenin was and that he was the only one forever.

I am happy that I was born in our wonderful country. I

might have been born in that dark and cruel America and lived, starving, in slums. Here I can take part in creating and building communism for the happiness of mankind. I, a young Pioneer, by my small deeds, help that great work of the Soviet people.

I wish I could talk now to Lenin and ask him: "Vladimir Ilyich, what do you think about our life, about our people? Do you think I am working enough and acting in accordance with your behests?"

I am sure he would have been happy to see what progress we have made in our industry, agriculture, and the way people live. I always feel that he is watching me and I try to do everything better. I recently learned a new song which says: "Lenin is always alive, Lenin is always with you, Lenin is in you and in me!" Yes, Lenin was so great that a part of him is in every Soviet citizen and in me also.

A month ago I visited Lenin's mausoleum. I like to visit Red Square and the Kremlin. It inspires me. But this was a special visit—I wanted to talk to Lenin. The weather was not very good, but I like gray days—this time it suited my mood. The line of people waiting at Lenin's mausoleum is always about 1,500 meters long and I had difficulty finding the end of it somewhere in Alexandrovsky Garden. The line moves constantly, but it usually takes three hours to reach the mausoleum. This was my first visit and it seemed to me of great importance.

I kept looking around, examining the people in the line, trying to get some clue to their thoughts. But they were all so different that I could get no response or understand them. I preferred to look at the Kremlin Wall, the dark red building of the Historical Museum, the Kremlin Red Stars.

The line kept moving and I found myself in the middle of Red Square. The square was empty except for the line, for it is closed from all other sides when the mausoleum is open. Militiamen around the square and all along the line kept order.

When I was only three hundred meters from the mausoleum, I noticed some uneasiness in the line and soon understood the reason. A heavy drop of water struck my nose. I looked up and saw that the sky had become dark gray with low swollen clouds which moved slowly and threateningly. One gust of wind and all the heaviness came down on the square.

I covered my head in terror. Heavy drops struck like bullets. The impact was so sharp it was unbearable. Floods of water beating on my face, shoulders, legs, going through my clothes, cold, wet, painful. I looked around desperately for escape.

But nobody in the line moved. It turned into a line of huddled shoulders and bent heads. It was as if they did not dare move. The square was empty and the Kremlin Walls and the Red stars in the towers and the militiamen—all were looking at the line to see if anyone would move. Maybe even Lenin himself was peeping through a secret window. What would they all do if we moved? Fear was more powerful than execution by rain. Nobody moved.

The next day the newspapers reported that this had been the heaviest storm in many years and the power in the city had been off for half an hour. But there had been one line in the whole of the city—out of hundreds of other lines—that didn't break up. And that was the line to Lenin. A picture in the newspaper showed the line of huddled shoulders and bent heads in the dark square. I had not been mistaken. Somebody had been watching and even taking pictures. Everyone was delighted at this story. We hadn't moved. . . .

When I reached the mausoleum, the storm had stopped. I was gradually recovering and doing my best to get my breath back. I was approaching the two famous Lenin guards. These are two soldiers with rifles who stand on both sides of the entrance. They stand, I think, for an hour or two without moving until two others come to relieve them. The changing of the guards is very beautiful. Now, while I was passing them, I saw with disappointment that both of them were blinking.

I remembered my last visit to Red Square the month before. It was the fortieth anniversary of the All-Union Pioneer Organization and I was elected as one of the best Pioneers of one of the best schools of Moscow to stand on the guest platform next to the mausoleum and watch the Pioneer parade. I was standing there among foreign guests and other Pioneers together with the director of my school. Suddenly all the Pioneers began to push and stretch their hands forward. The first cosmonaut, Yuri Gagarin, was passing us and all of them crying out his name were trying to touch him. He was smiling his famous shy smile. I started back with horror and disgust. It always made me shudder to see my ideals from portraits and books alive and so very close. The reaction of the crowd strengthened my disgust. The great first cosmonaut was as disappointingly alive as these two Lenin guards.

I entered the mausoleum and began to go down the staircase. Everything was of dark red marble. Then we all turned to the right and continued to go down. I was expecting to see Lenin after each turn, but instead, I found myself again and again at the beginning of a staircase going down. I became nervous. I had always thought that Lenin was lying in the marble cube that is seen on the square. But that, it seemed, is only a big gravestone. Lenin was like everyone else, lying in a grave. But I didn't want to go down to the grave. I didn't like it. It seemed to me like a trap.

We made one more turn and I realized that we had entered a big, dark hall with light coming from the center of it. I peered through the bodies surrounding me and saw a large glass box and, lying in it, a little man in a black suit. He looked like Lenin, but he seemed too small. Small head, small fist lying on his chest, small feet. . . . I felt sick. "Comrades, pass! Comrades, don't stop!" I heard many low voices mumbling. It came from men in military uniforms standing along the walls. I again felt surprised that Lenin's grave-mates were alive and even could talk. In a few seconds more I found myself climbing the endless marble steps and soon bright sunlight from the clear, wet sky blinded me. I turned my face to it with relief, screwing up my eyes against the sun's bright rays. It was all over so quickly.

I hurried past the marble blocks with the names of the Soviet great that were buried in the Kremlin walls and hastened to leave. I was hungry and wanted to go home.

On my way home I decided I would never go again. Of course, Lenin was alive and sacred, but it was his teaching and not this small body in the glass box. And that terrible storm had spoiled everything. It seemed to me like a personal offense, as though someone were mocking me. I remembered that I had heard someone's terrible screams of laughter coming through the noise of the storm. And the merlons of the Kremlin wall were like teeth bared in a terrible grin.

Laughter. . . . Do I deserve laughter? It is not often that I suffer from it, but I fear it because it means humiliation. And I hate humiliation. It is like when I am late for my classes and the teacher on duty looks at me. . . .

Yes, in the very same way that she is looking at me now. I am again late for the first lesson.

Anguish. . . . I can't get out of this state. It is always with me, it has become a part of me. What am I yearning for? I don't know what I want. I feel an emptiness in my mind, in my life. And I despise myself. This anguish is without end. I feel it like a snake somewhere near my heart or in my lungs.

All is rotten. All this: school, Komsomol, the institute, my job, people. All this social work, socialist competition, red flags—all is nonsense and lies. It is like a large billboard which I look at from a distance, but when I approach I realize it is only a canvas daubed with slogans and fat faces.

I alone am foolish enough to believe all this. All the others mock me and they are quite right. One must live only for oneself. There is no such thing as collective mutual love and respect, responsibility. There is only you and, maybe, your family. If you take good care of yourself and mind your own business, you will do better in and for this society.

But I cannot live for myself and I have no family. It is all my own fault. Now there is only this emptiness, this terrible anguish. I have lost my way. I feel like a robot who was suddenly left without a program or one whose program turned out to be all wrong.

Maybe if I read, educate myself, learn more about literature, music, art, the world, improve myself, I'll find the way—or someone will find me useful. But who?

* * *

I graduated from the school I used to love so much and never went back to visit. In the last years I understood it was all lies and grew to hate it. After I finished school, I felt so tired that I didn't dare go to the Technical Institute, as I had always dreamed. I went to the Foreign Languages Institute because it seemed easier. But the four examinations turned out to be four executions by humiliation. There were no human examiners there—just pigs sitting at the tables with their cloven hooves holding documents, grinning.

English: They entrapped me very quickly. I made some mistake and they smiled in satisfaction. *Four* (good). You may go.
Russian: I spoke on Turgenev. The pig interrupted me. "You don't speak good Russian. Where are you from?" She looked at my registration card. *Four* (good). You may go. (I don't speak good Russian! I always received very good grades in composition. And am I not Russian? Russian? I have to repeat it to myself in order to understand the meaning. Of course not. I am not Russian, I am Jewish. How could I forget?)
History—Composition: both *fours.* I was not accepted. I received only a sixteen instead of an eighteen.

It was all done so quickly. I decided to smile and went to work as a secretary at a research institute.

A few weeks later I learned that I had been accepted in the Correspondence Department of the Institute. That meant I could study by myself or attend evening classes and come to the Institute for my examinations. The authorities had taken into consideration the recommendation of my school, which couldn't bear the fact that I hadn't been accepted into any institution of higher learning, and they also considered the fact that I was an orphan.

An orphan? I am not an orphan. My mother is in a hospital. But they consider me as being an orphan.

It happened during my final examinations. My sister and I were sitting in a room and mother was standing on the balcony. She always stood there for hours looking down into the yard from our third-floor apartment. We thought it all right because at least she was in the fresh air. She hadn't been able to go out for she was very weak. After the terrible winter of 1961 when she was in a mental clinic, she began to develop a dreadful sickness. Her hands and then her legs refused to move and her face became like that of a statue. Her whole body gradually became paralyzed. She shrunk and her hair turned gray. It was Parkinson's disease.

That afternoon she was standing on the balcony when we heard her call us. We rushed to the balcony door and stopped short. Mother stood on the other side of the balcony railing on a narrow cornice, holding on to the balcony with her weak, white hands. It took us a few seconds to realize the situation and we rushed to her and seized her by the hands. How had she gotten there? Then I noticed a chair standing on the balcony. We tried to raise her, but she was too heavy and cried with pain. The railing of the balcony was sharp and cut her breast. We didn't know what to do. I thought of her age, her weight, and the yard down there. The houses in the yard were all seven-storied and gray. Now they looked like children's bricks with daubed windows, and every window had a man or a woman in it. One with hands in his pockets, another with his arms crossed on his chest, all silent, without expressions on their faces. So we stood—the world, indifferent and curious, and we three, embracing. Two of us were standing on the balcony and the third was outside over an abyss. In desperation, groaning, not paying any attention to her pain, we raised her once more and she fell over into our arms. Once back in the room, we couldn't talk. The next day I took her to the hospital.

I could never believe that mother was insane. She was so reasonable even when she talked of suicide. She couldn't accept her dreadful disease, she would say, she didn't want to be a burden to us, she hated this life, all her past, the Party which left her without help. . . . We never thought she really meant suicide. But the doctors said that an attempt at suicide meant that a person was insane. Maybe they thought there just couldn't be unhappy people in our country.

On the way home from the hospital, I felt relieved. Mother's illness was always a reproach to our youth and health. She would sit completely motionless, only her large green eyes moving, following us around the room. And when she walked, she moved like some slow, awkward insect, turning slowly, the movement of her eyes outstripping all her body movements. She rarely smiled, but when she did—I would gladly give anything just to see her smile once more. Her smile was wide and light, like the sunrise over a lifeless desert, innocent as the smile of a baby. She often reminded me of a baby by her awkward movements and that wonderful smile which only babies and old people have. Her head was beautifully shaped with long, straight silver hair—it once had been curly. She looked old and still so beautiful in her disease. Yet she was only fifty-six. In her younger years she had enjoyed waltzing and we often took her by the hands and danced a waltz around her, she turning around with us. Then she would smile.

This happened all too seldom. The rest was pain, suffering, talk of suicide, and eternal reproach in her big eyes. And now it had happened. She was in the hospital and I was going home exhausted, but relieved, after a sleepless night. It was shameful to feel relief, but I had to be honest. I needed a bit of rest.

The sun was gentle and caressing as in early spring. It had been raining during the night and the whole world was wet and clean. And the sun was also wet and smiled at me as through happy tears. I liked the streets with their puddles and wet trees, weeping clean shop windows, and the smell of damp, breathing earth in the air. I felt myself a part of it.

Seventeen, sun, spring. . . . I am slender and my arms are long and thin. I am like one of those young trees. I have big brown eyes and my smile is mysterious. This young man is following me. Yes, he smiles at me. He likes me. Yes, I also like myself. Am I not a beautiful little part of this wonderful world? Well, then there must be some place for me in it. I shall find it. I must wait a little.

* * *

Anguish. . . . Eighteen is a terrible age. I am so sick and tired of this work—eight long hours, working like a dog. And yet I like to work, whatever or for whomever I do it. If I begin, I can't stop, and work until the last moment and come home exhausted.

And, of course, they like me very much there. Everybody. So what? My teachers also liked me, and they were lying to me.

I cannot understand this world. I am in complete discord with it. Perhaps *I* am insane.

"Alla, what do you want to be when you finish at the Institute?"

"I don't know for certain, Chief, but I like the work here. I like active work, dealing with information."

"Oh, yes, you're a capable girl. Even now you could do the work as well or better than most of these dozens of graduates. You could have made a wonderful career here."

"But?"

"But your documents are not good. You know, I want to be frank with you. Is it written in your passport—Jewish?"

"Yes, of course."

"And can't you change it?"

"Why should I? I was born with it."

"Well, of course, it is your right to think that way. But it will always handicap you."

* * *

"Dina, tell me, please. We are both Jewish. You are my friend. Was it difficult for you to find a job?"

"I can't call it difficult. I am used to it and take it for granted."

"What?"

"That I am a second-class person."

"But why?"

"Because I am Jewish."

"I can't believe you. Aren't we all citizens of the Soviet Union? I can understand that there are some anti-Semites, but we don't depend on them. We are governed by a just and progressive State. I cannot be anti-Semitic. We should be able to achieve what we want."

"You think so? Well, I don't believe in what is taught. I believe in what I experience. But you'll see for yourself."

"No, no, no! I can't believe you."

* * *

"Well, Chief, what is going on here? The personnel department has fired so many useful engineers from our department. Does the fact that they're Jewish have something to do with it or am I mistaken?"

"Maybe not. But look. There are thirty percent Jews working in the whole Institute. And among the fired employees there were thirty percent Jews. It seems to be just."

"What kind of justice is this? You know you can't afford to lose these people. You need them."

"Well, if we keep those whom we need, we shall make a Jewish bazaar out of our Institute."

"Are the Jews to blame that they are the most capable and diligent here? Where should they go?"

"I never told you I could solve the Jewish problem, so don't ask me. You know I'm not an anti-Semite. Although I don't usually like Jews. There is something about them, I don't know what it is . . . well, typically Jewish. Please, don't be offended. I don't mean you. You are not like them. I am sorry you are registered Jewish."

"I am not sorry. I belong to them."

* * *

"Dina, I still can't believe there is no way out. I can see that many of the Party people are narrow-minded, undeveloped, and often cruel."

"Oh, don't exaggerate. They are just simple, good-natured people who come from the village and treat people as if they were cattle. They are just not in the right place."

"That is the point. And that is why I think there is still hope. Our duty is to get into the Party and change it from the inside, change its ways and methods. But the idea itself is right and we must try to realize it."

"What idea?"

"The idea of socialism and a Communist future, equality."

"And dictatorship?"

"But this is a dictatorship of the proletariat!"

"Words, words, words, and nonsense. The main thing is that it is a dictatorship and of one party only."

"What is wrong with that. There cannot be other parties in our country. Everybody thinks the same."

"Are you sure?"

"If somebody doesn't, then he is wrong."

"Oh, God! Alla, are you sure you know what is right and what is wrong?"

"I don't know . . . any longer. Forgive me, Dina. I always ask you such stupid questions. You must consider me a complete fool. People at my age have usually formed their points of view, whatever they are, and I am still groping."

"It is good you have begun to ask questions."

"You know, Dina, I am afraid I don't want to come to the conclusions you have come to."

* * *

"Chief, I can't believe this. You've applied for membership in the Communist Party! You! You, who have always been so cynical about it and talked about the corruption in it."

"I have no way out. I am Chief of a Department. If I want to advance in my career or go abroad on business, I have to be a member of the Party."

"So you will take part in the corruption. Those old fools are gradually dying out and soon the Party will consist of career-makers like yourself. And this is the Party that rules over hundreds of millions of people. Don't you understand that by our indifference and conformism we add to the crimes?"

"I don't think I shall add to the general corruption by my deed or change anything if I don't do it. I don't think anything can be changed in the near future. I have ceased believing in all these 'justices,' 'freedoms,' 'equalities.' "

"What do you believe in, then?"

"In nothing. I just don't waste time in thinking about it. Or, maybe . . . I do believe in something—in my two children, in my apartment, comfort, salary. I want to keep them."

"What will you say to your children when they grow old enough to ask questions?"

"I shall see. Why should I think about it now? I want them to have a happy childhood and then . . . maybe . . . they can live through their lives like me—without problems."

* * *

"Dina, I want to ask you a very strange question. But, please, don't take it as the question of a girl at her 'awkward' age. I just want to know your opinion. What is the sense, the purpose of life? Why do we go on living if we don't believe in anything, if we consider ourselves powerless? Can you answer that?"

"I think so. It's only my opinion and I'm not sure you'll accept it. We live for the sake of our children."

"I was amazed."

"Yes, to give birth to children, to keep the generations going, to keep life in this world and, if possible, to make it better. But in general we are born to live and to continue life."

"You know, it is so terriby simple that I cannot but believe in it. It is fantastic, but you've made me feel better."

* * *

Anguish. . . . There is no end to it. Yesterday Dina told me that the meaning of life is in children. At first I thought it a revelation but then. . . . It doesn't solve my problems now. I still don't know what to do. I feel I must read, read, read, but I don't know by what system to go, where to begin. And I have no strength, no will. I am so weak, I despise myself.

Just to go to some other place, to see new cities, historical places, people. Maybe the truth is hiding from me there. At least I shall have some fun. Why not accept this invitation from our second cousin in Riga? This family gathering is, of course, nonsense, but Riga must be an interesting little place.

It will be awfully expensive. But it might be worth trying. Myra also wants to go. It will be easier to go together and then we shall discuss what other places are worth visiting. One a year, at least. And during the year, we shall save our money. I think we can make it. Meanwhile, Riga in August. It feels good to come to a decision and to have a plan.

I am going on a long trip in search of happiness, like a young son of a Czar in search of a bride. First stop, Riga.

The train arrived in Riga in the afternoon. We were already late for the ceremony and we hurried. It was exciting to come to a new place.

We entered an old apartment—two rooms and a kitchen—on the second floor of a shabby house. Every room and the corridor was filled with people, about eighty of them.

The religious ceremony was just over and the young couple met us at the door. I kissed my second cousin, a girl with huge black eyes and short curly hair. We congratulated the bride and groom and entered the crowd. I was sorry to have missed the marriage ceremony with its canopy, the *chuppah*, held over the wedding couple. But the noisy crowd was so interesting that I soon forgot my loss. Entering the first room, I glanced at a strange thing standing in the corner of the corridor. Four tall, thin sticks were wrapped in dark red velvet inscribed with some yellow figures or letters, which had been golden many years before. An old man with a black beard and a little black cap on his head was taking his leave at the door. It occurred to me that the scrolls and the old man had something to do with the ceremony, but this thought was lost in all the new impressions crowding in on me.

There were some relatives known to me and I joined them, wanting to feel at ease in this strange crowd. I was struck by the number of Jewish faces. In fact, there was not a Russian male at this wedding. The black and red curly hair, big dark eyes, large noses, and delicate features of the small vivid women made me smile joyfully. I really felt something for these people who were so bright and original and yet the pitiful remains of something great which was never to be revived. And I belonged to these people.

Yiddish was heard from all sides. Why do they talk so loudly? A real Jewish bazaar!

Everybody was invited to sit down at the tables. Two rows of tables covered with picturesque Jewish dishes occupied the whole room. There were hardly enough places for everybody, but it was fun. At last all the guests found their places and the host called for attention.

He asked the oldest man present to be the toastmaster of the evening. Everyone joined in his request by applauding. The man sitting near the young couple smiled and slowly stood up. "He has been in Israel for three months as a guest," one of my cousins whispered.

In a hoarse, low voice, the old man began: "My dear friends! I am happy to be given the opportunity to be the first to congratulate the beautiful young couple upon their wedding, to wish them happiness and love for the years to come. I am happy to congratulate all of you, my people, on the birth of a new Jewish family that has been united according to the laws of our people, of our Torah. This fact is even more important now when our brothers defend our State thousands of kilometers from this place. And though we are so far from them, we feel our shoulders and elbows together with theirs."

I didn't hear the continuation. Lightning had struck my world. It swayed and turned upside down. A red transparent shroud stood before my eyes and behind it I saw those whom the old man was talking about. "Pitiful remains?" a voice inside me asked. "Impossible to revive?"

And I remembered. On the 6th of June on my way to work in the Underground, my glance fell on the opening pages of the morning issue of *Pravda* in the hands of the man standing next to me. "Israeli aggression." "The clouds of war over the Middle East." Oh, God! That country with such a Jewish name. It must have something to do with Jews. Then why did they do this? How did they dare? Is it not enough that everybody dislikes them all the same? Annoyed and frightened, I had turned aside from the burning words and made myself forget the whole thing. It was not difficult. I never read newspapers. I was tired and busy and had no time to think.

How could I fail to understand? Aggressors, capitalists, agents of American imperialism—all the junk the government had said about them had blinded me. My Jewish people was actually defending itself, and for the first time in thousands of years in its own State! My own people struggling there for life! I needed only this small word "brothers" to realize it. I began to feel how an indefinite "they" was turning into a strong definite "we" in my mind.

I clenched my teeth in order not to scream with the emotion that filled me. I managed to gain control when the second speaker stood up. He was a young man with red curly hair, blue eyes, and an aquiline nose. When he began, I couldn't understand a word he said. "What language is he speaking?" I asked my cousin in a whisper. "It is Hebrew!"

Hebrew—the ancient language. It is so different from Yiddish, the language of "pitiful remains." Strong and distinct sounds and syllables struck my heart like a hammer. This is the language of a proud and strong people. Proud and strong. Yes, we are. I feel it now. I bent my head, unable to look into the faces of the others. I was ashamed, but I was happy too.

The wishes of happiness and love continued. The guests demanded that the young couple kiss each other again and again to the shouts of "Bitter!" demanding that they sweeten the party with their kiss. (These Jews couldn't avoid this typical Russian custom which gives everyone such pleasure.) The room was filled with the clatter of glasses and forks, the fizzing of champagne, and laughter. I didn't take my eyes off my red-headed Messiah, trying to imbibe his energy and his inner fire.

When the table ceremony was over, the guests gathered in groups, their hands flying up and down, to the left and to the right. The Jews were talking: women gossiping, young people telling anecdotes, men noisily discussing something. I joined the group of men gathered around the red-headed one. He was speaking:

"This is a wonderful book. By an American Jew. Listen to just only one episode from it. There was a pogrom in a small Russian town. Many Jews were killed and among them a pious old man, a father of two sons. He was killed with a Torah in his hands which he had saved from the burning synagogue. One of the sons came at night to the house of the gymnasium director, the organizer of the pogrom, and killed him. The same night the two boys, Yossi and Yaakov, escaped the town and decided to go to Palestine.

"The police were already searching for them and they walked only at night, hiding days in the forest or in the houses of Jews. They went from one Jewish settlement to another, from one rabbi to another, maintaining only one direction—to the south. More than three years passed before they reached the Holy Land.

"Grown and tempered, they were standing on a hill and a beautiful valley was spread beneath them. 'We shall build our state here!' they swore. And they did it."

The men around me were listening silently with some kind of nervousness in their eyes. I shamelessly stared at the speaker with delight and eagerness. He noticed it and, having found a convenient moment, came up to me. "Let's get acquainted! We must be relatives." Having found out that we were ridiculously distant relatives, we came to the point. "Are you interested in what I was telling everybody about?"

"You can't imagine how much I am. I don't know anything, but I want to learn everything, everything. What can I do? I came here only for five days."

"There are Jews in Moscow."

"But I don't know anybody."

"I'll help you, don't be afraid. The main thing is that you want to learn."

"Yes, yes, of course!" I assured him once more.

"Look here. I have a friend. She is a girl of approximately your age and she is very interesting. She knows what to tell you. More than that, in a month she is going to study in Moscow and she will help you in everything. I'll arrange your meeting tomorrow."

Everything was happening as if by magic. Some force was pushing me onto a new road. I was nervous, but eager to undergo this change.

Next day I met Ruth in the street and she took me to her home. She was only two years older than I, but I felt myself a little girl compared to her. And she treated me as if I were much younger, but there was nothing humiliating about it. I felt as though I were being caressed and led along the new path with care and consideration. She didn't have to talk much in her house. I could see everything on the shelves, in the bookcase, among the records. I looked through everything, and touched everything. All of this had come from Israel. I handled every picture postcard, trying to penetrate into the world of each one. The names Yaffa Yarkoni and Simon Dubnow, the blue sky and yellow sand on the pictures—everything was a revelation. I was horrified by the thought that I might have missed all of this and was reassured by the knowledge that I had found it.

Ruth was one of the divine discoveries—her mass of curly hair and her deep serious eyes, even her name, which came from Israel, all had a special meaning for me.

We arranged to meet in Moscow.

She gave me the book about which the red-headed Messiah had been speaking. It was in English. I didn't see anything of the city I had come to visit or any of my relatives. I didn't see my new friends. The whole of that week, I lay on a bed, reading Leon Uris's *Exodus*.

I returned to Moscow and to myself as if from a fascinating and frightening dream. I felt as though I had sinned against. . . . Against what? Against whom? My former point of view, those who taught it to me, the State? I began to feel the State all around me and above me like a huge, tight box. "But I haven't done anything," I told myself. "It is just in my mind." But the system had so strongly possessed my mind that I felt any change in me must be noticed. I felt watched and trapped. I sat at home, biting my knuckles, thinking.

By daring even to think "against," I had become an enemy, and all the Communist irreconcilability to enemies, which I had been taught and with which I had agreed, would be directed against me.

I was afraid and yet I felt confident there was no way back. I couldn't forget about that tiny piece of land or about the small street in the center of Moscow where there stood a building with a six-pointed star on it holding my newly discovered identity. All this was fact and I could only be ashamed for being a coward. What will be, will be.

I returned to my work and began my second year in the Institute for Foreign Languages.

On Saturdays my apartment was filled with new acquaintances, young Jewish boys and girls, a noisy and gay company. The Jewish holiday of Simhat Torah was approaching and I felt it would be my first step on the new path and waited for it with excitement. I wanted to give to my new life everything I possessed. I could sing—I would sing Jewish songs. I knew English—I would read and translate literature on Jewish subjects. I was energetic—I would give my energy to these new activities.

Ruth brought us the words of the Israeli songs known in

Riga: "*David—melech Israel*" ("David—the King of Israel"), "*Eretz Zavat Halav u Dvash*" ("The Land of Milk and Honey"), "*Havah Nagila*" ("Let Us Rejoice"), and we learned them. My sister played the piano for us and the learning seemed easier. With her accompaniment we also learned to dance the *hora*, our whole house trembling under the feet of ten to fifteen leaping young people. Every day the company gathered.

I reveled in these noisy meetings and in the fact that four KGB men were watching my house. And, just as in my Komsomol past, I wanted the meetings to be effective and productive. I begged my guests not to waste time on chattering and the telling of anecdotes, but to thoroughly prepare for the coming holiday. It seemed as though the change in the objective of my pursuits did not matter provided my thirst for activity that would express my vanity was satisfied.

One day Ruth introduced me to her close friend, a man who was to play a very important role in the strengthening of my point of view. At that time I was not yet sure of my opinions and had many unanswered questions; the accusations against Israel in the press and on the radio affected me. I was feeling rather than thinking during this period.

When I met this man, I understood that he would answer my questions. "David," he introduced himself, looking at me with interest and welcome. Ruth looked proud, as if she were showing him some special kind of gift.

David was a short, thickset man over thirty. His heavy eyelids, which made the shape of his deeply set dark eyes very irregular, his prominent aquiline nose and his small mouth radiated strength and confidence. He reminded me of the leaders of the Judean war in a book by Feuchtwanger that I was reading. And I was not mistaken. He was really a very strong and devoted man with years of Soviet camps in his past for his Zionist point of view. I became attached to him very quickly and he responded with a warm, paternal attitude.

He used to come to our weekly meetings, bringing his recorder with Jewish tapes, and he would sing and dance with us. I appreciated his selflessness and felt that he was giving up his time and efforts to help us, the kids, because he thought the youth the most important ingredient for Jewish rebirth in Moscow. When everybody left, he used to sit in our huge old armchair and I sat at his feet on a small stool, asking my endless questions. This position seemed most suitable considering my attitude toward him.

"Please, David," I begged. "Don't think I have any doubts. No, I am sure because I feel we are right. But I would like to have some factual proofs for myself and perhaps for those to whom I may want to prove something. What is this all about, this problem with the Arabs, the refugees? Do we have the right to be in Israel?"

And he would tell me the background of the problem, the history, and the facts about the Six-Day War.

"Don't worry," he would comfort me after that. "Israel is strong enough now to defend herself. All this fuss in the United Nations about the Middle East problem is nothing but the fighting of politicians over spheres of influence. You can't judge by this who is a friend and who is an enemy, and you can't rely on anyone. We had to become strong enough to defend ourselves. Just imagine! Our people, those eternally unhappy Jews now have their own state and army, and they win victories. If the fighters of the Warsaw ghetto had foreseen this, they would have known they were not dying in vain.

"What should really worry us here is that we are not in Israel and cannot take part in defending and building it. We must be as strong as Israel to withstand everything and to live until the moment when we shall be able to realize our dream."

"Yes, I understand, to withstand everything. . . . I haven't done anything yet, David. But I want to and will do everything I can. But if some day I am called by the KGB, what shall I say?"

"Tell the truth."

"What do you mean?"

"Yes, tell them that you want to emigrate to Israel. And always remember that it is your right, recognized both by the

Soviet Constitution and international law. Try once and forever to get rid of the feeling that you are committing a crime by that wish. No, you have the right and you are right."

He was more than a friend and a teacher, he was the embodiment of everything he taught. Every Jewish hero I learned about, every Israeli leader, Israel herself, had for me the image of David.

The KGB never took their eyes off David, and were doing their best to entrap him again. But he seemed to know the limits of what he could do and was keeping within them. If he was working with the youth, then he made sure that it looked like harmless meetings over a bottle of wine and sandwiches; if he received and passed on materials, no one could ever suspect they had come to or from David. The KGB understood everything, but they could never catch him. At last in 1969 they decided to get rid of him in another way. They let him go to Israel.

For three days hundreds of people from different parts of the Soviet Union came to say good-by to David. His house trembled with songs, dances, loud talking, joyful laughter. I understood then that what he gave to me was only a tiny part of himself. There was enough soul, heart, and strength in him for all these hundreds of people. And they all came to thank him and share his happiness. But he was not very happy. He felt as a soldier feels, leaving the battlefield at the beginning of a great battle, leaving his friends, leaving the whole of still blind Soviet Jewry behind.

And at such a moment: when activities were for the first time beginning to be organized; after the first meeting in Moscow of representatives of different groups from various cities, in which he himself took part; after his proposal about writing collective petitions was at last accepted. No, David was not happy then. He ran from one person to another, introducing them, distributing tasks and materials that had been his, trying to fill the gap he was leaving. No, he would never forget them, he would keep in contact with them from Israel, he would try to help as much as he could, he would try to be useful to them even there.

He repeated all this dozens of times. He talked to everybody about his love, and then rushed into the circle to dance. He was completely drunk, but the famous kosher wine which his loving friends from Georgia brought in a small tun didn't help him to get rid of his sorrow, his feeling of guilt.

This was in 1969, but in the autumn of 1967 I had only just come to know David.

Together with David, Josephus Flavius, Judas Maccabaeus, and Bar Kokba entered my life. I began with *The Jewish War* by Feuchtwanger. I read it with frenzy and despair, imbibing the new sounding names, visiting the newly discovered places, acquiring the new spirit. When the scene of the destruction of Jerusalem came, I lay on my bed, covered myself with a blanket, and read the chapter slowly and attentively. When everything was over, I covered my head with the blanket and began to cry. It was a long, ritual-like weeping of relief. Suddenly I realized that I was crying about myself.

On the day of Simhat Torah that autumn, I put on a white scarf with a blue six-pointed star embroidered on it, which I had made specially, and went to my classes at the Institute. Before the end of the lessons, I went up to the teacher and asked for permission to leave.

It was our national holiday, I explained, and I had to go to the public celebration. She looked at me as if I were mad and allowed me to go, having understood nothing. Since when did Jews begin to have national holidays and, more than that, celebrate them publicly, I saw in her astonished look.

That scarf and the frank declaration were typical of the young people who had just become aware of their Jewishness. We always began by overdoing and exaggerating and had to learn gradually to be cautious. The older people who joined the movement had, on the contrary, to learn to be more free.

The day was cool and rainy, but I didn't wear my coat for it would prevent me from dancing and, in general, from feeling free. I was not late, but could not help quickening my steps; my heart beat violently.

I took the direct train in the Underground from Sokolniki to Dzerdzhinskaya, the center. Each stop marked an increase in my excitement and by the time we reached Dzerdzhinskaya I could hardly control the trembling of my knees. The train stopped, the automatic doors opened, and I saw Ruth waiting for me on the platform. We looked at each other silently and walked toward the exit.

On the escalator I felt joy and relief. I saw people singly, in couples, and in small groups with the signs of holiday on their faces. They were all silent, but their eyes were like a password for me. Once somebody had compared those eyes to the eyes of a cow—big, warm, brown, and sad. It was true, but only partially. Those eyes were not slow like those of a cow, but were easily frightened and quick to sense danger. The eyes of a gazelle.

We reached the top of the stairway and went out into the huge, dark square. All those going in our direction avoided each others' eyes, but quickened their steps as if drawn by some great magnet.

The square was one of the biggest in Moscow, with a high monument in the center of it. The stone leader of the Soviet Tche-ka, the secret police under Lenin's government, fearful and fearless Felix Dzerdzhinsky, one of the ideals of my Pioneer childhood, gave me a strange look from his pedestal. It suddenly occurred to me that his hand in the pocket of his long military coat was holding a revolver. Ruth didn't pay any attention to him. Maybe she was on different terms with this guard of the Soviet system.

We passed the huge building of the KGB headquarters, then the building of the Central Committee of the Young Communist League. All this had acquired a different meaning for me, but I tried to shake off those thoughts. Only those lighted windows in the KGB building didn't leave my mind. What could possibly be going on there at this hour? Interrogation, discussing the destinies of people, gray anonymous men preparing their punishment for me? Nonsense, it has nothing to do with me. Nothing! Not yet. . . .

After we crossed Dzerdzhinsky Square, we went along side

streets. No, not went—ran. And people near us also ran until we all at last reached a narrow street on the right. We turned into it and the sight took my breath away. The street went downhill and all along it as far as the eye could see there was a sea of dark heads. Thousands of people. A hollow hum rose from that moving mass, reminding me of boiling lava. "Too many Jews together," I thought with horror. The fatal figures flashed through my mind: six million, tens of thousands at Babi Yar, tens of thousands in Rumbula. . . . I stopped, but Ruth pushed me slightly, and I plunged into the boiling sea.

We found it hard to move in that crowd, but Ruth wanted to find our friends down near the synagogue. The weak light from the street lamps fell on the faces and they stayed in my memory like snapshots. Where had I seen all these faces? Again hazel eyes, pale skin. I remembered thumbing the pages of a book of pictures taken in the ghettos. The faces behind the barbed wire, in a long line of people going to—I had closed the book immediately, feeling sick. And now they appeared before me again—alive.

The expressions were different, laughing, delighted—and frightened, inspired—and attentively listening. It was hard to move. I saw faces and faces and felt that I was walking on them.

At last Ruth found our friends and we joined a group of young people singing Hebrew songs. David was among them. I was introduced to those whom I hadn't met before. Their names delighted me: Mordechai, Yoseph, Dan, Moshe. . . . The names themselves sounded to me like a challenge.

"And what about you?"

"My name is quite Russian—Alla."

"Choose for yourself a Hebrew one."

"I shall be delighted to. What names do you know that sound like mine?"

"Ayala."

"Ella."

"No, no, this is all nonsense." Ruth interrupted. "I have a brilliant idea. How do you like Aliya?"

"Aliya. . . ." I remembered *Exodus*. Aliya "Alef," aliya "Bet."

Aliyah means rising, *aliyah* means returning to our motherland Israel. Aliya is my new name and I shall have to live up to it.

We formed a large circle. Most of the boys and girls came from the institutes, so the bags with books were piled in the center. We embraced each other at the shoulders and began to dance a *hora*, singing "*Hava Nagila*." The circle grew and grew. Other people broke in and joined the line. And with every newcomer, joy grew in my heart. I wanted to leap up to the sky, to sing as well and as loud as I could, and my voice didn't fail me. My new friends began to leave the circle one by one and to form circles in other places. Soon I found myself alone among strange people. I hesitated, but seeing their longing looks, continued to sing. They clapped their hands and repeated the words after me. I finished all the songs I knew and began from the beginning. It was hard to stand. People were pressing from behind. I didn't notice how I became the center of the circle without stopping my song. The chorus around me grew and grew. I couldn't see the end of the crowd surrounding me. I was frightened, but I couldn't stop, and sang and sang and explained the words to the strange people around me and sang again with them. When it became impossible to sing, I began to dance.

Freilachs! The dance of wild joy, just be happy and dance, forget everything and dance, dance as well as you can. No one ever taught me this dance. My heart prompted me. The people around me clapped and sang the melody. Suddenly David rushed into the circle and joined me in the dance. Oh, David, I shall never forget how we danced *freilachs*! Leaping high, his arms flying up, he danced as if striving toward the heavens. His burning eyes came out of their deep sockets and fixed on the heavens. He begged, he demanded something from the heavens, he danced the dance of praise to the heavens. Cries of joy bellowed out from his chest. I couldn't check my own cries of happiness and whirled and whirled endlessly. One by one people began to join us and the circle was filled with dancing Jews. Exhausted, I stepped aside. Some one suddenly seized my hand and kissed it.

"I shall never forget you. Thank you." I saw a middle-aged man with tears in his eyes. He immediately disappeared into the crowd, but other people surrounded me, touching my scarf, wanting something from me.

I heard Ruth's voice and made my way through the crowd. She was standing in a tight circle, leading a chorus of voices.

"*Mi ata?* (Who are you?)"

"Israel!"

"*Mi im'cha?* (Who is your mother?)"

"Israel!"

"*Mi avicha?* (Who is your father?)"

"Israel! Israel! Israel!"

The answering voices roared, screamed as if they wanted the whole world to hear them. They were not satisfied that the stone guardian on the square certainly heard them through his hundreds of ears moving here and there through the crowd.

Why are they not afraid? Why am I not afraid? Because it is dark? Because we are together? Because we are near the synagogue? Or . . . because no one yet has been punished? Do they come here after they have been called to the KGB? Shall I come here if I am called and threatened?

No, enough questions. Not on this night, which in recollection seems to be happening again.

The circle becomes narrower. Everyone stands shoulder to shoulder showing each other by finger to lips that the next song will be without words. Hand in hand, with clenched lips, swinging, boys and girls start to sing. The melody begins very quietly, then grows louder and louder as if there is not enough room for it in our throats. Slow and solemn, it becomes aggressive and demanding, threatening and promising. It tears Jewish hearts, flows through our burning eyes, makes our hands clench tighter. The melody without words drowns everything around and swells into a hymn over the city. "Hatikva"* . . .

Now the crowd turns the world upside down. This narrow street is the world. It is without size. The noise and tension have reached such a point that they threaten to break through the sky. The crowd cannot bear even this limit above it. No limits! Freedom! Freedom!

* The Zionist hymn and the national anthem of Israel.

We are trying to make our way through the mass of bodies. This group is dancing a *hora*, that one is singing *"Shalom Aleichem,"* this one is screaming with laughter at a joke.

"Kids, go home, it is late," the cautious voice of an old man mumbles.

"Home? Ech, *papasha*, it is a long way home!"

The crowd is applauding.

This group is singing Yiddish songs. It is not very large. The young people do not know Yiddish and do not want to return to it. Hebrew and the spirit of Israel are reigning on this planet, the term of life of which is six hours—from 6 P.M. to midnight.

Again we find ourselves in the middle of a circle. There is no end of strength and will. Only *hora* can express what is burning inside, trying to escape. And the dancing circle is growing. Soon a big square is formed in the crowd. People rush inside it and form a second circle, then a third. The whole world is whirling in *hora*. *"Hava nagila v' nismecha-ah-ah-ah!!!"* "Let's be glad and rejoice!"

What a feeling it is to dance *hora* on this night. Your hands are on the shoulders of strange young people. Strange? No, on this night there are no strangers. Dear, beautiful faces are passing you in the whirling dance. Where shall I meet you next? In the Hebrew study group? In prison? In Israel?

And again I sing: "It is so simple. Repeat after me, '*Le shana habah b'yerushalaim . . .*'—'Next year in Jerusalem.' "

And more: *"Yerushalaim shel zahav"* ("Jerusalem of Gold") *"Sharm-el-Sheikh."*

"Where did you learn it? Do you know Hebrew? Do you have a textbook? I want to meet you. Please call me."

A hand bearing a paper with a number on it reaches above the heads.

"And me! Let's all get together."

But some people stand silent looking at you with devouring eyes. What possesses them? Shyness? Fear?

Several times my sister tried to get me to go home, but I didn't even hear her. Then she found a way of bringing me to my senses. She, together with her friend, seized me by the hands and shoulders and made me stand still for a few moments. After half a minute, I felt a terrible giddiness and a weakness in my knees and almost fell. Six hours without stop!

They took me home. I was silent, able to produce only coarse, inarticulate sounds. The silence all around pressed in on me. I was half dead, but really happy after so many years. There was again something to live for.

Dina dear,

I am so sorry I failed to find time to visit you, but I really couldn't. Almost every day after my work is over, I go to my classes in the Institute and they are not finished until 11 P.M. *As I travel home, I struggle to keep my eyes open. I'm afraid that if I close them I won't be able to open them again. And when I enter the subway I feel terrified; I know that I will not be able to resist and will fall asleep in the car. But due to some kind of instinct, I always awaken at my stop, but feel terrible.*

My life seems to me then so black and unhappy. I damn everything—the Institute, the subway, myself—and go swinging, struggling again to keep my eyes open, to my house. The street is always completely dark and empty. It is already after midnight and I think with irritation that even drunkards and dogs are asleep at such a time. And what is it all for? No sense at all in anything—in my work, in my studies, in the whole of my life. To work in order to have money, to study in order to have a diploma, to live—in order to live.

But enough of complaining. I should stop torturing you with it, at least in written form. I should remember the advice of all clever and experienced people—wait.

I feel very lonely in our department since they fired you. Berman has also been "relieved" of his position "due to reorganization." Gurvitz was advised to look for another job the same week and Aronson decided to leave himself. The snob decided to make a fine gesture—to leave, being sure he would be sacked soon.

I never told you that I spoke to him once. I could not resist the temptation to stir up a Jew. You know what he told me? That he is a man of the Universe, he does not classify himself as Jew or Russian. He was born here and therefore he is a citizen of the Soviet. Well, now he is gone like other good Soviet citizens who just happened to be Jews. I am sorry for him now. There had been a real pogrom. The next week they began to hire Russian engineers.

And only I am left—alone—like a chinchbug that stays in a house no matter what happens to it—fire, flood, earthquake. I know the reason I am left. My chief said: "You are lucky to be almost an orphan. They cannot fire you, according to the law. I know they would like to."

So you see, I am lucky. Why should I complain? By the way, mother is very bad now, worse than ever. We hope to get her into a hospital, but until now they have all refused us. Her disease is incurable and they don't keep people in the hospitals who are considered hopeless. I don't know what we shall do. Last time, she was taken to the hospital from the subway station. It is terrible to think about, but it is on my mind all the time.

We had left her sitting on a bench in the yard. When we came to take her home, she wasn't there. Hours passed and she didn't come home. We ran our feet off looking for her, but couldn't find her. You cannot imagine the feeling of losing your mother in the street. Children can be lost—they are helpless. But your mother? The evening came, the night passed—I was obsessed with the thought that she was wandering somewhere in the night, not far from us.

Neither the militia nor the Central Ambulance Service knew anything. At last in the morning when we re-called all the hospitals, she turned out to be again in that mental hospital. She had been taken from our subway station where she was standing on the edge of the platform looking down on the rails.

We rushed to the hospital. She was lying on a bed in a corridor of the overcrowded hosptial, her face as white as the pillow, her hair completely gray. She looked at us silently and we could find no words to ask, to scold, to beg. Her eyes moved from Myra's crying face to mine and there was such suffering and despair in them.

Why is it so? I constantly seek for an answer. Why is she suffering so much? What for? And then I cannot get away from the fear that this may turn out to be hereditary. No! No! No! I shall resist it. Just be calm and avoid nerve-wracking situations. Of course, I shall overcome it. The main thing is that I know about it and it won't come unexpectedly.

On weekends I sleep late and then do my homework for the Institute or something about the house, though, as I told you, I don't see any sense in all the routine I continue to go through. I feel that I must do it or I will be completely lost.

I'm sure you didn't expect to get a letter like this from me and you're probably wondering where all my new friends are; whether I'm disappointed in everything I found out about my national identity. No, I'm not disappointed and everything is in its place, except perhaps for the friends. I'll try to explain it to you and maybe it will help me understand what has happened.

I had never met so many people as of late and I had never known they could be so different and interesting. And, speaking frankly, I would have preferred they be more simple, but good, than so many-sided in their human faults. I understand that I am just one of this menagerie, but the contact with them turned out to be too difficult for me.

The young people who used to gather at my place seemed to be interested only in dancing, singing, and just getting together for the sake of fun. I became tired of learning Hebrew songs in Russian transcription without understanding a single word; of looking at beautiful picture postcards without knowing what was on them; of talking about Israel without learning about it. I know it is possible to learn a lot, but they didn't seem to be interested.

You know, since my school years, I have always tried to choose for my friends people who were better than I—better in everything: in character, in intellect, and especially in erudition. I always preferred to take rather than to give. I have always thought and do think I do not possess enough to share with anybody. I wanted and do want first to accumulate knowledge and learn human virtues and then maybe I shall be able to give something. You will probably object to the possibility of borrowing virtues. But I really think that if one feels imperfect and wishes to become better, one can learn to be kind by rubbing shoulders with kind people and by studying their relationships to the world.

You showed me a lot in this respect, but I learned much more of the virtue of kindness after meeting a really wicked human being. He was among those who interested me most among my new acquaintances. He was the most interesting specimen in this large menagerie of human beings. He is a middle-aged man, a husband, a father, a Jew, and a good doctor. But all this is not as important as that he is a collection of several traits which are expressed in him in their highest possible degree.

I met him first at one of our Jewish gatherings. David introduced us and from that moment, our many months' long conversation didn't stop. I was highly flattered by his attention to me, which was probably due to my talent as a good listener, and I listened eagerly for all those months. In his book-lined study he introduced me to the worlds of Freud, Kafka, Joyce, and Proust, Chagall, and Mann, Greek mythology and the Bible, Aznavour, and Joan Baez.

In his home I discovered a whole world and in him—human nature. Because to know and understand him meant to know one half of humanity. While listening to him, I was learning logical thinking and self-expression, emotional perception of the world around me, of art, literature, and music. I was learning to understand and to see through human nature—and I was learning to hate and despise people. Yes, because that is what he preaches, not by direct words, but through his whole expression of himself.

Oh, if you could only have listened to him talking scandal about people. His whole logical thinking, wit, erudition, knowledge of human nature and the psychiatric vocabulary were summoned for his talking which he usually did after meals while wearing a pleasant smile under his bristled moustache. It was one of his numerous vocations. One would probably call it mere gossiping, but he did it with such skill that you could not help being delighted by it and learning it subconsciously. And I could not deprecate anything about this great Lilliputian with such a simple human word as "gossiping."

Why Lilliputian? He existed for and in a tiny Lilliputian world that he created for himself. This world was limited by the walls of his apartment and consisted of himself, his wife, and his two children. All his acquaintances, his patients, his relatives, including his only brother, an old and sick man, belonged to the other world which he hated and despised.

And side by side with the qualities of a great intellectual, he possessed also the features of a man in the street, a fussy little Jew. He was delighted and jumped like a schoolboy with every new success in his psychiatric practice which any other talented doctor would have taken for granted. He did not like to give help free of charge to his patients whether they sought it at his home or at his place of work—a state district dispensary—and like a diligent ant he took everything he got from his patients in kind or cash to his home, to his two Jewish children—his creation, his sense of life. It was for their sake that he built that closed world in the center of Moscow, a world inhabited only by his dear ones and art, literature, philosophy, the Muses, and a spirit of intellectual meditation.

I took delight in this expression of parental love. Everything for his children. For his children he would step over dead bodies. I saw that he read, listened to music, enjoyed art with the thought that he would immediately pass his riches on to his son and daughter. Everything he had acquired in forty years he wanted to put into the heads of his seventeen-year-old son and his beautiful twelve-year-old daughter. And he did. When he first told me about his son, he exclaimed passionately: "My son is a refined intellectual." Those words produced a tremendous impression on me. They shocked me. I did not really understand the word "refined," though I knew about refined sugar or oil. "Refined intellectual" was something quite new to me. But I believed it must be something great.

The two offsprings' heads were filled with a tremendous amount of the world's intellectual treasury. They spent all their days reading, with the sounds of music in their ears, or talking with the only clever persons in the world, themselves and their father. All the rest of the world, these little sages hated.

Well, that is not completely true. There was one thing in the world the doctor, and accordingly his children, loved. And that was Israel. They listened to the broadcasts of "Kol Tzion" five times a day, five broadcasts of one and the same program. They dreamed of this wonderland where people must walk along the streets emanating rays of intellect. And they were all so thirsty for intellect in others. They were sure that Israel was that lost world, that lost planet of supermen to which they belonged. And if it had not been for their Lilliputian quality of "cautiousness," their great love for Israel would have made them heroes in the movement which is being born now. During our more than a year's acquaintance he was extremely kind to me and even interested in me. At the same time, though, everything that was behind me—my family, my former friends, my job and studies—was entirely dismissed. I did not resist, but on the contrary gladly submitted to this.

I just silently worshiped the doctor. One would probably expect some romantic side of the story and would not be mistaken. It was there, with the doctor's son, and it was as great and as disgusting as everything else about this time.

At last, one day, I was banished, very quietly and simply, by telephone, just a moment before I was going to leave my house and fly to them as I had every day during these long months. These months had been like a whole life to me, but the lifetime was over and the unexpected death came. I died there by the telephone and I spent a whole day and night in another world.

During this day and night, I didn't think about the death or how unexpected and cruel it was. I was just trying my best to be born again, to return to the world, to life. And to this end I used all the methods of psychiatric analysis I had learned in the doctor's school; I summoned the effort of a drowning person. And, indeed, I was like a person who had just been taught to swim and then thrown into the sea without help. And I knew there was no one to save me if I failed to save myself.

That night I spent sitting on the sofa with my legs crossed, looking at the white wall opposite me. I didn't dare move for fear of pushing myself into a deeper abyss from which return would be impossible. I clasped myself in my arms to keep myself from moving and sat so all through the night. In the morning I went out and walked along the streets. Then I bought an airflight ticket to a distant town and continued wandering about the city waiting for the flight. Finally, I made the first successful effort—I returned the ticket and slowly went home. I had no more strength to struggle and when I reached home, I lay down on the floor. But when I returned to myself, I knew that I had returned to life. Yet I ate almost nothing for several days and felt terribly sick and weak. But I was alive.

So much for the story. It can be as long as a lifetime. I haven't given you the doctor's name, for the Jewish name he bears does not suit such a person. Let him stay in your mind as "Homo sapiens" wicked. Yet I admit that he taught me to see and appreciate the richness of the world and he taught me—in the end—to love people. He also taught me never to stand with both of my feet on one board, but always on two, so that if one breaks under me, there will be a second one to support me—and the second one should be myself—never to give myself completely to someone or something, so that if he or it betrays or leaves me, I shall still have something left.

The lesson was very difficult and dangerous, but I passed the final exam and now I can safely re-enter the world.

I did not really tell you about my relations with other people, but this story is already too much for one letter. I shall write about others some other time.

Yours sincerely,
Alla

Dear Dina,

How are you? Did you find a new job? Please, come to visit us some day.

Mother is at last in the hospital. Now she will be thoroughly examined, as her intestines do not digest food well. I think her primary disease has now begun to paralyze her internal organs. Anyway it is better when she is in a hospital, especially now that an epidemic of grippe has spread through the city. At least she will be isolated from that. And, of course, we shall both be freer and calmer, although it is like covering your head with a blanket and imagining that the world has ceased to exist. I know that we do not help her enough and this feeling of relief when she is not at home is shameful. But what is the use of knowing it and shaming myself if I continue to behave in the same way?

How do you like this weather? Every day is like a fairy-tale New Year's holiday. I just love it. The soft white carpet muffles me up and protects me from the whole world. It is like the heavy rains of autumn which I also love because they put a protective wall between me and the world. I like to be at home alone in such weather. Yes, I am again alone. And I like it, as always. I think loneliness is the most productive state for a person. I hate anybody interfering with my studies or with my being face to face with myself.

I use my loneliness to the fullest. I use every free minute for reading and studying Hebrew. Every Saturday and Sunday, I go to the Foreign Languages Library where I discovered a large collection of literature on Israel and Hebrew textbooks. That is what should be done instead of wasting time in aimless dancing and singing in the streets and holding forth that Hebrew is forbidden for studies and there are no books on Jewish history. This is all true, but at least the first steps can be taken—to find old Russian and foreign books in the two central libraries. And this I do now. I found a dozen American Hebrew grammar books which I compare and extract from them everything I need on a certain question, and little by little the Hebrew grammar becomes clearer and clearer to me. The hours that I spend in the library make me happy for the first half of the next week. The second half I feel happy looking forward to the coming weekend.

Frankly, sitting in the library over the Hebrew file, I hoped I might meet somebody who was also working with this catalog. The meeting came very quickly and turned out to be more important for me than I had expected.

One Saturday I did not find the file in its usual place. With a rapidly beating heart, I began to look around the room. At last I saw an old man looking through my file. (By this time I was already calling it "my" to myself.)

"Will you please give me the file for just a moment?"

"Yes, here you are." He moved the box to me without taking his eyes off my face. I kept on looking for the necessary card as long as I could until the man broke the silence. "Do you know Hebrew?"

"No, but I am studying it now."

"What books do you use?"

I explained my system to him.

"Who helps you?" he asked.

"Nobody. I do it myself," I answered proudly and didactically. "Do you know Hebrew?"

He smiled sadly and answered, "Hebrew is one of my professions. I have just finished a textbook on Hebrew."

I jumped and could hardly keep my eyes from popping out. "Will it be published?"

"Well, that is a question. If you need any help in Hebrew, I shall be delighted to help you. My book will never be published, but you can use it."

We made an appointment for the next week.

My Hebrew teacher (what a wonderful thing to be able to

write these words!) is a soft-spoken old man with big dark eyes. Never before have I seen an old person with such large, open eyes, but Morduch Lazarevitch Roodshtein has a big, open heart also, and you feel you have an access to it through his eyes.

During the entire week, I wondered how I was going to pay for the lessons and, as I could not find any possible solution, I went to my first lesson with the determination that I would pay any price he asked and just give up one of my meals. But the problem was solved much more easily. When he heard my question, my teacher looked at me with sad surprise. I understood immediately and felt ashamed. Lessons in Hebrew in the Soviet Union are free, at least with such people as Morduch Lazarevitch.

My teacher gives me lessons in Hebrew grammar and tells me to enlarge my vocabulary by myself. At home I work on the grammar exercises from his textbook.

He has worked on this textbook for many years. It consists of grammar paragraphs, exercises, and short texts. Many texts are on the theme of life in the Soviet Union, but this has not helped in getting it published. The Council of the Institute of Asia and Africa gave it a very high appraisal, but the question of publishing it remains open. The teacher understands that this policy of delay means that the authorities have decided that the publishing of such a book is inexpedient. He does not hope any more. He teaches. Besides me he has several other pupils, but he works with everyone individually. It can be explained both by pedagogical principles and by cautiousness.

The textbook is accompanied by a supplementary book called The Destiny of the Language. *It tells about the history of Hebrew from the biblical period up to its miraculous rebirth in the State of Israel. He has given the manuscript to me to read at home and has asked me for my comments. I shall have the book for a week. Perhaps you'll drop in one day and look through it.*

I sit enchanted at his lessons. Very often he takes out the Bible or a book of poetry containing the expressions we have just learned. This makes me feel at the beginning of a long, unknown, and wonderful road. I am anxious to continue along the road as swiftly as possible.

The teacher lives very far from me, at the opposite end of Moscow, but I do not notice the cold, the crowd in the subway, or the hour and a half for the trip.

I am terribly happy now and hope this lasts longer.

Yours,
Alla

The teacher never talked to me about Israel or about applying for an exit visa. I knew nothing about his private life and never dared ask him. But in 1971 he arrived in Israel during the mass emigration from the Soviet Union. It had been the dream of his whole life, and it was now coming true. He went to Israel with his wife, leaving behind his only son and beloved granddaughter. When his son was small, this Hebrew scholar did not talk about Jewish problems or anti-Semitism in his presence in order to protect him. When the son grew up, he didn't want to hear about it.

This teacher of a new generation of young Hebrew scholars in Moscow spent three wonderful months in Israel, reading to the public his Hebrew poetry and meeting Israeli poets and writers. He died of a heart attack on the stage in front of his Israeli listeners at one of his performances. God bless his sacred memory!

Dina dear,

I have just learned that the KGB is concerned with my person and has been for quite a long time. No, I am not at all frightened and even feel intrigued and a little proud. But I have to tell you everything from the beginning.

One evening when I was already in bed, Myra came home and, without taking off her coat, sat down on the bed near me. Her look seemed very strange.

"I was there," she said.

"Where?"

"There."

I understood. I suddenly grew cold and felt a terrible headache. Myra was smiling. You know she always smiles that stupid smile when she is excited. But the corners of her lips were trembling. I didn't say anything, but waited for her to begin.

"It happened yesterday. After I had finished my lesson in the sixth class, I left the classroom and saw a man standing near the door. He said he was waiting for me and asked me to go out with him to the staircase where we could talk quietly. At first I thought that he was a parent of one of my pupils, but his bold manner surprised me. When we reached the staircase, he showed me his identity card—KGB. Can you imagine what I felt? I knew immediately it had something to do with you."

"Stop, Myra. What did he look like?"

"Well, nothing special. Very ordinary, colorless face, middle-aged, green hat and gray raincoat. Very polite, soft-spoken."

(Dina! Remember this description. This is he who follows you, who stands near you in the synagogue, who watches near your house for hours. Dina, if you see a man who seems very much an ordinary man-in-the-street, without anything special about him, take care! He is the KGB.)

"What did he ask you?"

"Better ask what he didn't ask. From the very beginning. About parents, school, friends. And he knew everything about our family: that father had died, that mother is ill and that she is a veteran member of the Party—everything. You know, it's a terrible feeling when you meet a strange man and he knows everything about you. There was nothing special in this talk at the school, but at the end he said that he had more questions, but did not want to interfere with my work. So he invited me to come today to his office in Lubianka Street. When I heard this name and remembered that building on Dzerdzhinskaya Square, I nearly fell from the stairs.

"So now I have just come from there. At five I went to Lubianka Street and went in through the side door. You know—those huge black doors. There was a pass for me at the entrance and a man took me to the room which was indicated on the pass. We walked along long, narrow corridors, then turned and walked again, and again turned, until I couldn't orientate myself. There were doors on both sides of the corridors; some were open and the rooms were empty. Others were closed. The building seemed completely empty, but somewhere at the end of those endless corridors my visitor of yesterday was waiting for me. When I was finally shown into a room, the man who brought me left immediately.

"My visitor of yesterday seemed happy to see me. He greeted me and invited me to sit down. In the room there was just a table with a chair on each side of it. He began again to ask the same questions, but this time he put down my answers on paper. At last he began to ask about you. What are your interests? Who are your friends? Who influences you? I answered who else can influence you but I, your elder sister. Then he asked who used to come to our place during the young peoples' parties. I said I didn't know the surnames. He asked me the first names. I began to think of all the Jewish and popular names I knew, except of those who came to us, and gave him some. He asked if there was anyone by the name of David. I said I couldn't remember everybody who used to come and maybe there had been a David among them.

"He showed me several pictures and asked if I could identify anybody. There was nobody I knew on them. He asked whether you were going to the synagogue on Passover. I said that as far as I knew you were not going. At the end of the conversation, he asked me for permission to bother me once more if they needed more information. He said they did not call you because you are so young and they did not want to frighten you. He was very polite. Then he showed me out."

We sat silently for awhile. I wanted to say that I was sorry that she had become so involved in this. She has nothing to do with my activities. But I saw she did not need my apology.

I have never understood my sister completely, nor my mother. We, three women, have lived all our lives together, but have never come to know one another deeply. Mother had her own life, and her way of thinking is completely strange to me. We two daughters are also going different ways in our lives.

In the summer of 1967 when we were both in Riga, she became more interested in Israel than I. But when we returned to Moscow, she forgot everything, resumed her usual way of life, and did not want to be bothered. My noisy company antagonized her. She saw people's faults, but refused to see the important idea that was behind them. Nothing could reawaken her interest in Israel.

But she never disapproved of my point of view. She agreed that I was right and was proud of me and, in some way, even envied me my obsession. But she herself was bound by a love for the country in which she was born, and to give up her life to go to a country she didn't know was strange to her. And a hypocrite she could not be.

During the telling of her story, my fright had subsided. I was able to consider everything quietly. It had been several months since I was in the synagogue or a large group of Jews had come to my place. The KGB definitely wanted to intimidate me. Well, to a certain degree, they did. I am afraid, but just a little. I was not going to be in the synagogue on Passover. But now two feelings struggle inside me. One is fear and the second is the wish to go there to spite them, to show that I am not afraid.

But, in fact, I do not want to go to the synagogue. I do not feel like dancing or singing now. And I have an unpleasant aftertaste from my meetings with some people.

I shall try to explain this to you as I have already promised to do, and you judge me, please. After that trip to Riga, I became acquainted with a lot of people, all very different and interesting. I thought they belonged to a heroic movement for the rebirth of our nation, and they must be courageous and idealistic if they dared to defy our system and give up their lives to their historic motherland. So they were heroes to me and I was proud to belong with them. But after a certain period of rubbing shoulders with my new friends, I realized that they were all human beings and were not strangers to human vices. One shocked me as an outrageous liar, a second was full of jealousy, and a third was a fool. But what made me completely unhappy was the discovery that grown-up men, heroes in the Jewish movement, married and fathers, were very unreserved in their relations with women and young girls, behavior from which I myself suffered more than once.

I began to feel uneasy, to put it mildly. I had always thought that people who are involved in one holy cause cannot be immoral or dishonest in other things. Or, if they had not been perfect before their involvement in the holy cause, it made them better in all things. I never thought people could be heroes in one regard and immoral in another. And maybe there are no heroes at all but only heroic situations which make people behave in a certain way. So these people whom I had thought to be heroes are no better than I am. So why, therefore, should I feel uneasy if people turn out to be only human and not monuments of heroism? Because I must have somebody to look up to? Have I the right to demand that other people be better than I? And, if they are no better, to reject them?

So, you see, you don't have to tell me anything. I answer all my questions and reason with myself. But still I cannot get rid of the unpleasant aftertaste of the discovery and prefer again to be alone.

I am happy that this disappointment has not influenced my belief in Israel as it did Myra's. She saw Israel through the people who brought her the idea and, having been disappointed, lost it—maybe forever. I have remained face to face with Israel without mediators. And I shall keep this bond.

And yet I sometimes wonder whether this, too, may not be another of my mistakes, a new food for my boundless idealism. I really think idealists are dangerous people. Since people have not found absolutely true ideals, they find something else and are eager to serve their idols. Idealists are active, tireless, selfless. They are ready for heroic deeds and crimes. They will step over anyone in the implementation of their ideals. Richness, glory, individual power—are they not ideals? But there are ideals which can be more dangerous—social justice, communism, equality, internationalism, racial purity—for their sakes idealists step over millions of dead bodies, over whole nations.

I myself very nearly became an accomplice to the crime that is being committed here. So I am afraid of making a second mistake and am trying to understand what is happening to me.

There are variables and constants in this world. Variables are political points of view, social orders, opinions, and those still undefined concepts of ideals. They are all subject to change in the course of life.

The constant is that which is given you by birth, belonging to a family, a nation. You can be proud of it or you can be ashamed of it, but you can never change it. And you must be responsible for your belonging. That is my point.

I belong to the Jewish nation. And this is a constant. Israel has been reborn for the sake of our nation and someone must go there. And who is that someone if not I. It is simple and, I think, true. I admit again that there is some kind of idealism in this: I want to give up my life to the country, to the nation. But besides that I feel that Israel needs me. I also feel that I need Israel much more than she needs me. And that makes me think that I am beginning to depart from that class of dangerous people.

Yours,
Alla

Mama!!! I wanted to scream in pain and despair. If I could give one long scream, maybe I would feel better. But the scream was only inside. It tore my head and chest apart but would not come out. Ma-ma-a!!!

It happened on the morning of January 16, 1969. Myra and I were at home and both in a very good mood. The sun shone brightly over the soft snow and we told each other something very funny. I remember Myra was jumping with laughter on the sofa when the telephone ring interrupted her. She took up the receiver, listened for a few seconds, and burst into sobs.

Mother had been in the hospital for a month. For the last week we had not been allowed to visit her, since no one was allowed to visit the hospital because of an epidemic of grippe. Mother also had a cold.

Myra put down the receiver and I could hardly hear her through the sobs: "Mother died. . . ."

The sun went out, the snow turned yellow. The floor was swinging under me. I had no tears. I was too terrified to cry. But Myra was crying and I did not want to see it. We had never known how to comfort each other. I went to mother's room, knelt in front of her bed, and put my head on it.

There is no more mother. The world remained as it was, life

goes on and there is no "mama" in it. How can it be? How stupid and unimportant everything that has occupied me is now. All those ideas, plans, people—everything. How stupid and unimportant if there is no more mama. What shall we do now, how do we live now, if there is no mama? How can it *be* that there is no mama?

She had died the night before at 9:00 P.M. and nobody had noticed it. She was as quiet as always, but dead. They saw her only in the morning. There was nobody beside her at the moment of death. She was alone, as always. What did she think? Or did the fever that wracked her weak body not permit her to think? Nobody had been beside her for a whole week and perhaps she had wanted to say something to us. How could she leave us without saying anything? We must have had a talk, we must have understood each other at last. I am sure she had something very important to say.

She must be very calm now. She is at rest at last. I am happy for her. There will be no more pain in her eyes. She is sleeping quietly now for the first time during all those years. There are some people who cannot be ill, who can never accept illness. Mother could not and, after she became a complete invalid, did not want to live. But she didn't want to die. . . . Death came. Mama, was it painful? Is it painful to die of pneumonia? However it was, she is better now.

But what shall we do now? How could you go without forgiving us our sins against you? Our relatives have always warned me that after your passing away I would never forgive myself for being rude to you. Maybe they were right. But I shall not think of my behavior now. What is the use of it if you cannot forgive me? And God will not forgive me.

But there is one thing I shall never forget. And I do not ask God to forgive me for it, for I shall never forgive myself.

That terrible night. I sat on the sofa, half insane, and you did not sleep in the next room. You felt something had happened to me and you wanted to help. You felt I was suffering and you forgot about your sufferings. You called me many times, "Alla . . . Alla. . . ." And I was silent. I was afraid to move. And you called to me. You wanted so much to help me, to talk to me. And I rejected your help. I forced myself to say only: "Please, mama, don't." All the next day your nervous glance followed me, but I avoided it. I should have come to you and cried out everything. You would have told me how to be heedful of people and I would have been myself again. Instead I rejected your help, struggled alone, and came out cold-hearted and strong. But I missed that moment when you wanted to talk to me and I lost you forever.

Who were you? What did you think? Did you really mean it when you used to say, "Don't trust people"? Were you serious when you told me, "Try Israel. Maybe you will find happiness there. Here I did not find it." But then you denied your words and demanded that I stop my activities. And there was so much fear in your eyes then. What made you—who was so strong and proud—be afraid? What would you say if I decided to leave Russia now?

But I do not want anything now. I just want you back, to try to understand, to feel each other. Please come back!

I passed my hand over the bed. It was empty. No. . . . And you are right. You are better off there. You will have a new bed now. Not yet. We shall have to buy it. How much does it cost? Where shall we buy it? Ah, the relatives must decide it. Let it just be as quickly as possible. You must already have been taken to the morgue. It is so cold there. You must be freezing there, lying naked on a cold marble table. I do not want you to lie there, I hate even to think about it. Wood is warmer. And we shall bring you your favorite blue dress. . . .

I have a headache. I shall go to sleep. Mama. . . .

* * *

In three days everything was ready for the funeral. We went to the morgue. There was a round hall with a long table in the center. We sat on chairs near the door. Soon the side door opened. I closed my eyes. When I opened them, the coffin was already on the table. I looked at mother from where I sat. Very pale, her facial bones covered with white skin, gray hair, very unnatural. We did not move.

"Shall we take the deceased to the bus?" the huge Russian

attendant asked. "The deceased." The words struck me. There was something old-church Slavonic in it. They do not use the phrase much now. But what could be better than these quiet comforting words? The coffin was covered and taken to the bus. It was a very small wooden coffin, the cheapest. I did not mind. I knew that there were coffins lined with black and red silk or with white silk inside and tassels on the ends. No, I would not have insulted mother with tassels. Death is superior to all this.

The bus moved quietly along the Moscow streets. There were Myra and I, a few relatives absorbed probably in thinking about their own ends, and mother lying at our feet. I suddenly felt a strong feeling of tenderness toward the coffin and wanted to stroke it. But the relatives watched our reactions to the death intently during the intervals between their philosophizing, and I did not move.

We arrived exactly on time. Coffins were entering the crematorium—relieved mourners coming out. The crematorium is a dark gray building with a tall tower breathing out black smoke. It must have been built by sadists to spoil the life of the whole neighborhood and all the passers-by. There was no more space in the ground and urns were put into specially constructed cement walls. Some of these walls were inside buildings and looked like incubators. I once saw there a young woman whose mother's urn had been put on the very top of such a wall. She was crying bitterly and I understood her.

We were lucky. We had got a place in the ground for mama, the old grave of a second cousin.

Our turn came and we all entered the hall. The coffin, which had been placed on a black velvet platform, was opened and musicians began in a businesslike way to play something sad to help people weep. Mama's hands were covered by a white sheet.

For the first time I began to cry. I cried and cried. The tears washed my tired thoughts and wet the fur collar of my coat. Myra was sobbing beside me. Trying to catch a trembling of her eyelids, I did not take my eyes off mother's face. My relatives insisted that I kiss her, but my face was very wet and I didn't want to let my tears fall on her, lest she raise her hand to wipe them away.

A woman attendant came in and said, "Your time is up!" She closed the coffin, turned some invisible lever, the coffin went down like an elevator, and two black velvet doors closed. The music stopped. The end. As we went to the exit, the next coffin was coming in.

* * *

Several months later we got a small white urn in the shape of a flower pot. I held it without fear, feeling the same tenderness toward it that I had felt toward the coffin. A worker took the stone off the grave, we put the urn in there, and arranged the ground again.

I seldom found time to go to mother's grave, but when I did, I never felt sad. I was quiet and comfortable and talked a lot to mother, telling her all my news.

And in 1969 I had more news than I had ever had in my life.

Today, September 22, 1969, I was expelled from Komsomol. Yes, I have to write these words and try to believe them. The girl who wrote my diary for 1962–63 could never have believed them. But they are true.

After what happened today, I rushed to a bookshop, bought a pen and a little notebook. I could not wait to get home. I am afraid I shall lose what I feel now, this feeling which makes my head burn and my heart beat violently. In two hours perhaps this will not seem so awful and in two days perhaps I shall forget it, just as Anne Frank got used to her life as a prisoner and the inhabitants of the Warsaw ghetto passed corpses in the streets without paying any attention.

Not that I compare my situation to theirs. I just want to remain clearly aware of what is happening to me. Let me recall everything from the beginning.

After mother's death, I could see no reason to delay applying for an exit visa to Israel. There was nothing to keep me in this country. I had lost everything that tied me to it. I saw my future life as being in Israel. I knew the struggle to get there would be long and I had to begin it as soon as possible. One of my distant relatives in Riga had been allowed to leave Russia and I had asked him to arrange an invitation from a relative for me. In two months the invitation arrived. I took it from the postman and just sat looking at the envelope without opening it. Until that moment my plans had never seemed real, but now this document with the red seal of the Israeli Foreign Ministry was a signal for me to begin. With the invitation in my hands, I realized for the first time that there was no way back.

Next day I went to the Department of Visas of the Interior Ministry and was instructed on the procedure for making application. I had to provide: two photographs, a document from the housing authorities, two copies of a filled-in questionnaire, stamps of state taxes for four rubles, and a character reference from my place of work. That was it! I had already heard that the last item would cause all the trouble. It would be a signal for all your colleagues to bait you and finally to throw you out. Does the Interior Ministry really want to know whether you are good enough at your work to go to Israel? No, this is just one of the more refined methods of torture. In my case it took them five months to give me the character reference.

I asked for it one day at the end of April. My Chief said, "I know, you want to catch a millionaire there and become rich. But look at yourself. Don't you think there are enough really pretty, sweet-scented girls there?" I didn't argue. People think in different ways and if I had begun to tell him of my ideals, he would have made fun of them. He was witty enough to do it rather cruelly.

Two days later a member of the Party Committee of the Institute, a handsome middle-aged man, a Jew, invited me for a talk. He began to tell me a lot about his travels abroad in Western Europe, how side by side with wealth he saw terrible poverty there, how strongly he missed his motherland during these trips. I listened silently and very attentively. When he finished two hours later, I said: "Will you please try to hasten the giving of my character reference? I want to leave as soon as possible." He shrugged his shoulders and let me go.

A week later the secretary of the Committee of Komsomol, a young handsome Jew, came to talk to me. He began to tell me about his numerous trips abroad, how people of a Communist point of view were persecuted, how members of Communist parties could exist and publish their newspapers only with the help of the Soviet Union. I listened to him silently and with understanding. When he finished, I asked: "When will my character reference be ready?" He shrugged his shoulders and said: "You cannot be given this document without being expelled from Komsomol." I had expected this but wanted to resist to see what would happen. "I cannot agree with this, but as you will have to convene a Komsomol meeting I shall explain my point of view on this question at the meeting."

The meeting was not convened for three months. In the meantime I was on leave for two weeks and when I returned I found the whole of my department changed. The moment I arrived at the Institute, I was called to my Chief for a talk. He preferred to talk to me in the corridor.

"Do you take the salaries of our workers from the cashier?"

"Yes, I usually do it and give them out according to a register."

"Did you ever take money from the salaries of some people?"

"What do you mean?"

"No, please, do understand me correctly. Look here, last week someone reported to the Director that you used to take a ruble from the salaries of all Jews in the department and gather them for Israel."

"Do you believe it?"

"Of course not. I just wanted to make sure."

"Did they ask the Jews themselves?"

"Yes, all of them were called to the Special Department and they all denied it."

"Thank them for nothing."

"I think it would be better if you didn't sit in that room any more. Your presence will make their imaginations work harder. Move to my room. You will be alone and no one will bother you."

He hurried to his room, worried that he had already stayed too long with me in the corridor. I remained alone, people passing me by. I felt terribly tired though the working day had just begun. I thought:

"It is only the beginning. What else will they invent against me? Dozens of grown-up people against me. Have they forgotten everything for which they used to love me and take care of me? That I am young and an orphan, that I have been kind and am a good worker? Now they consider me a traitor. No, they are afraid themselves. Well, if you are afraid, I shall not be; if you try to destroy me to save yourselves, I shall despise you."

I entered the room. Everyone immediately became silent and absorbed in his work. I gathered my things, looked around the room with a sunny smile, and left it. I wanted to cry.

People passed me looking down at the floor or up at the ceiling or just aside, each to his own liking. But a few people who had never greeted me before began to utter a short "Hello" while passing me quickly, looking aside. This was enough to make me strong.

Time passed. I reminded them every day about the character reference, but they postponed it from week to week. They seemed to be consulting someone in higher echelons. Mine was one of the few cases in Moscow and the Party authorities were not yet experienced in handling such situations.

At last the date of the first meeting was set. On that day I worked as usual at my files, trying to avoid thinking about the meeting. But when I was at last invited to come down to the Party Committee's room, I felt I had never for a moment stopped thinking about it. Yet I also felt as if I were going to an exam unprepared. I couldn't even imagine what kind of questions would be asked. I went downstairs slowly, trying to overcome my nervousness. I succeeded only as I opened the door. It was just like an examination where my nervousness disappears the moment I take the examination ticket.

There were about ten people in the room, the members of Komsomol, and two Party members. Everyone seemed to be feeling uneasy and I thought to myself that at least one person should be at ease, and it might as well be I.

I sat down in a chair in the center of the room. They were all sitting along the walls. The necessity of turning my head to answer each question made me feel peculiar. I knew only one thing for certain. I would not be aggressive or give them any possibility of accusing me of anti-Soviet convictions.

"You want to apply for an exit visa to Israel. What is the reason for it?"

"You know I am an orphan and in Israel I have relatives."

"But do you know what kind of a state Israel is?"

"That doesn't change anything. Whatever Israel is, my relatives happen to live there and I want to be reunited with them."

"You have a good job, you study here, the State took care of you, and at last you are a grown-up person. Whom are you trying to deceive with your story about relatives?"

"I want to be reunited with my relatives," I repeated distinctly and loudly.

"But do you know that this desire of yours does not conform to the principles of Komsomol?"

"No. I do not see any connection between these two things."

"Read the Rules of Komsomol. In the first paragraph it states: 'The member of Komsomol must be loyal to his Soviet motherland.' "

"Who says I am not?"

"But you want to leave it."

"That does not mean I am not loyal. I can even remain loyal to it after I leave it."

"How can you if you want to leave for Israel, an aggressive, nationalistic, imperialist state, the enemy of the Soviet Union?"

"There are Communists all over the world. All of them are

loyal to the Soviet Union. Israel has two Communist parties. Maybe I shall work for communism there." (God forbid!—I could not help saying to myself.)

"But you are leaving the Soviet Union, so you cannot remain a member of Komsomol. It is simply unnatural."

"Of course it is. As soon as I am allowed to leave the country, I shall resign. But I am not leaving yet and who knows when I shall be allowed to go. And just for having the desire to leave, you cannot expel me."

"Who said we cannot? We shall." This was said by one of the Party members, the Deputy Secretary of the Institute's Party Committee, a middle-aged Jew.

The questions were pouring in from all sides. It was like a game where one person stands in a circle and the other players throw him a ball and he returns it. I enjoyed it and tried to behave according to my understanding of the game—to be logical and not aggressive.

"But do you know that our state supports the Arab countries with armaments?" the pretty Secretary of the Komsomol Committee, who used to travel a lot, asked.

This was a blow below the belt and I couldn't help throwing the ball back with hatred, "Unfortunately, I do." Now they had caught me.

The Party member jumped up. "What do you mean by 'unfortunately'?"

I looked at him with disgust and didn't answer. "I think, comrades, the case is clear," the Deputy Secretary pushed forward. "All this argument is useless. A member of Komsomol dares to apply to leave the Soviet motherland to go to a capitalist and, I would even say, fascist state."

"I'm sorry," a voice behind me interrupted. I turned around. It was my colleague, a young Jewish boy who had never seemed enthusiastic about my ideas and was one of those who had assured me that he belonged to no national group but to the whole world of people. I listened to him with surprise. His voice trembled with his inner struggle. "I am sorry, comrades, but I do not think we can say this. All of us know very well that there are some really fascist states like Greece, for example, and the imperialist United States that is waging war in Vietnam. And yet our country still has diplomatic relations with them, though none with Israel."

("Thank you for nothing," I thought.)

"Our state," the Party man answered in an irritated voice, "defines its diplomatic relations according to its interests and current policy."

Everybody was dumfounded at such idiotic frankness. Silence fell in the room.

"Let's start the voting," the Komsomol Secretary hurried to break it. "Who is in favor of expelling Alla Milkina from the ranks of Komsomol for behavior not in accordance with the Rules of Komsomol?"

The hands began slowly to rise. One, two, three . . . nine. My unexpected supporter was last. He hesitated, but having looked convulsively around, he slowly raised his hand. Unanimous!

"The resolution will be confirmed at the Institute's Party Committee meeting and then at the District Komsomol Committee. Only then will you be given the character reference."

I stood up and left the room.

* * *

I left the Research Institute and went out into the street. It was late summer: stuffy, dusty Moscow. I looked to the left, then to the right. Where should I go? How I wished there was somebody to whom I could tell all this. But I have nobody. So why are you standing here indecisively? Go home, enjoy your loneliness. Talk to yourself. You chose to be alone. You neglected friends. But if I had them now, would it be any better? Don't they have the same troubles? Would they be interested in listening to the same story? Who really needs me? Nobody. And why should I mix with them just to make myself believe I am not alone? No, I'd better go home, cook a good dinner for myself, wash something, and just be by myself.

* * *

The second meeting didn't differ from the first. After it I was deprived of my quarterly premium which I needed to help make ends meet. The atmosphere around me grew more and more tense. Two Jewish engineers left after they had been called to the Special Department and asked about their contacts with me. Someone had reported to the Department that one of them was the leader of the underground Zionist organization and I was his assistant. Poor men! And they had nothing to do with me!

Though I was not afraid, the baiting made me more and more exhausted. I returned home half-dead with fatigue, tension, and hunger. I stopped taking care of myself, didn't arrange my long hair, dressed slovenly. In one month I began to look like an old hag.

Finally the day of the "complete solution of the Jewish question" arrived. And it was today, the 22nd of September 1969.

In the morning I began to feel very nervous and could do nothing. I was certain this meeting would be more businesslike and less terrifying than the previous ones. This time I would be meeting with professional Communists who are more careful in dealing with people than are those Party members who feel they must constantly prove their loyalty.

Our Secretary of Komsomol accompanied me to the District Komsomol Committee. Walking beside him, I thought that I could never have gone out with him socially although he was rather good-looking. He was a terrible fool and a coward. He was afraid not only of his chiefs, but of me. When he was alone with me, he was very polite.

We had to wait in the reception room, for there was a long line of young boys and girls who were being accepted into Komsomol. I sat there remembering the day in 1965 when I had been accepted into Komsomol. I was not yet fourteen, but because of my good grades and behavior and my activities in social work, I had been recommended for membership in Komsomol. I remember how disappointed I was when we were accepted not individually but in large groups and when all the pupils without exception, including those who did not deserve it to my mind, were accepted. I had thought membership in Komsomol a great honor, but it had been given to everyone. I remembered how I had looked every minute at my Komsomol badge—a red banner with a golden profile of Lenin—and how I took my Komsomol card everywhere with me.

Now, a little more than five years later, I am again in the office of the District Komsomol Committee.

When my turn came, we entered the big hall of the meetings of the Bureau of the Committee. There was a large portrait of Lenin and a tall, thin, neatly dressed man sitting under it at the head of a long table, covered with a green velvet tablecloth. There were three other members of the Bureau, the representatives of the larger enterprises of the District: a man who resembled the pictures of workers on placards and two women who looked like weavers, those old women of about thirty who do their hair only in buns and wear neat white blouses—anything else would be considered "imitation of the capitalist West."

They met me with a broad smile as though I were the next candidate for Komsomol and invited me to sit down at the end of the table. My Secretary hastened to dispel their illusion. The mask of welcome left their faces, to be replaced with a very real expression of dislike. My illusion, of having to deal with business-like professional Communists, was dispelled.

Then I suddenly became deaf. I saw their shouting mouths, but could not make out one word from the flood. I sat with my hands on my lap under the table, trying to hide the short and threadbare sleeves of my old sweater. But as soon as I understood that they were insulting me, I forgot about that. I lifted both hands and stretched them forward with coupled fingers on the table. My back straightened. I raised my head and looked directly at them. Scraps of their words began to reach my mind.

"You have eaten Russian bread. We gave you an education."

"Who is that aunt of yours, a capitalist?"

"You hid your real face for five years, you deceived Komsomol!"

"Your parents are buried in this land." (I remembered the death of my mother, the Party veteran. This made me open my mouth.)

"I want to reunite with my family."

"We, the Soviet people, are your family."

"Please, let me choose my family myself."

"Shut up, don't you dare speak in such a tone or we shall arrange things so that you never go to your Israel."

I was silent.

"Ah, let her go to the devil himself. Give me her card." My Secretary ran up to him and handed in my Komsomol card. The Secretary of the Bureau looked at it with disgust.

"I don't understand," cackled one of the weavers, "How can *they* do it?"

"Don't you know," the worker explained, "that *they* always betrayed us and will always betray. Who do you think betrayed us during the war?"

I am silent! How happy I am to hear this. For all of my twenty years I have waited to hear these words and now they have been said. Never before could I really understand what anti-Semitism was and here it is. Now I have no more doubts. I know that I am right because I have seen what is wrong, what is evil.

I clenched my teeth and forbade myself to open my mouth. The shouts continued until the Secretary said at last: "Go away. We hope to see you no more."

"Thank you," I smiled at him, stood up, and went to the door.

"You've already prepared an anti-Soviet article, haven't you?" the worker sent the last shot at my back. My back answered him with silence and disappeared behind the door.

I neither noticed how my Secretary took leave of me nor how I passed the big park in front of the Committee's building. Even the drizzling rain could not put out the flame which was burning inside me and in my face. I wanted to do something. I was almost running, although I didn't know where to go. Then I decided that in spite of what had happened or rather because of it, I must go to my classes at the Institute. I would continue to study, I would continue to live in spite of them. I bought the notebook and a pen in a bookshop, went down into the subway, and began to write in the subway car. How right I was to begin then. Now, as I am finishing, I feel much quieter. I have already lost the shock at feeling the hatred directed against me. My holy indignation has combined with a feeling of happiness that I am on the right path. But I shall never forget the hatred.

* * *

A week later when I had gathered all the necessary documents, I went to the Interior Ministry to hand in my application. The official, a red-headed dried-up woman, was not very welcoming. She looked through my documents and, having found nothing wrong, she provided me with "discouraging" information about military service for girls in Israel. When I did not respond, she concluded: "I accept your documents, but I assure you that you will be refused."

"Why?"

"Because you haven't any close relatives there."

"What if I haven't any close relatives at all?"

"Then you should stay here."

I stood up and left the room. I had finally gone through the seven circles of Hades, and felt terribly relieved. But I shall be alone no more. There are people doing the same thing I'm doing and thinking the same way. I must be with them.

At David's "going away" party I saw many new people of different ages, professions. They are all together and I shall join them. I'll find friends my own age, I'll be young again. And I'll start the same way I came to Zionism two years ago—at the celebration of Simhat Torah in the synagogue. Next year in Jerusalem.

* * *

On the 4th of October, I approached the synagogue with mixed feelings of happiness and the remorse of a prodigal daughter. The narrow street had become even more crowded than two years before. I passed through the dancing, singing, shouting, and laughing crowd without seeing a single familiar face. But I hoped to meet my old acquaintances in front of the synagogue.

That day in the morning a man had called me on the telephone: "This is Yosif speaking."

"What Yosif?"

"I came from Riga."

I searched back in my memory and fortunately it didn't fail me. "Oh, yes, how are you and when did you come?"

He was one of the boys whom I met in Riga. I hadn't known him well, but I remembered him as a tall, very handsome boy with curly black hair. We arranged to meet in the evening in front of the synagogue.

And now I ran into him there. We turned aside. At twenty years old he only slightly resembled that teen-ager of 1967. He gave me regards from my Riga acquaintances and asked about me. I suddenly felt that I wanted to tell him everything. All that had happened in the last two years poured out of me. There was something of Riga in him and he looked at me with the eyes of Riga. And those eyes were sad. Yes, Yosif, I know that I look awful. Yes, Riga, I know that I have changed a lot. But I have come back and that is the most important thing.

We joined one of the circles and soon lost each other in the crowd. I met some of my old acquaintances. They greeted me and asked no questions. I was grateful to them for this. New dances, new songs, new boys and girls dancing their ritual dances of the reborn Jew in circles. How much I had missed!

A foreign-looking but clearly Jewish man was standing in the center of one of the most active circles. There was a tape recorder in his bag and he spoke constantly into a microphone, translating the meanings of the songs. I prompted him with the translation of one of the lines in order to show that I knew English. I was not mistaken. He seized me by the hand: "Do you know English?"

"Yes."

"Would you consent to answer some of my questions in English?"

"Yes, with pleasure."

We stepped aside and I told him my story. One of his questions was: "Why are you all not afraid to be here?"

The question was difficult and I replied with a joke: "We fear nothing near the synagogue."

I don't know whether he was satisfied with the answer, but I was not. It was not true. People can be afraid in any place. I was not afraid then because I had never yet been punished, because I did not realize the real danger of it. I think the majority of those who were there were in the same position. When I came to realize the danger, I became very much afraid, but I still came to the synagogue.

A week later my aunt told us with excitement and fear that her friends had heard on a Yiddish broadcast from Israel an interview with a Moscow Jewish girl who had been expelled from Komsomol and had applied for an exit visa to Israel. Myra looked at me then with a smile.

I left the synagogue alone and went home. I was full of excitement after my interview with a foreign correspondent, joy about my return, and dreams of new friends, parties, activities. The long way home in the subway passed very quickly. I did not even notice how I reached my house in the darkness that usually frightened me.

Suddenly I saw that a man in a gray raincoat had entered my house before me. When I entered, I noticed him standing in the doorway. He stepped aside and let me pass. I began to climb the steps and it immediately occurred to me that he wanted to see which apartment I lived in. I climbed slowly trying to think of something, but the safest thing was to enter my apartment and be at home. I opened the door, closed it behind me, and stood near it holding my breath. The steps came up and then approached my door. The moment was so tense that I stopped being afraid and became all ears. The man lit a match and was probably looking at the number of the apartment. Then he hurried down the stairs. As soon as he reached the ground floor, I opened my door and ran up to the window in the staircase from which I could see the street. Three men in gray raincoats came out of our entrance. I followed them with my eyes, smiling: "You haven't forgotten me, have you? O.K. I shall try my best to live up to your suspicions."

10

What a marvelous idea. We are going to Riga in December. Natasha, Basja, Olja, Bettie, and three boys. We decided to go at one of the last parties—just decided and that was that. None of us has any idea of how we will make it, but we all know we'll manage somehow.

It sometimes happens that an idea takes you so strongly that you feel if you don't carry through with it, you will not forgive yourself. For example, I cannot imagine now where I shall get the money for the trip. Then I think that by the end of the month I shall get my two weeks' salary and this will be just enough for the tickets to Riga and back. What shall I do when I come back to Moscow? I don't know. It will have to work out one way or another.

Maybe I shouldn't go. Oh, no. I must get away for a time. I must see something new. I am sure it will mean a lot to me. And then think of the fun with the friends. Cannot I give myself this pleasure? Just to dream about the trip makes me happy.

I shall go in my red velveteen suit and take Myra's black and white dress. She doesn't wear it any more and it is so becoming on me. All the girls are wonderful. Bettie is going with her husband, Zeyev. Two years ago when he used to come to my place he was Vladimir. Now he has become very religious and has learned a lot of Hebrew. She does not know what to do with him. He refuses to eat meat because it is not kosher. Where can she get kosher meat in Moscow? A funny couple.

Pretty, plump Basja will make us laugh all the way. She is so funny with her typically Jewish mannerisms. Olja has not changed much since 1967 when David first brought her to one of my parties. She has remained very bashful. Natasha is new. She is the youngest among us, only eighteen, but she is quite mature.

It is pleasant to have these friends. I think about them and it helps me not to pay attention to the situation at my job. And now the trip to Riga completely possesses my thoughts.

We are going for four days—December 4, 5, 6, and 7. The 5th of December is the holiday of the Soviet Constitution, so there will be no work. And the 6th and 7th are the weekend. But the most important thing is that these days are the Jewish holiday of Hanukkah. That is what really made us think about going to Riga. In Moscow almost nobody really knows how to celebrate Jewish holidays. And if they do celebrate, then they do it very symbolically in a Zionist way. But in Latvia all the rituals are carefully observed, and young people of our age know them as well as their parents. The whole of Jewish Riga will celebrate Hanukkah in families or in groups, but certainly according to all religious rules. And we want very much to see and to join in this celebration.

So we are going. We have decided and at least nothing can prevent me. All the others have to ask permission from parents, to ask them for money. I go when I want and where I want. I am free and independent. Is it good? I don't know. When I see problems between fathers and sons or when I watch a family quarrel, I want to close my eyes and ears and run away. But sometimes I feel I want someone to say "stop" or to advise me. But would I obey? I doubt it.

Are we really going to Riga? I cannot believe it! How happy I am!

* * *

The trip is over. We are flying back to Moscow. Every minute of those four days was happiness. Every moment was full of meaning. But I am not sorry it is over; such concentrated joy could not and should not last too long. Moreover, I feel that there will be a continuation of everything we found there. I saw it in the faces of our friends who saw us off at the airport.

We arrived in Riga just in time for the lighting of the first Hanukkah candle. (Now I know something about it.) We went to beautiful Ruth's apartment where the party was going to take place. Ruth has changed a lot since 1967, but she is still the same hospitable and easygoing girl. We are both a little reticent. It is so difficult to get rid of the unpleasant aftertaste of what separated us two years ago and was one of the reasons for my retiring. But we shall try our best, shall we not, Ruth? Isn't the idea that unites people more important than all the trifles that occasionally separate them? And I shall never forget that you were the first to tell me about Israel and what it meant to be Jewish. You brought me salvation in your beautiful hands saying: "Look . . . Listen . . . Read!" I remember your hands holding picture postcards with a blue sky and orange trees or thumbing a volume of Dubnov's *History of the Jews* or showing me a record of Yaffa Yarkoni. You gave me part of your great love for Israel and for this I shall always be grateful.

Ruth's mother rushed to us with questions in Hebrew. I hastened to escape. Her Hebrew, learned in a prewar Hebrew high school, was too good and too fluent for me to understand it. Zeyev would have to uphold the honor of the young Moscow Zionists.

The apartment was already full of people and many more were expected. They all knew we were coming and came earlier specially to meet us here. My dear friend since 1967, Tsvisha, everybody's pet; serious and mature Lev and his younger brother Yehoshua; Yosif, whom I had met in Moscow on Simhat Torah. I didn't expect to see him, for he had not been sociable in 1967. I felt very free with everybody else, but he made me nervous. He was too handsome and every time he spoke to me I began to talk very quickly and stupidly, avoiding his eyes. I certainly didn't want any emotional involvement now and there must be many girls in Riga who were interested in him. But he was so handsome, that I involuntarily sought him in the crowd.

Natasha was already talking to the brothers, Lev and Yehoshua. Lev was very clever and erudite. I wondered what they were talking about. Probably the eternal problem of Russian Jews, whether it was more important to revive Jewish culture in the Soviet Union or go to Israel. It seemed so stupid to argue, when everyone had already applied for visas to Israel. Anyway, what would be the use of reviving the culture when it had been deliberately and cruelly destroyed over and over again throughout the centuries? Well, Jews love to discuss. I could imagine the flood of facts, quotations, and Hebrew sayings Lev was throwing at Natasha.

The group in the corner seemed to be on the brink of a quarrel. Of course, Yiddishists and Hebraists. The Hebraists seemed self-composed and calm, confident of their victory. The Yiddishists were very aggressive, but Yiddish has no importance among the new generation of Russian Zionists.

The evening had not yet begun. We discussed the new songs we had learned. For us songs were a main source of inspiration.

"Let's have a contest—one song from Riga, then one from Moscow. Then we'll see who knows more."

"O.K." Riga began with a Hasidic song: "*Yossis alayich Elochayich, kimsos hosn al kalo*" ("The Lord will rejoice over you [O Israel] as a groom rejoices over his bride"). A wonderful song! But I winked at Natasha; we answered with one of our best "*Lo yisa goy el goy herev, lo yilmedu od milhama*" ("Nation shall not lift up sword against nation, neither shall they learn war any more"). They were delighted. The contest continued. Riga won. Many more songs, nearly all of them in Hebrew or in Yiddish, while most of ours were in Russian. But "*Lo yisa goy*" was recognized as the best song of the evening. And we knew something else that nobody, I was sure, knew in the Soviet Union—three Israeli folk dances. We had learned them from American tourists on the night of Simhat Torah. We danced and Riga admitted defeat.

Then someone spoke. A middle-aged man told us the story of Hanukkah. He was excited, looking at something far away. He was there then, fighting together with Judah Maccabee, cleansing the Holy Temple, lighting the oil in the small jug. He had quite forgotten that he was in the twentieth century, thousands of miles away from his Holy Land, among young people born in Galut, and that he was telling the story of their ancestors—a story some of them had never heard before.

A thoughtful silence fell in the room full of standing people. And then one of Ruth's family began to recite the benedictions and lit the first candle. I could not follow his biblical Hebrew, so

I looked around. I looked at the Jewish faces in the light of the candles. Their eyes reflected the glimmering flame, or perhaps it was their inner flame, aroused by the story of Hanukkah. Every time I see Jewish faces around me, I feel happy and safe. I touched Natasha's hand, "Look, aren't they wonderful, these people? They look like Israelis." But how could I know, having never been there? They were beautiful and that was why they looked like Israelis.

And Jewish eyes—eyes that can tell you everything, eyes that reveal, eyes that beg, demand, but seldom laugh. Eyes that live their own lives separate from their faces. Eyes that make me strong and sad, proud and frightened.

The boy, Leib Khnokh, could be described in two words—eyes and beard. Huge, black, sad eyes and a curly black beard. I wondered if Mary, his pretty girl friend, was not afraid of his eyes. There was one boy who was always laughing and couldn't stand still for a minute. He was full of energy, joy, and youth. His name was Izja Zalmanson. He was very young, good-looking, strong. Why shouldn't he be happy and gay? Why should we always carry the burden of our history? We might be the first generation of Happy Jews. (*Leib Khnokh, aged twenty-six, an electrician, was arrested on June 15, 1970. Sentenced to ten years of imprisonment in a hard labor camp. Mary Khnokh (neé Mendelevitch), twenty, student, arrested on June 15, 1970, pregnant. Released at the end of 1971. Arrived in Israel with her newly born son. Israel Zalmanson, age twenty-two, student. Arrested on June 15, 1970. Sentenced to eight years in a hard labor camp.*)

I looked at the Jewish faces. My dear people, I love you, I love my distant motherland. I wish that all of you will soon be in Israel and we will celebrate Jewish holidays at home. All of you are struggling for emigration to Israel, but I don't want you to become heroes because heroes appear when the people are in trouble. Pharaoh, let my people go without making them heroes!

The benedictions were over and I finished my prayer. Wine, cookies, jokes, conversation. The Riga boys helped us to learn the words of a new song. They wrote them down easily in Hebrew. Unbelievable!

It was already late at night when one of Ruth's best friends arrived. Always late, always busy, and tired, he was completely unaware of and uninterested in his good looks. He came to gatherings like this and sat in an armchair half-asleep. But at least he spent an hour among friends. I greeted him. I had met Misha in 1967. *Michael Shepshelovich, age twenty-seven, engineer, arrested in November 1970. Sentenced to two years in a hard labor camp.*

Pinchas, Leib's brother, with a deep bass voice, sang "Let My People Go." This song, by an unknown author, is so moving that we in Moscow could not help but sing it aloud at the synagogue. And now in Riga everybody joined in his singing with an aggressive readiness—bearded boys and slender girls, sad men, and vivid Jewish women.

I say to Pharaoh
Let My People go;
Let the Jewish People go
To their homeland.

Never shall I tire of repeating:
Let My People go!

Into God's way
Let My People go!

For your own safety
Don't keep My People
Let My People go home.

Ruth introduced us to a boy from Minsk. She said he was famous for his wonderful Russian, Yiddish, and Hebrew songs about Israel and about us, the Russian Jews. I had noticed him but would never have thought he was a composer and a poet. I would have characterized him as a mixture of Odessan Jewish hooligan and a *yeshiva* student. He was thickset with a wide neck and short beard, which set off his wide face. His sharp eyes were sometimes indifferent and often mocking. He looked out through round glasses which constantly drooped on his nose and which he automatically straightened with his middle finger. His rapid speech was interspersed with Jewish *hochmas* and his jokes could make even statues blush.

But how he changed when he sang his songs about Israel, beating the tempo with his right foot and swinging his right hand. Then he looked like a praying Hasid.

"*Nu*, Isroel, did you bring something new?"

"You know, I never come to Riga without new songs. This time I have two. One in Russian and one in Hebrew. I have called the first song 'The Nearest East of Mine.' Listen to it:

I live so far from you
In a distant and strange land
But in my heart I am from my birth with you
The Nearest East of mine.
The land calls me
In which I never have been
My land—my star
The Nearest East of mine.

When war came to your land
I suffered together with you
And together with you I burned in its flame
The Nearest East of mine.
And together with you after all troubles
I was happy with the victory
*I am your soldier and I am the same age**
The Nearest East of mine.

There the air is mine and the sand is mine
And all the people are my friends
My land, my country
The Nearest East of mine.

I believe I shall cover all these thousands of kilometers
And I shall come to you
And I shall come down to your land
The Nearest East of mine.

My dear fatherland,
It is lost in strange sands
My shield with six points
The Nearest East of mine.

No one moved or uttered a word. Nothing could express better the thoughts of everyone than this song. And these thoughts were sad. I had felt a lump in my throat at the words, "I

* Isroel was born on the 14th of May 1948, the Independence Day of Israel.

shall come down to your land." How could young people be so sentimental? But we are young only in age; in mind we are all two thousand years old.

Isroel broke the silence with his second song which was in Hebrew. It was called: "*Kahol velavan*" ("The Blue and the White").

The blue and the white
These are my colors
The blue and the white
The colors of my land
The blue and the white
These are my colors
For all my days, forever.

The blue and the white
There are no other colors.
The blue and the white
I repeat and repeat
The blue and the white
Like a song, like a dream,
The blue and the white
A hope and peace.
The blue and the white
Hermon and Kinnereth
The blue and the white
My heart sings.
The blue and the white
The sky and the snow
The blue and the white
This is so wonderful!
The blue and the white
These are my colors
For all my days—forever.

By the second couplet we had all joined in singing the magic line "The blue and the white." The chorus grew and grew and the song sounded like a hymn. We had been waiting for this song for years, the song of our faith and hope, our oath of allegiance and love for our motherland. Now it came and in the language of our distant past and near future—Hebrew.

* * *

Next morning we went to the Riga suburb of Rumbula. Thirty-six thousand Jews from the Riga Jewish ghetto had been shot and burned there. Until the sixties the bones had lain unburied. Then the Jews of Riga came with their children, made several huge graves, and put the bones in them. One grave was for the children. Each season the Jewish youth of Riga go there to clean the graves and to plant new flowers. On the anniversary of the destruction of the ghetto, thousands of Jews come there to pray for the memory of those slain.

In 1967 Ruth had brought me there and I took part in the summer maintenance of the graves. During heavy rains, little white bits of bones appear again and again on the ground—there is no end to them. The earth itself seems to remind people of the tragedy. At that time I had gathered some of these little pieces with black traces of fire and brought them to Moscow. Every time I felt fear, tiredness, or despair, I looked at those bones. They helped me to gain strength. The fire that had burned them nurtured the flame that had been lit in me.

And I remembered. One day at my friend's house I happened to see an album of photos from the Warsaw Jewish ghetto. The book was published in Poland and was a very rare thing in Russia. In fact such literature was "unadvisable" for a Soviet citizen. I had never seen it since that time. But every picture stamped itself upon my memory forever. During the whole week after I saw the book, I could think about nothing but those pictures. I was frightened, deadly frightened.

What if it comes again? They will take me. No, I shall escape. I do not look Jewish. They will not recognize me as a Jew. But Myra? They will catch her immediately. Then that will be the end. I shall go wherever they take her.

Stop it! I am going mad. This will never come again. Never. And then I have nothing to do with this. I was even born long after this. I am just imposing these thoughts on myself. They are unnatural.

Unnatural? But do not I belong to them? Do not even fingertips feel when the whole body is suffering? If they don't, then they are sick, their main senses are atrophied. But the fact is that they will die if the whole organism dies whether they feel it or not. But I feel and this is natural. This was my pain, my fear, my Holocaust. Can I forget all this?

This time we all went to Rumbula. The Jews from Moscow, far from all Jewish mass graves, went to swear that we also would not forget.

The remaining days passed in careless happiness. We went to the seashore and danced a sunny *hora* on the snow-covered shore of the northern sea. We retold Jewish jokes and fell into snowdrifts with screams of laughter. We threw snowballs and drank coffee with whipped cream in empty seaside coffeehouses.

The stars shone in the black sky and the moon threw its silver light over the snow carpet and the fairy-tale fir trees especially for us. And for us beautiful medieval Riga became more majestic.

Tsvisha, Lev, and Yehoshua were with us all the time. Yehoshua, with his silent girl friend, Rochl, and Lev with Natasha, continuing their endless conversation and he looking attentively into her serious eyes.

But Yosif surprised me more than anyone. He seized every free minute to join us and went with us on our trip to the seashore. Every time I saw him joining our evening Hanukkah parties or running to us along the shore, joy swept over me, but I showed it to no one and hardly to myself.

Generally we were all in love with each other and could hardly imagine parting. We promised that we would use the New Year holiday to meet. It was beyond all reason in respect to money and time, but they promised to come to Moscow.

On the 7th of December, they saw us off at the airport. We had paid our last silent visit to the Rumbula graves near the Riga airport and went slowly to the terminal. Until the last moment we could not imagine that we were parting, but the moment came. We shook hands with all the boys except Tsvisha to whom we could not help giving a kiss. Yosif was the last to whom I came to say good-by. I put on the most careless air I could and smiled:

"Please, Yosif, come to us on the New Year."

"I doubt it, but who knows."

We all ran to the plane, waving good-by. I looked back at Yosif and stood dumfounded. I could barely see his face, but his glance pierced me. There was such sorrow in his eyes that I was ready to rush back. "How could you not understand?" his eyes seemed to say. But I could not believe it and ran to the plane.

When we were airborne, everyone was sad. Then someone said, "Do you remember that joke about. . . ."

"Leave us alone."

The New Year was coming and we decided to welcome it in a circle of young people no older than twenty-five. The Zionist community had grown greatly during the past two years and we could afford to divide into two groups for the New Year's night.

It had long been our dream to form a youth group and to feel that we were not only Zionists, but young people as well. Later on we would be able to develop different kinds of activities for this group, different from those of the older people. We wanted generally to get together, go on trips, dance, drink, make new friends, and fall in love. If we were to live under such conditions for many years, we should develop and live naturally, according to the laws of Nature and social life.

The celebration of the New Year was the first step in this plan. Forty boys and girls wanted to come and we had a problem about a lack of space and food. We were not acquainted with the majority of our guests, who had all been invited through a chain of acquaintances. It would be interesting to see new people, but our happiness on that night depended on the coming of the boys from Riga. We were waiting for their call with bated breath. The boys had only three or four days of holidays before their examinations. They had to spend two nights on a train or pay a lot of money for airplane tickets. Therefore, we felt, their decision to come or not come would show their real interest in us: Lev's in Natasha, Tsvisha's in all of us, and Yosif's in . . . me.

No, I can't believe it. It is all nonsense. I am not a little girl to get myself involved in this childish game. But who is talking about love? I am waiting for all of them. I am interested only in useful and interesting friendships and further "business" ties. Do you understand this, you big fool? In order to make the suggestion more effective, I knocked three times at my forehead.

The call came very unexpectedly. All four of us—Natasha, Basja, Olja, and I—were at my place discussing the problems of the coming party. After I lifted the receiver and heard the words, "Riga is calling you," my hands began trembling, something jumped in my stomach, and I turned to the wall to conceal from the others the color of my face, which I was certain must have been green or even purple.

It was Tsvisha on the phone, as usual. He had only three minutes to talk, so, after the usual first "Hi, how are you?" he immediately said that they were all coming. "Who? You?" I asked, stammering. "What do you mean 'Who'? We. I, of course. Then, Lev and . . ." he was mumbling for at least half a minute "and Yosif."

The girls couldn't hear all this so they were sitting like runners on their marks with their mouths open. I discussed in short the date and the hour of the boys' arrival, the weather, and the three minutes were over.

"Nu?" the girls breathed out.

"They are all coming."

"Who, 'they'?" they shouted at me.

"All three."

"And Lev?"

"And Tsvisha?"

"And Yosif?" they all asked at once. We laughed, we danced, and then suddenly we all rushed to do something for the party.

There were only three days left.

* * *

On the 31st of December, we were on our feet from early in the morning, cooking, washing, and decorating the apartment of our friends, Bettie and Zeyev. They were one of the first Zionist couples to be married in the synagogue. I was not present at their *chuppah*, but they say that Rabbi Levin was unpleasantly surprised to see the newcomers, carried out the ceremony very quickly, and, when all the guests began to sing Israeli songs, hurriedly stood up to show that the ceremony was over.

Bettie was still having terrible problems with his *kashrut* (kosher diet) and Zeyev was wasting away. He was stubborn, like all mathematicians, and no less stubborn in Hebrew than in *kashrut*. During the two years since I had last seen him, he had turned into a walking encyclopedia of Hebrew.

So we were preparing for the evening, and our friends from Riga, who had already arrived in the morning, were walking around the capital. At last, when they couldn't stand the frost of — 30° C, they came. All three of them with black curly hair, tall and slender in black suits, white shirts, and black neckties. With beating hearts, we all pretended as much indifference as we could and extended all our affection to Tsvisha.

One by one, by couples and groups, the guests began to arrive and we were soon packed in like sardines. I was rushing from the kitchen to the room with dishes and bottles, having no time to talk to anybody or to take part in the general discussion—which was already flaring up.

"Have you heard about the universal census in January?"

"Sure. We have already discussed it."

"Are you really going to write that your mother tongue is Hebrew?"

"Of course, I am."

"But it's a lie, it is not true."

"Are you afraid to lie to them? Didn't they lie to you all of your life?"

"But we can't use their methods. And besides the census is statistics, not politics."

"No, now it has become politics. They'll show the results to the whole world and say that we forgot our language. We don't need it."

"That's why we have to learn it, but not lie in the official documents."

"One doesn't interfere with the other. We have to declare that we do exist."

"Ah-ah-ah-ah . . . !"

"What are you shouting?"

"I want you all to shut up. You are shouting like crazy."

"Excuse me for interrupting all of you. I have heard that you don't want to lie. Wonderful! But first we have to define what a mother tongue is and then see whether it is a lie to say that Hebrew is our mother tongue."

"As far as I am concerned, Hebrew has nothing to do with me. My mother tongue is Yiddish."

"How do you do! Where did you come from?"

"Why not? I also consider Yiddish my mother tongue."

"But Yiddish is a dying language!"

"Yiddish is the language of European Jewry and American Jewry. The whole of Jewish literature of the last centuries was created in Yiddish. Six million people were speaking Yiddish."

"But they will never return. And Yiddish in fact died together with them. Our reborn people speak Hebrew, our real language, the language of the Bible, not a jargon of German."

"I see that you talk according to Lenin."

"Hey, you, this is not a place to mention the classics of Marxism-Leninism."

"Jews! I heard a very interesting suggestion. It will surely put an end to all this argument. We will write neither Hebrew nor Yiddish. We shall write—Jewish language."

"That's fine!"

"No, I don't like compromises. I shall write Yiddish."

"You are all crazy! It is three minutes to midnight."

"Where is my glass?"

"There are plenty of them on the table."

"What is that in the bottle? It smells nice."

"Stop shouting. We must hear the striking of the clock over the radio."

"But don't forget to switch off when the hymn begins."

"Be sure I won't."

"Listen, it is already five. . . ."

"Six, seven, eight. . . ."

"Eleven, twelve!!!"

"L'chayim, l'chayim, l'chayim!!!"

We all—Natasha, Basja, Olja, I, and the boys from Riga—found ourselves, as if not intentionally, in one place. At that moment we wanted to be together. Though not yet daring to say anything aloud, our glances at that moment were clear enough. "I love you all! And I really wish you great happiness and that it come very soon . . . this year in Jerusalem!"

There was a hidden irony in our saying it, but we could not know it. We said it with a bitter smile and without the slightest hope.

Behind us were the echoes of *"L'chayim."* "To life!"

The argument was beginning again when we heard somebody's sad voice from the window:

"Look here, people are already having a good time and we are still arguing."

We all looked out of the window. A Russian man was trying to walk, swinging from one side of the road to the other. At last he met with a telegraph pole, embraced it, kissed it, and sat down in a snowdrift. "Their" New Year was already in full swing.

We decided to put on some music in order to avoid another argument. We had gathered Israeli records from all of our friends. A modern Western record would have offended most of the young people and they would have begun discussing our acceptance of other cultures.

The soft velvety voice of Yaffa Yarkoni filled the room. She sang *"K'she haynu yeladim"*—"When we were children." Everything of this kind, as for example, *"Hayu zmanim"*—"Those were the times"—strongly appealed to us. We felt it had something to do with us. We dreamt about the time when we would be able to say these words about ourselves in a different world.

Yaffa Yarkoni helped us not to go beyond the Israeli culture and to feel young. She helped us to fall in love. The boys embraced the girls' waists and the dancing couples began to mark time in the semidarkness. Nobody could really dance well and there was no mood to shake the floor with modern dances. We were all "serious people."

In my rushing from the kitchen to the room, in joining different groups for singing or discussion, I didn't lose sight of Yosif. I could not help admiring him. Tall and very broad-shouldered, though not unreasonably huge, he seemed too big for this small apartment. When it became very hot, Riga's boys shocked us by asking permission to take off their jackets. This was unheard of among young people in Moscow. So now Yosif was sitting in his white shirt and I suffered from the desire to touch his shoulders which emanated strength that seemed almost tangible under the delicate fabric. He rarely spoke and when he did, his face and lips scarcely moved, which added some special charm to his manners. His dark serious eyes would say a lot. He was unquestionably handsome, but what was more important was that he was not aware of it. Usually such an awareness spoils a man's manners, gives him some stupid superficial self-confidence. There was nothing of this kind in Yosif. He was perhaps even too modest, which made him sometimes seem awkward.

I had to admit that he was fascinating to such a degree that girls were afraid to build any hopes about him and left him without attention. Late at night, terribly tired and hardly moving, I found him sitting alone near a wall. Having explained to myself that I ought to be polite and engage him in conversation, I sat down next to him. He seemed glad to see me, which I immediately interpreted as being caused by boredom.

"Why are you not dancing?" I asked—the most stupid question I could think of.

"I am not a good dancer."

Silence.

"I didn't expect to see so many people here," he said with a note of disappointment.

"This was a very good opportunity to gather all of them to make friends and then to act together." (I hated myself for being so terribly businesslike at that moment.)

"I see you are eager to do something."

"And you are not?"

"We have always been doing something," he said evasively.

"I am not going to lose time. Two months ago I applied for the visa. The refusal will come in January. Time passes and, if we have to vegetate here, we must use this time for a good purpose. When I get this damned refusal, I am not going to sit idle."

"What are you going to do?" he asked sadly.

"I don't know yet, but something."

"How many times have you applied?"

"This is the first time."

"Ah-ah. We have applied for eight years."

I felt ashamed. "Did you try to do something else? Did you write to somebody in the government?"

"Better ask to whom we didn't write."

"Well, tell me, what can be done? Can we live like this through our young years? To wait is not the best form of living."

"Last year when some of the families in Riga got permission to leave, we were sure that our turn also had come. Everybody congratulated us beforehand. And when we were again refused, I was sure I would collapse, I would not live through it. But, I did, you see that I am still alive. And now I am more ready to wait than ever. This year I can't apply at all because now they expel us from the university for applying. Then, the Army, and after that there will be no hope at all. There can be no end to it, but still we have to remain alive."

I was terrified by his words, which sounded like a verdict. I could not accept it. I needed some hope. And I felt this hope. So I was quite serious and sincere when I predicted something great would take place in the coming year:

"Still I have a definite presentiment that this year of 1970 will be special. Something great, bad or good, I don't know, is going to happen. I am sure. You will see."

"Maybe, but don't expect too much," he said. "You can be easily disappointed."

There was tenderness in his tone. I felt that he cared about what I felt, but I immediately attributed it to the general kindness of his nature. To end this difficult conversation, I asked, "Whom do you have in Israel?"

"My father's mother and sister are there and also my mother's brother."

I felt stupid. He had not only political or national feelings, but must be yearning for close relatives, the more so since his grandmother was nearly ninety years old, as I learned afterward.

"And whom do you have in Israel?" he asked.

"An aunt from Tel Aviv!"

"What do you mean?"

"Don't you know the song? It's a new joke song in Moscow. A Jew from Moscow says that he loves his Tel Aviv aunt most of all and he can't live without her. In answer to a strict lady's question in the OVIR he answers that he wants to go to his beloved aunt. And he tries to prove to everybody that he must go to his Tel Aviv aunt and that she is impatiently waiting for him on the Mediterranean shore. So now we call all these second cousins twice removed who send us invitations Tel Aviv aunts. I have something of this kind."

I didn't want to interrupt our talk and was ready to sit with him all through the night, but the evening seemed to be over and I had to say good-by to the departing guests.

For the first time since we had started our long talk, I dared to look straight into his eyes. I looked and drowned. So deep they were, so much they wanted to say. They were like open gates to the soul, calling, calling. . . .

I felt my heart beating in my throat. No, I can't believe it! Does he really mean it? And why? Who are you? Where did you come from? Who or what created you and brought you here to me?

12

The 20th of November 1938 was a wonderful sunny day, untypical for Liepaja in late autumn. Everyone said that it was a good sign for a happy marriage. The wedding that was to take place that day was on everybody's lips. One of the wealthiest and most respected men of the Jewish community of Liepaja, Yosif Rusinek, was marrying off his twenty-four-year-old son Ezra. The bride was the twenty-three-year-old beautiful daughter of Yeshiahu Baron-Rosa. The match seemed perfect on all counts—bride and groom were young, handsome, well-to-do, and the object of envy and delight of the whole community.

Ezra had recently returned from France where he had studied at a technical school for watchmakers and he was now working in his father's watch factory. A true Zionist, Ezra was one of the founders of the "Herzlia" Zionist organization in Liepaja and after his return from France he became the leader of the local "Beitar" Zionist group. Calm and effective, he won everybody's respect, managing the camp for training youth for settlement in Palestine, getting certificates to Palestine, and gathering money for those who were emigrating. Certificates were valid for two persons, so those who were ready to go had to marry. Thus many artificial couples were able to enter British-ruled Palestine, some of them remaining together afterward, others parting as soon as they reached the Promised Land.

To go to Palestine was Ezra's dream, but he thought he could do it more easily than those from poor families and he was needed in Liepaja. Besides Yosif Rusinek was not very interested in leaving all his developing business to emigrate to Palestine. His wife, Rachel, businesslike and strong in character, had been trying to persuade him to go, since she felt the approaching danger from Germany, but when Rusinek bought new equipment for his factory and started to build his fourth house, she realized that further effort was useless.

Rumors of the Nazi threat became more frequent and threatening, but the Jews of Liepaja thought that if such people as Rusinek did not leave, there was no need for them to hurry. Many of them preferred to stay for the time being.

The brilliant and handsome Ezra had been the object of the hopes of many girls and their parents in the town and it was unexpected when quiet, modest Roza Baron became his choice. She had been living for three years in Palestine, studying at the Hebrew University in Jerusalem. The summer of 1938 she came to Liepaja on vacation with her friend and roommate Miriam, Ezra's younger sister.

They had both come especially to be present at the wedding of Ezra's second sister, the town's beauty, Hadassah. Before anyone realized it, Ezra, who was generally free with girls, was courting Roza and in November the town was taken by surprise by the announcement of the marriage. The young couple asked their parents not to make a large celebration, but just a small dinner for the family circle. They preferred to have the money go for arranging their move to Palestine.

The night before the wedding, Roza could not sleep. She had no doubts about her marriage. No, everything pointed to a happy life—they loved each other passionately, they were both from well-to-do families, and they both wanted to move to Palestine. There was nothing to worry her, but she had to follow the eternal custom of all young brides and spend a sleepless night in exciting dreams over the coming day and approaching happiness. Then the 20th of November 1938 dawned as a wonderful sunny day, which seemed one more sign that the marriage would be happy and unclouded.

The ceremony took place in the morning at the Barons' home and the two families contributed all the magnificence that was possible for such a small wedding. In the semi-darkness of the hall, the beautiful women in long, elegant silk and velvet dresses with high shoulders and men in tail coats and top hats discussed admiringly the slender bride and handsome groom. The glimmering candles, the sparkling silver of candelabras, and the women's diamonds were the only light in the hall. Tall, old Mr. Rusinek, with a large candelabrum in his hand, led his son to the *chuppah* as a father confident and proud of his heir. An aged, bearded rabbi recited the benedictions to a respectful silence. Everything—the beauty and love of the young couple, the elegance, the solemnity of the religious ceremony—added to the greatness and symbolism of the moment.

The young husband and wife left the same evening for Estonia to spend their honeymoon and to send from there one thousand English pounds to the British bank in Palestine.

This money, as proof of capital, would provide them with the right to obtain a special bourgeois entrance visa to Palestine. But soon Great Britain issued the "White Paper" which limited the number of entrance visas even for capitalists. So the young Rusineks had to wait for a regular certificate, which was delayed from month to month. Meanwhile Roza became pregnant and gave birth to a baby daughter whom they called Ilana. At last in June 1940, the long-awaited visa was received.

But it was fated that the moving be delayed once more, and this time not for months, but for tens of years. The second time the problem came from another quarter. On the 17th of June 1940, several days before they received their visa certificate, the Red Army occupied Latvia, and the people there found themselves in a large prison called the Soviet Union. Now the problem of an exit visa arose, but this proved insoluble. The Russians had their own plans with respect to the population and these plans were put into operation very quickly. One day the workers came to Rusinek and took the keys of the factory. Now it belonged to them. Everything was done quietly and quickly. Factories, shops, buildings were taken over and the owners did not resist. An iron fist bound everybody's hearts, wills, and minds.

Old Mr. Rusinek was appointed director of his own factory and Ezra worked there as an engineer. They still lived in their well-furnished, comfortable apartment and, watching little Ilana growing rapidly, the whole family forgot their troubles. But then a terrible rumor began to spread among the former propertied people. No one spoke of it aloud, but everyone grew fearful at the thought of it. No one could run away. Before long the rumor became a reality.

On Saturday, the 14th of June 1941, at four o'clock in the morning, a long ringing sound awoke the family. Ezra jumped out of bed, but everyone else seemed paralyzed with the one frightening question in their minds. Ezra stroked Roza gently, asked her to be quiet, and went to open the door. When he returned, he was terribly pale and told Roza to dress quickly. In a minute the house was full of policemen who began to search in all the drawers, wardrobes, kitchen. The family was ordered to pack in an hour, taking only the most necessary things. What was necessary? The women began to take everything that was at hand and throw it into suitcases.

The hour passed. They took the small, sleepy baby, the suitcases packed every which way, and left their home for good.

They were taken to a distant railway station with long rows of freight cars standing in it. The men were separated from the women and children and all were loaded into the cars. There were already many other people there—all pale, tired, and frightened. The torturing questions were in everyone's eyes: "Where are we going? What will be the end of this?" But there were no answers and it was better that way.

The train with the men in it soon left. The women and children were kept until nightfall and only then did their train also begin to move slowly. After several hours, it stopped. The women had been sitting silent, afraid to say a word. Tired children were sleeping.

Suddenly one of the cars was opened and Ezra entered. The door behind him was immediately locked and all found themselves again in darkness. Nobody could understand what was happening, least of all Ezra. All of the men were in the other train. None of them knew in what direction they were headed. At that particular stop Ezra had suddenly been called out of his car by a soldier. It seemed to be a railway station in an unknown suburb. The soldier led him along the rails to the women's train.

Years later, they learned that a Soviet secret police officer who used to buy watches in Rusinek's shop saw Ezra in the first train. That train, with former capitalist and bourgeois political leaders, was headed for forced labor camps. Ezra was there not as the son of his father but as a Zionist leader. The unexpected savior sent a soldier to take Ezra to the second train with the members of the families of the former capitalists, which was bound for Siberian exile. Thus Ezra was reunited with his wife, mother, and daughter.

In a month they reached the Yenisei River and were loaded onto a steamship. The families were being distributed among different kolkhozy (collective farms) on the banks of the river. No one wanted to take a family with an old woman and a baby, so the Rusineks were left until last and sent to the distant village of Yefremovka. While standing on the ship and looking at the wild forests and empty villages on the banks of the river, old Frau Rusinek said, "They brought us here not to live but to die."

But the Rusineks and thousands of other Jewish and Latvian families were brought there to struggle for life. Some of them won—others perished.

The Rusineks were at first lodged in an old stable. There was no work and no one knew what to do with them. They exchanged the clothes they had with them for food. The peasants, who were dressed in rags, were glad to give bread, potatoes, milk, and even meat for dresses, jackets, and trousers. Once a week the family was obliged to register with the authorities so that the latter should know that their "exiles" had not run away. But where could they run to? The Taiga? After several weeks, their living conditions improved. They were settled in a room with another Jewish family. They even had a Russian stove. But no stove could cope with the Siberian winter and icicles grew in the upper corners of the room. Little Ilana would lie in bed watching these icy monsters. There were beds in the room and a table which served as a bed for one of them at night. Life went on.

The Siberian women neighbors were intrigued by Roza. "They say you studied at the University. What did they teach you there? You don't know how to do anything. You cannot even wash the floors or milk a cow." When they heard that in big cities the toilet was in the house, they threw up their hands: "My God, what a stink must be in the house!"

And the Rusineks lived there, learned to wash floors made of boards, to milk their cow, Zorka, to bring water in two big pails from a distant well, to use the wooden toilet several tens of meters from the house.

At last they discovered that somebody in the village had a clock and the commandant of the district owned a watch. Ezra repaired them and got food for the family. Then Miriam, who was living in Palestine, discovered where they were and began to send parcels. Someone advised Miriam to send them an invitation to come to Palestine, which by a miracle reached the family. Ezra took it to his commandant. The man proved to be very kind.

"Take it away immediately," he said, "or I shall have to report you. I have not seen this. Forget about it."

Ezra asked permission to move to a city where he could earn more by his work. And after a while they were loaded onto a steamship and went to Krasnoyarsk.

Years passed. Life in Krasnoyarsk was better. In 1943 old Yosif Rusinek was released from the labor camp as unfit for work. Though he had seldom been employed in hard labor but had repaired watches for the authorities of the camp, the harsh regime of the life had undermined his health. He went back to his family with a serious heart condition.

Still he was anxious to return his family to life and to their home. In 1947, when the time of their exile expired, he went to Riga, registered himself in its suburb (the capital of the Union Republic was closed to former exiles then), and began to arrange things for the return. Meanwhile, the family still lived in Krasnoyarsk, waiting for news from him.

One day while Ezra and old Frau Rusinek were out, a postman brought a telegram from Riga. Roza was at home and at that moment was teaching the seven-year-old Ilana how to wash the floors. The little one felt very important and was upset when the postman interrupted them. Roza took the telegram, read it, and with a scream dropped into a chair: "Father suddenly died of heart attack," said the telegram.

When Ezra came home, they both had only one thought over-riding their own grief and despair—to protect their mother. They ran to the post office and begged the telegrapher to type another message that should simply speak about father's illness. Several days later they showed Frau Rusinek the real telegram. Rachel lay in bed and did not talk or eat for several days. Meanwhile an old family friend buried Yosif Rusinek in the Riga cemetery.

That same year the Rusineks were finally able to return to Riga. What happiness to come back, to see old friends, all of whom offered their help, their rooms. This time the tears were of joy.

But Hadassah did not come to meet her mother and brother. She, her husband, and their two-year-old son had perished in the ghetto. Roza found none of her large family. All were gone. Only brother Mulja was living in Israel. And there were not even graves over which to cry and pray for them. Roza shuddered as she remembered having considered leaving little Ilana with her family.

But they had come back to live and again to hope. They had many friends; they had Miriam and Mulja in Israel. They now had their long-dreamed-of motherland, the State of Israel. For this it was worth coming back to life. Roza found that she was pregnant, and when the baby arrived in its due time, it was a beautiful strong crying son, demanding a happy life. He was given his grandfather's name and became a symbol of the family's rebirth.

Yosif was only nine months old when the family again had to escape. In 1950 the Soviet authorities began sending to Siberia all the families that had returned from exile. This time the Rusineks did not wait for the night guests, but packed the necessary things and left Riga. After a few months of wandering, they settled in an old southern Russian town on the Azov Sea—Taganrog. The first years were difficult, but they passed. Ezra began to earn more by his work, the family was gradually adjusting to the environment. They now had peace and safety. Riga friends did not forget them and came almost every summer to see them. Friends of their Zionist youth, who had returned from exile or from the ghetto's half life, came, aged and quiet. How much can a human being endure? A lot, if they are all still alive. They came now with their late little ones, big-headed, big-eyed, big-eared Jewish children, and for their sakes' their parents would not lose hope.

Every year Ezra and Roza quietly celebrated the Jewish holidays and their clever Ilana and little Yossi knew that there were things that should not be mentioned at school.

Miriam was the first to learn that old people in Latvia were being allowed to reunite with their children and immediately sent an invitation to her mother, but the Russian authorities of the Taganrog District refused the application. Then Ezra thought of another way. He registered his mother in Riga in his friend's home and the application was sent to the Riga Department of Visas. It worked.

The entire family went to Moscow to see off their eighty-year-old mother and grandmother, who was making her long-awaited *aliyah*. All were silently crying. Rachel held her beloved grandson by the hand and didn't let him go until an airport servicewoman separated them at the barrier. From there she went alone. Miriam met her in Vienna. It was 1961.

And in 1963 the entire family moved back to Riga.

They immediately began to apply for exit visas with Miriam's invitations. All were refused. After the first application, Ilana was expelled from the fifth year of the Medical Institute and began to work as a nurse. That blow was unexpected, but it strengthened all of them. They would not give up now. In 1964 Ilana married and in 1965 little Hadassah opened her large dark eyes to the world. Yes, they would live. Live . . . and struggle.

13

The first days of the New Year, 1970, passed with a carelessness and joy which we were all trying hard to hold on to. We went skiing and tobogganing and just walking along the streets. In the evenings we went to the fanciest cafes and spent much money. We could not deny ourselves this pleasure which added to the happiness of being together.

We tried not to get involved in any of the Zionist activities because of the visiting boys from Riga; we just wanted to have a rest from everything. But suddenly on the 3rd of January, we got a note saying that an American rabbi was visiting Moscow and that night he was having dinner in the synagogue. We immediately rushed there.

The dinner had already begun. A gray car was standing near the entrance of the synagogue and two gray civil men were idling about. We entered the synagogue, hoping to see the rabbi coming out. One of the synagogue men, in black rags, a mumbling hunchback, rushed to turn us out, but a second one, blackbearded, but no better dressed, shouted at him: "Don't dare, you spy! They came to see the rabbi. It is their right. Didn't they come to their home?"

The scene amused us. We felt stronger. But when the hunchback retreated hastily, we understood that we could easily be fooled. There were other exits to the synagogue. One by one we penetrated into the backyard and stood near the window and door of the dining room. We could hear the clatter of crockery and low voices.

"They are eating," we said to each other.

"Yes," we answered each other.

We knocked at the door and excused ourselves for interrupting the dinner. Another hunchback appeared. It seemed that the rabbi, being himself a tall and handsome man, liked to surround himself with dwarfs.

"What do you want?" the hunchback asked rather inhospitably.

"We want to see the rabbi."

"What rabbi?"

"The American one."

"Go away!" he suddenly said rather illogically. "Go away or I will call the militia. You are hooligans."

The door closed. We looked at each other and then knocked again.

The hunchback appeared again. This time he was supported by a long, bony old woman who shouted at us in a whisper through the hole in the window.

"We are not hooligans. We only want to talk to the rabbi. We are also Jews."

"You are not Jews, you are hooligans. I told you that once already. So don't bother us." He pulled the door, but this time it didn't close. The strong foot of one of the boys was holding it.

The hunchback became furious. He thought we were going to rush into the room, but we were very careful not to make noise, lest we find ourselves in the hands of the militia.

"We want to speak to the rabbi!" we repeated three times loudly, once in Russian, once in Yiddish, once in English. The rabbi didn't come out. We let the hunchback close the door.

We again looked at each other and suddenly a brilliant idea struck one of us. We began to sing. "Let my people go," "*Artsa Alinu*" ("We went up to our country"), "*Shalom Aleichem*," "*Palmach*"—anything that came into our heads.

The rabbi did not come out.

We continued our concert until we got a signal that the hunchback was calling the KGB. We divided into couples and dispersed through the nearby backyards.

The rabbi did not come out. . . .

A few days later an article appeared in *Izvestia* that an American Rabbi so-and-so had visited the Moscow Choral Synagogue. His visit took place in a friendly and cordial atmosphere. The Chief Rabbi of Moscow told Rabbi so-and-so about the happy life of Jews in the Soviet Union. Rabbi so-and-so left for the United States with a feeling of satisfaction at having received a full and exhaustive picture of Jewish life in the Soviet Union.

The rabbi did not come out to the Jews. . . .

* * *

All four days passed under a constant dread of parting. We tried our best to forget it, but the end of every wonderful evening reminded us of the end to come.

On the second day of January when we went tobogganing I hit my foot violently. It became terribly swollen and I could hardly step on it, but nothing could prevent me from taking part in all our gatherings, and I spent the rest of our days leaning on Yosif's arm. Every evening he took me home and in the morning he came to pick me up. We usually walked in silence or talked quietly on general subjects. When, in the evenings, we reached the door of my apartment, I hastened to say "good night" and disappeared behind the door. He was left noticeably disappointed and upset, but I made certain not to be responsible for what had to happen sooner or later anyway.

On the evening of the 3rd of January we went to one of the best Moscow restaurants, Pekin. Its Chinese waiters had long since left Russia, but the menu was still Chinese. We were not acquainted with the dishes and decided to order those that had the funniest names. Thus, trepangs that didn't want to be chewed but slipped immediately inside appeared on the table; then followed a pork ball and the seed of a lotus tree and other different "mao-tze-tungs." We all helped to spoil each other's appetites by suggesting other dishes like "gefilte" snakes or cocktail of flies.

At last, having nourished ourselves with Homeric laughter, we all went to dance. While everybody else was dancing, Yosif and I sat at the table, but at the end of the evening I asked him to dance with me. He was surprised but game. He was really a bad dancer, but I enjoyed feeling myself in his arms. On my part I did my best to move gracefully on my one good leg.

We couldn't all part just like that. We had to promise something to each other. And we promised to go together in four months to Tallinn, the capital of Estonia, a small but very beautiful city which has managed to preserve its Middle Ages character and looks like the scenery for a knight's ballad.

The next day we saw off our boys. Tsvisha and Lev were leaving by train in the morning. We stood on the platform, not knowing how to express how much we would miss each other. We sang our favorite song "*Lo yisah goy el goy herev.*" The girls tried to keep back their tears. I didn't cry but I was ready to hang myself.

The train began to move. Tsvisha began to kiss all of us on our cheeks. We all turned our backs on Natasha and Lev to give them time to say their own good-by to each other.

The train left. Yosif was to leave in a few hours by plane. We went to our friend's house to spend these hours. Time mercilessly passed. When we got to the friend's house, I retired to a small room to lie on a bed and to give Yosif an opportunity to come to me. He came immediately and asked about my leg.

I was very excited. I stood up, tried to walk, and looked for something on the table. He asked me to sit down. I did. There were pictures scattered all over the floor. We had used them for decorating our New Year's party. One showed dancing Hasidim, the second dancing young Indians, and the third seemed made especially to depict our friendship. A girl and a boy are sitting on a swinging rope, kissing. One end of the rope holds the Kremlin tower with a red star and the other the tower of the Dome Cathedral of Riga with a rooster on it. Both towers are bent to each other under the heaviness of friendship and love of the boy and the girl.

"I shall take it with me to Riga," Yosif said, showing me the picture.

"What for?" I asked and shrugged my shoulders.

His face fell at such lack of understanding or unwillingness to understand.

"It was all childish, and not serious. This picture is not true." I did my best to worsen the situation. "I wish it were you who had hurt your leg, not me."

"Why?"

"Then you could stay longer in Moscow."

"What for if everything was childish?"

"Just so. It is very nice to be all together."

"Didn't you understand that I didn't come to be all together?"

It was already too much. I didn't answer.

The talk continued like that all during our trip to the airport until, seeing the lights of the terminal in front of me, I understood that I was playing games with my own destiny.

"Don't pay attention to me, Yosif, I am just trying to sound very clever."

"What for?"

"I don't know. Perhaps to keep myself safe."

"Safe from what?"

"Safe from disappointment."

He did not understand. He was to learn many things before he would be able to understand what I say. But at that moment he was patient enough not to ask any more questions.

I just added, "Everything will be O.K. Tallinn will solve everything, I promise you."

Standing aside, I gave him time to say "good-by" to everybody. Then he ran toward the boarding bus, embraced and kissed me on his way, and climbed aboard the bus. I found a small piece of paper in my hand with his address. I looked at it. I liked his handwriting, but his second name, which I saw for the first time, sounded very strange and out of place: Rusinek.

And Yosif Rusinek was sitting in the bus which hadn't yet moved and looking at me with his torturing gaze. There was a big question in his look. I couldn't answer it yet, so I avoided his eyes.

* * *

We were left alone with our thoughts. Natasha couldn't understand herself, and Lev's "attack" frightened her and put her completely at a loss. Lev, it seemed, was not going to lose time and was as swift as a tank. He was going to write frequent letters and in March he planned to spend three weeks of his annual vacation in Moscow. At the end of March, he wanted to go back to

Riga with Natasha's love ensured and definite plans in mind. I was delighted with his purposefulness and swiftness and wished him success.

For me, the four months that I had to wait until our Tallinn meeting seemed more than an eternity. I was happy and proud to have deserved attention from such a boy as Yosif and yet sad that I had let myself become involved in a love story which was such a good nutrient for my bacilli of craziness. We were each to wait alone for the great thing that I had predicted had to happen this year and for Tallinn. But deep in our hearts, we prayed that the second would take place before the first.

The day after they left, we counted and told each other that we had 116 days to wait and each day we counted again and informed each other of the number of days left. We thought and talked only about Tallinn. We saved every kopeck to gather money for May. We all had new clothes made that were as fancy as possible. We were crazy. Natasha and Olja, who worked together in a Research Medical Institute as laboratory assistants, would be standing at the dissection of a corpse looking somewhere ahead. Then they would nudge each other and whisper, "Stop thinking about Tallinn." I was sitting at my table over papers for hours, thinking, then scolding myself, and again thinking. We were all crazy.

I gave myself and Yosif two weeks before I wrote him the first letter. In the meanwhile we all took our exams in the Institutes, but we cared nothing about our marks. We felt our studies in Russia were purposeless and useless, yet we continued because you don't simply leave a university.

* * *

On the 13th of January, I, like all of us, received my long-awaited refusal. It came, as to all of us, in the form of a postcard saying, "Please call us at Tel. No. so-and-so." Like all of us, I called the given number and, like all of us, I heard the words, "Your application to leave for permanent residence in Israel has been refused." Like all of us, I asked: "When can I apply again?" Like all of us, I heard, "In a year." Not like all of us, I said, "Thank you" because I am usually polite over the telephone. To make the conversation more amusing, I answered myself before the woman-automaton and proved to be always exact. But it seemed to me that I heard in her tone something special concerning only me. She seemed to be saying: "You crazy girl! We don't even pay any attention to your application. You think we don't know what kind of an aunt you have in Israel. Stop interfering with our serious work! You will never be allowed to leave, but you will be punished, like all of you Jews!"

But maybe it only seemed that way to me. Not like all of us, I was quite alone after this telephone call. I couldn't describe it to anyone, so "like" it was and I didn't expect any special reaction in myself to this "news."

I finished my long working day and dragged myself home. I felt exhausted as never before. On reaching home, I threw my bag somewhere, didn't wash, didn't go to the kitchen to make something to eat, but sat down dully on the sofa. My whole body was tired. Every finger, every bone was aching. I leaned my head against the wall and turned it left and right, right and left. The electric light bothered me. I felt sick to my stomach.

And my eternal companion, who had been silent since "the doctor's lesson," my inner Satan, the author of all my bad thoughts, was immediately there: "What have you done? You have made your bed, now lie in it. People who were fond of you now hate you and are afraid of you. You could have made such a brilliant career there and now you are nothing. Your life is senseless, it is nothing but emptiness. Israel?!!! It is your imagination. What do you know about it? A few postcards and a number of songs. Is it worth sacrificing your whole life? And if it *is* something, you will never get there!!!

"What have you got instead? Loneliness. Yes, yes, complete loneliness. You try to play games with your new friends, try to feel young and don't really get any satisfaction from it. Don't deceive yourself. And from me you can't conceal anything."

"Shut up!!!" I cried to him. "Don't you know there is no way back and there's no use in such talk?" But this was all I could tell him, as he was not the kind of person to accept fine words. He was the other part of me.

And suddenly a feeling of terrible guilt swept over me. I thought about those good comfortable Jewish people whom I had been "stirring up" all those years. Besides having deprived them of their equanimity, I may have pushed them to the same abyss of hopelessness and baiting. Did I have the right to do it? Is it in my power to judge people, to decide what is bad and what is good for them, to change their destiny?

But I was bringing truth to them. And by no means do I blame those who had once brought it to me. I am grateful. If there was somebody to blame, it was only myself. I had free choice and I had chosen my own destiny.

But those people on whom I was trying to impose my new truth. . . . Yes, that was it. New truth, old truth, my truth, his truth, their truth. What is more important—all these truths or happiness and peace of mind?

My glance passed along the shelves of my bookcase: the box with the bones from Rumbula, a textbook on the history of the Communist Party, an album of pictures of the State of Israel, a typed brochure from the Underground democratic movement in the Soviet Union. I closed my eyes. I was dizzy. I shall answer no more questions. New answers—new truths.

I looked at the clock. It was 11 P.M. I had been sitting in thought for four hours. All the Russian programs of the "Voice of Israel" were over, but I switched on the radio. I heard Israeli music and then a low, strong, man's voice speaking in Hebrew. I smiled, seeing my poor devil, Satan, flying away through the window as devils are supposed to escape at the sound of a cock at dawn.

I stood up, stretched myself, and went to the kitchen. I had been unexpectedly and easily saved.

14

Natasha suddenly had a great many troubles.

I had met her mother at one of the Jewish parties in September 1969, the first one I had visited after my "voluntary retirement" for two years. I hardly remembered her face, but when I suddenly ran into her at the Committee for Standards which I often visited on business, I recognized her immediately. At that party she was playing the piano and her father, a hale and hearty man, was dancing *freilachs.* She was very happy to see me and was eager to introduce me to her eighteen-year-old daughter, Natasha. At that time young Jews had begun to have very specific problems and badly needed the friendship of their own people. I was pleased to learn that they lived only three minutes' walk from my office and I should be able to visit them even during my lunch hours. Soon I became their frequent visitor, as well as a very good friend to Natasha.

Natasha and Inna, her mother, who was thirty-seven and looked very young, were more like two sisters than mother and daughter. And they treated each other as sisters, with all the shortcomings and advantages of such a relationship. They lived in a big room in an apartment of several other rooms, each being occupied by another family. The apartment didn't have a bathroom and the house seemed to be falling apart. It was one of those beautiful houses in the center of old Moscow with a view of the Kremlin, a house which once had been owned by the Russian bourgeoisie and every apartment had been rented by a respectable family. After 1917 the apartments were each crowded with several proletarian families and since then left almost uncared for.

The room now occupied by the Slepyan-Kamzel family was divided by a large cupboard into three parts: entrance, a corner for a bed, and "the hall." The grandfather slept on the bed, Natasha and Inna on a sofa, and the grandmother made for herself a folding bed at night.

I liked the family very much for their intelligence, vividness, and hospitality. They compressed in themselves Jewish and Soviet history.

Abram Kamzel came from a well-to-do Jewish family, with all the children following different paths in life. One son was an Anarchist, the daughter was a Socialist Revolutionary, and Abram became a Bolshevik. In the saddle on a fiery horse, he had galloped through World War I, the Revolution, and the Civil War, fighting for communism, defending his young state, and brandishing his saber against the revivals of the old order, among them religion in the Jewish *shtetl.* And just so, in the saddle, swinging his saber, he had burst into a Jewish *shtetl,* fallen in love with sixteen-year-old Ronja, stood for a few minutes with her under the *chuppah,* then lifted her into his saddle, and galloped off.

Keeping pace with the breakneck course of history, he had been in the diplomatic service and various Party posts, always active, indefatigable.

Then in 1938 he fell out of his saddle, was expelled from the Communist Party, and sentenced to be shot. He was "an enemy of the people," "a traitor against the course of communism." Some miracle saved him. He jumped again into his saddle and rushed to fight against fascism, but this time his horse was lame in one leg.

In 1952 he again fell, was expelled from the Party, and lost his job. He was reduced simply to being a Jew. Soon he again saddled his Communist horse, but this time it was lame in both legs. It limped for some additional kilometers of time and then fell down and died.

Abram had a son and a daughter. His son had his own life with his family and, in addition, was a good Communist. His daughter, Inna, with a mass of curly red hair and burning eyes, inherited his idealism and activity, and viewed life as her parents saw it. Together with her father's horse, her fiery foal had been gradually becoming lame, but she was not afraid to look truth in the face.

When she was nineteen, she married a young Communist, Leonid Slepyan, a promising scientist, but in five years they parted, for his horse galloped through life without a single slip. He couldn't see deeply into things and in general they were quite different. Four-year-old Natasha had never since seen her father.

So three generations were lost in an open field when the idea of Israel found its way to them in 1967. Together they abandoned their dead Communist horses and went their new way, but this time on foot.

In 1969 the Party Organization of the Krasnopresnensky District of Moscow celebrated the 50th anniversary of the Party service of eighty-year-old Abram Kamzel, a recipient of a special Party pension. With a bitter smile, Abram received his golden diploma and sat down to write an application for a Party reference, the document which was demanded by the OVIR—the Department of Visas—for an application for Israel. In some months Abram Kamzel was for the third and last time expelled from the Communist Party.

At the same time Natasha was expelled from Komsomol at her Institute of Electronic Machine-building and was given sick leave for a year under the condition that she never come back to the Institute. Inna had gone through her own seven circles of hell in the Committee for Standards and had obtained her employer's reference.

They needed only one more document to be able to apply for the exit visa to Israel. Among other numerous documents, the OVIR demands a written and legalized permission from the parents of those who want to leave for Israel without them, irrespective of the former age or family status. This permission is required to indicate that the parents have no objection to their children leaving them without material support and, in general, that they are aware of the children's desire.

The OVIR didn't really pay any attention to this useless

scrap of paper and was ready to accept not only written permission, but also written prohibition. But without this paper, one could not apply.

And this was Natasha's problem. She had to find the man, unknown to her, somewhere in the Soviet Union, who was her father and ask for something he would not understand. The Jewish circle of acquaintances helped to find Leonid Slepyan in Novosibirsk and spoke to her father. He was very polite and largest universities, a respected Communist of a high military rank. He had a second wife and a young son.

On January 2, 1970, in the presence of Lev, Natasha called Novosibirsk and spoke to her father. He was very polite and surprised, at first could not understand anything but then, having grasped the character of the matter, interrupted and said that he was flying out immediately to Moscow and would speak to her personally. One step had been made successfully.

In a week he arrived and turned out to be a plump man and, by his face, definitely Natasha's father. This fact filled Natasha with disgust more than anything else.

The talks took place during three days in a hotel with Inna present. She did not interfere, but just looked at him victoriously. "Did you expect your daughter to be so strong, beautiful, and clever?" her stare was saying.

At first, of course, he refused definitely to give any documents of the kind and began holding forth about loyalty, Communist ideals, and the like. Natasha was ready for this kind of talk, but she was not going to argue with him on his terms. From requests she turned to demands, providing him with very clear explanations. She suggested that he should write that he had not seen his daughter for fifteen years and that he had not been responsible for her upbringing.

He could not do it and flatly refused. How could he, a Communist, confess that he had not seen his own child for so many years and didn't even take any interest in her. All kind methods having been exhausted, Natasha turned to the last one —threats. She told him that if he didn't give her this paper, she would certainly continue her struggle for the exit visa and write an official application through his Party organization, as well as write about the case abroad. Then he would hear his own name over the foreign radio program for the Soviet Union.

The stubbornness of the Communist was shaken. He made the last weak attempt. "And if I need your material help when I am old?" he asked.

"What did you say?" Natasha asked, horrified. Inna choked with anger. Her burning eyes reminded him of everything; that he counted with his own hands exactly fifty-two rubles and twenty-eight kopecks without adding a kopeck when she permitted him to send the allowance due his daughter on divorce instead of having it come through his place of work; that he never during these fifteen years had congratulated his daughter on her birthday.

The "father" was sorry to have said it.

At the end of the third day, he surrendered and wrote a paper with these words: "I have no financial claims on my daughter, but personally I do not approve of her decision." The same day he left Moscow.

During the entire three days, Natasha had been outwardly quiet but extremely nervous. On the third day in the evening I was sitting at home waiting for her call. She called and I heard her weak voice: "I am not well."

"What has happened?"

I did not receive any answer.

"Do you want me to come?"

"Yes, yes, immediately," I heard her sobs.

I put down the receiver and left at once to go to her. In half an hour I was at her place. She was lying on the bed like a little old woman, covered with an old warm scarf. She had already stopped crying, but she shivered and constantly rubbed her left cheek. She said that in taking leave he had kissed her on the cheek and she felt it was dirty.

I sat near her stroking her hand and said quietly, "You are a strong girl. You did something that not everybody would be able to do. It was a big victory. You should be proud of yourself. Now we shall be strong and persistent like you and we shall achieve everything that we want. And in 107 days we shall go to Tallinn. . . ."

Natasha smiled and soon fell asleep.

* * *

In March, Lev again came to Moscow. Natasha was very much excited and frightened. She was afraid of the big question because she could only answer it negatively or not at all. I advised her not to torture herself beforehand and assured her that the answer would come of itself in time. Two weeks after his coming, she was deeply in love.

They spent all of her free time together, he meeting her every day after work. They sat quietly in the dark corner of her room, whispering, telling each other many important things about themselves, getting to know each other.

Often I invited them to my quiet place, treated them to something tasty, and gave them good music to listen to. We sat together in the light of candles, dreaming of Tallinn. I had heard that Lev loved Mendelssohn's First Concerto for Violin and bought the record especially. We listened to it every day and we came to love it. The tension and excitement of the first part of the concerto reminded us of "the great thing" that was to come, and we became silent and thoughtful with its opening sounds.

One such evening was suddenly spoiled by a strange visit. A young blond, but Jewish-looking, man came and asked for me. I was astonished as I had never seen him before. And such a person could hardly have any relationship to me. He was dressed in foreign clothes in a pretentious kind of carelessness typical of those who care a great deal for their clothes. I was shocked by his Russian-style sheepskin coat of which we had only just begun to hear rumors from abroad. He was good-looking and I smiled to myself that such a visitor should come to see me, but soon everything became clear.

He said that he had heard about me from this one and that one (he mentioned some Jewish names which I had never heard before). I tried to tell him that I didn't know these people, but he answered quickly that it was not important and continued. He wanted me to join his company and also take my friends there. He was an artist and worked for the "Mosfilm" studio. He could introduce me to the cream of society, all of whom were interested in . . . Israel. They could get and exchange information and then, together with me, develop some activities. "We need your activity and energy!" he added. "If you help us, we can arrange later your escape to Israel, but only if you give your consent to work there for us."

"For whom?"

"For us." Poor boy! He got completely mixed up, I thought.

I looked at him with a smile, giving him time to say his say. I was really disappointed. I didn't expect the KGB to work so crudely.

My two guests were sitting in the second room as quietly as two mice. I was glad that they understood the situation and that this fellow would not see them in my apartment. I very politely saw the man out, took his telephone number, and closed the door behind him. I was not going to get myself involved in this provocation, even with my full understanding, but a week later I took one of our friends to the artist's place to show him the man and to remember him, just in case.

On the eve of Lev's departure, Natasha said to me, "You know, I love him. I really love him."

"Congratulations."

"No, I am very serious. It is so hard. You know, I can't tell you everything, but he is in danger. He can even be taken prisoner. It is so awful—I am so afraid for him."

At that time we hardly knew each other's part in the activities, but surely any of us could at any moment be arrested. I could easily believe her.

Lev was a typical Latvian Jew, as we understood these two words. He inherited from his parents an unusual delicateness of manners, politeness, love of his home and family. We attached these qualities to Latvian Jews because the Soviet morality, which ruins the family and coarsens outward relations among people, hadn't succeeded in doing there in twenty-five years what it had been doing in Russia for fifty years.

He was a chemist, not only by profession, but by nature

also. We always admired the way he set a table, when he took crystal or silver liqueur glasses and mixed cocktails like a new compound in a laboratory. He was outwardly reserved and exact and accurate in everything, including his relations with other people. He did not make friends easily, but when he did, he gave all his heart to the friendship. That was why, when I earned his friendship after three years of acquaintance, I valued it highly and was proud of it.

In 1969 he was expelled from the sixth year of the University for a "desire to leave for permanent residence in the State of Israel." Those who were not engaged in studies were taken into the army. In autumn 1970, during the draft, Lev's fate would be decided. He was very short-sighted, tall, slender, but strong. His being drafted depended only on the decision of the medical commission—or so we then thought, naïvely.

We could not imagine that our delicate, neat, brilliant Lev would go into the Soviet Army, which is a czardom of dirtiness, drunkenness, immorality, and humiliation.

When Natasha went to see Lev off at the railway station, I followed them at a short distance. I knew that she would be in distress after his departure and didn't want to leave her alone. I was afraid for her.

I was standing in a square in front of the railway station waiting for Natasha to come out, when I suddenly heard her voice calling me from behind. She was approaching from another side, deathly pale and walking as if she could hardly move. I ran toward her and had scarcely approached her when she began screaming. The passers-by stopped to look at her. I seized her head and pressed it to my shoulder to make her screams less loud. She choked and calmed down. Her hot tears mixed with the ice drops on my fur collar. It bothered her and she raised her head sobbing.

"I can't live like this any more. I am afraid for him. I want to be with him. I don't want to lose him. He is in such danger."

I was embarrassed and confused in the face of such suffering. In such cases I never know what to say or how to comfort a person.

"What do they want from her?" I thought. "She is so innocent, she can't have done them any harm yet. She doesn't deserve it."

Who "they" were, I didn't know. Maybe it was God himself or Fate, but we preferred "they" in thinking about our political enemies who were, of course, not responsible for our loves. But I had to say something to her and I began:

"Natulik, we are not at war. Nothing threatens his life. I am sure everything will settle itself one way or another. But if something happens, you must feel sure that you will always wait for him, however long it is. This confidence will help." I would have cut out my tongue if I had known then that I could evoke evil by making those evil prophecies. "By the way, do you know when Lev first became interested in you?"

"No," she said, suddenly becoming animated.

"He told me this. It was on Hanukkah in Riga on the evening of the first candle. He was reciting the benedictions over the candles when you suddenly raised your eyes and looked at him. He saw your deep serious eyes and immediately understood, 'This is she!' "

Natasha smiled and said, "You know how to comfort me."

I took Natasha with me that evening, as I had to pick up a typewriter and bring it to my house. At that time I had begun to type a lot—everything I was given and everything I myself wanted to type.

According to our main principle, "If you dance, you don't sing." I, having begun to type, should have stopped all my active outward involvements. But I could both sing and dance and I could talk to people and, moreover, I knew English. So I couldn't stop appearing at the synagogue every Jewish holiday where we gave our famous performances of Israeli songs and dances. Violating all the laws of conspiracy, I continued to do everything I found it possible to do.

Having decided to involve the girls in the typing, I arranged with them that they come to my place whenever they had free time and type as much as they could. We had quite a number of things to do. We typed collective petitions of Jews, historical selections, articles about modern Israel, as well as explanations for the Hebrew textbook *Elef Milim.* At the same time I was translating a guidebook of Israel by Zeev Vilnay into Russian and was preparing a picture album from 250 Israeli picture post-cards, with explanations taken from the backs of the cards. Having discussed and then checked the translations with our own "specialist" on Israel from Riga, I typed it.

This all helped us to feel that we were doing something useful and, if we had to wait, we were not wasting our lives doing nothing.

One day we were to meet a young American student who, according to his words, had something to say to the Jews. Natasha and I met him in the center of Moscow and we all went to a cafe. He proved to be unaware of anything and really wanted to listen more than to speak. He could hardly explain to which Jewish organizations he belonged and the only thing that we could get from him were two books on religion, several Jewish skullcaps, and prayer books. At that time we appreciated everything, but needed something else. At the end of the talk, he suddenly handed out ten rubles. He wanted to make his contribution to the cause and tried to prove that we could buy many important things with it. We laughed and said that we didn't need it, we had money and, in general, we didn't take money just like that. But he could not be dissuaded and at last forcefully put the money into one of our pockets. We were then in the street and didn't want to attract attention. He took his leave and we were left with his ten rubles, embarrassed and confused. We didn't yet know that this was the American way.

On our way back home, we suddenly found ourselves discussing not the talk, but the boy himself, his manners and clothes. Three things shocked us: he didn't help with our coats when we were leaving the cafe; he didn't pick up the coin which one of us had dropped; and, in saying good-by, he shook hands with us with his gloves on. We wondered whether it was generally like that in America.

Having discussed all this, we laughed—so unnatural it seemed to us. We were going down the escalator into the subway. I turned to face Natasha, who was standing behind me:

"Why not? Why should we always be clever and businesslike? Why is it not natural to discuss boys and clothes? Why should we go with a boy to a cafe only when we have to hide from the KGB? How old are you?"

"I am eighteen," she sighed.

"And I am twenty. And we are two old maids."

"But, Alka, some time, many years from now, we shall say '*Hayu zmanim* . . .' ("Those were the times") and people will say, 'Those are the women who were in prison in Russia.' "

"Yes, exactly. I don't know why, but we are sure that we shall have to go through prison."

"Because all this can't end well. We've turned your apartment into a real typing factory; we talk just like that with foreigners."

"But I didn't see any followers this time."

"Not this time, then next time. By the way, what about the article from Samizdat I brought you the other day, by Esenin-Volpin?"

"I've read it already, but he writes about what we should say when we get caught. I wish somebody would write about what we must do not to get caught."

"So do I. But let's forget about it. Let us dream instead."

"Of what?"

"Let's imagine that at this very moment we are told to leave."

"Just now, in the Underground?"

"Yes, what will you do?"

"I shall rush to the airport."

"Me also. But I shall call home and tell the folks first."

"O.K. And then we shall rush to the airport, just as we are."

"Without suitcases?"

"Of course. What do they matter then? Do we need them at such moment? We shall throw away our fur coats also and fly and fly. Isn't it great?"

"Fantastic. Take care, it is the end of the escalator."

Next day was Saturday. Natasha came early in the morning because we wanted to start typing as soon as we could. But, having adjusted our typewriters, we both suddenly felt that it was difficult to work without breakfast.

It was the end of the month and I had neither a penny nor a piece of bread at home. Having realized that we were both hungry, we could not forget about it and suffered terribly. The work didn't go well.

At the same time we couldn't look in one another's eyes, trying hard not to think about the American's rubles that were in my bag. They had already been allocated for two big albums that we had to order for our guidebook. But hunger soon proved to us that the work suffered from our stupid stubbornness and we began to think aloud:

"Isn't it better to have a good breakfast now and then do a really good piece of work?"

"But this isn't our money!"

"But what is the problem? In a couple of days, we'll get our salaries and buy the albums."

"And then we shall run out of money, not at the end, but in the middle of the month."

"Then we shall not buy them. Maybe this damned American gave us money to buy food, so that we could work. That would also be a contribution to the cause."

"You know, I am sick to my stomach and I have a headache."

"That always happens two hours before death."

"Thank you. O.K., there's no use wasting time. The money is

in the bag. Go buy something and I'll put some water on the stove."

In ten minutes Natasha returned with her hands full of packages.

"Anything left?"

"No."

"Fine."

We began preparing the food and soon were enjoying hot potatoes with herring, eggs, tea, and bread with butter. We noticed nothing until the food disappeared from the table and then we sat down immediately to type. Again we were avoiding one another's eyes, this time with shame. But the American fellow had made a good contribution to the Jewish cause in Russia.

I was corresponding regularly with Yosif, writing about everything except our "work." He was not only a bad dancer, but an awful pen pal. His letters were very short; everything in his life seemed boring to him and he had difficulty finding things to write about. But I could understand the main thought from his half-page notes. He missed me greatly, was dreaming about our Tallinn trip, and was thinking only of me. With every letter, I admired him more and more. He had already passed two of my three tests for a boyfriend: he was Jewish and he wanted to go to Israel. But did he take part in "the work," was he courageous enough to face the danger? Did he think about and want to help those who also wanted to go?

The answer came to me quite unexpectedly and filled me with joy and pride. One day I was approached by one of my friends and told that I might soon have a call from a man in another city.

"He will begin to tell you something which you will not understand. Don't be surprised. Just try to remember every word and then tell me. The contents will seem strange to you, but just try to remember everything. O.K.?"

I nodded. No questions asked. Two weeks passed and nobody called. Soon I forgot about it. Then one day Yosif called me from Riga, as we usually called each other every week, not being satisfied with just letters. "The work" played a very important part in our lives and it was extremely difficult to talk about anything else. We exchanged greetings, asked about our moods, studies, friends, and relatives. This time the talk was as usual. When all the subjects had been exhausted and I expected Yosif to say good-by, he suddenly began to tell me some nonsense. I asked him what it was. He was a little bit embarrassed, but repeated it. This time I caught the words and understood.

I was so happy to learn that "the man" was Yosif himself that I could not conceal my joy over the telephone. Yosif then for many hours cudgeled his brains to understand my extreme joy over the contents of his information. And I immediately rushed to my friend, passed the information on to him, and thanked him for the call, "the man," and the nonsense.

"Why?" he couldn't understand.

"Just so. You made me happy."

* * *

On the eighth of April, I was as usual working in my office. Twice when I was absent from the office, a man with a foreign accent had called me, my colleagues had said. I didn't want to miss the call the third time and was sitting in the room waiting. It came very soon. It was Yosif, with his Latvian-Jewish accent. I was surprised that he should call me at my job and that his voice was so near. He asked his usual questions, but I could hear a smile in his voice. Then he suddenly asked when I would finish work. A wild thought struck me.

"Where are you?"

"I am here, two minutes' walk from you."

I gave a cry of joy and jumped almost up to the ceiling.

"When? Why? For how long?" I asked wildly, not waiting for the answers.

Soon I was running to him. I ran into him and hid my face on his chest. He bent forward awkwardly, trying to find my cheek, and kissed me in the hair. I became frightened. We had seemed so close in our letters and now I felt shy before him.

He had to leave the same night and no one was to know

about his coming. We took a taxi to get home as quickly as we could. At home I changed my clothes and started to prepare supper. He became angry.

"Don't do anything! I didn't come to eat. Sit down for a little while. I'll have to go very soon."

I was in distress. Just a few hours and then again so far from each other. I sat down, but almost immediately stood up and began to walk to and fro in my tiny room. Yosif was sitting on the sofa with his feet set against the opposite wall. We were in a cage, in a cage of my room, in a cage of shyness and fear.

Something had to be done. We began to talk. Somehow we began to discuss the threat of the army for the Jewish boys and I said that if they escaped the Russian Army and went to Israel, there would be the army again, this time our army, but with danger to their lives.

"But don't you see it is something different? And why should you think about it now when we are still here?" The necessity for him to comfort me made both of us freer. He drew me to him and embraced me. I was so thin that he seemed to embrace emptiness. I raised my head and smiled at him and then he was kissing my hands, my face, my neck, and then suddenly stopped and began to smell my hair.

"What do you smell there?"

"Just so. It smells so good. So different. You are quite different."

All too soon we had to rush to the airport. His plane was leaving at midnight. We arrived on time and even had a few minutes to kiss each other shamelessly in front of people. At the last moment he rushed to the plane.

Suddenly a dark figure approached from somewhere at the side and stopped Yosif. I stood frozen with terror. But in a minute Yosif ran to the plane and it soon took off. It was a mistake. The man had just asked him for his ticket. But I understood it as a sign of everything that was awaiting us in our common future and that would not always turn out to be a mistake.

ALLA, 1972.

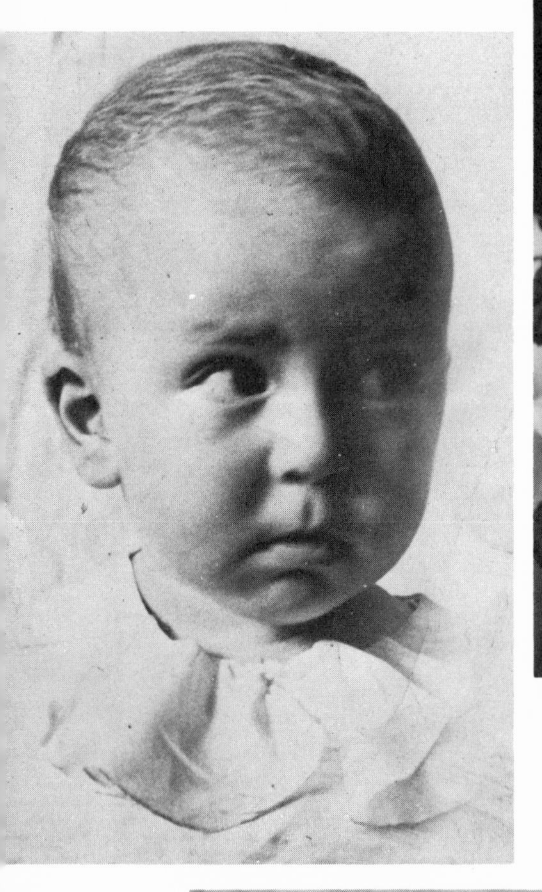

Far left: 1949. "I WAS A PLUMP CHILD WITH AN EXTRAORDINARY BIG AND BALD HEAD . . ."

Top left: 1956. "THAT YEAR I WENT TO SCHOOL . . ."

Lower left: FROM LEFT TO RIGHT: ALLA, HER MOTHER AND SISTER MYRA. "WE THREE WOMEN LIVED ALL OUR LIVES TOGETHER BUT NEVER CAME TO KNOW EACH OTHER DEEPLY."

Below: 1962. "I AM NOW IN THE SIXTH FORM . . . AND I AM A MEMBER OF THE EDITORIAL BOARD OF OUR CLASS NEWSPAPER."

Far left: 1966. "IN THE SUMMER I FINISHED SCHOOL . . ."

Top left: DANCING A HORA ON THE BALTIC SEASHORE, 1967.

Lower left: ALLA (TO THE LEFT) AND MYRA (TO THE RIGHT) AT A COUSIN'S WEDDING IN RIGA, 1967.

Above: ALLA WITH AN AMERICAN JEWISH TOURIST GIRL IN RED SQUARE, MOSCOW, 1969.

Above: THE WEDDING CEREMONY, OCTOBER 1970.

Left: "I LOOK AT YOSSI AND WE BOTH CANNOT BUT LAUGH OF HAPPINESS AND JOY."

Right: THE WEDDING CAKE.

Above: JANUARY 1971, AMSTERDAM. "I TRY TO EXPLAIN TO THEM WHAT A SOVIET JEW IS, WHAT HIS IDEALIZING ZIONISM IS, WHAT HIS HEROISM IS."

Right: ISRAEL, LOD AIRPORT, MARCH 1971.

НБ-

WELCOMING THE SABBATH DURING THE EIGHT-DAY HUNGER STRIKE NEAR THE WAILING WALL IN SOLIDARITY WITH THE PRISONERS OF THE LENINGRAD TRIAL, DECEMBER 1970.

MAY 1972. "IT IS SO WONDERFUL THAT WE ARE THREE NOW."

The official reaction in the press to the growth of Zionism was developing in proportion to the number of applications for exit visas to the OVIR. The officials could easily ignore us, but our mood was being reflected abroad in the speeches of Golda Meir, in numerous special meetings of the Knesset, and in the activities of American Jewry.

Not a single day passed without a long article against Zionism appearing in *Pravda* or *Izvestia*, which called the activities abroad political provocation aimed at the Soviet State. "Zionism, a Poisoned Weapon of Imperialism," "To Whose Tune Do the Zionists Dance," "The Provocateurs at Work," etc., etc. And new books appeared, published in "best-seller" editions—*Take Care, Zionism!*, *Judaism in Its True Colors*—both with a black cover showing a Jew with a large nose and burning, rapacious eyes. We, the young Jews, who didn't remember Stalin's anti-Semitic campaigns, realized that our turn had come. And we had to face it, to read it, and to swallow it. Our futile fury grew when similar articles appeared with Jewish names under them. The procedure of the 1952 campaign was being repeated.

Jews were beating their breasts trying to prove they were loyal, happy, satisfied. They hated Zionism and Israel and all imperialists of the world. "I have this and that, I don't need Golda Meir's protection," "I don't know what is Jewish in me except the word on my identity card," "Our Soviet Motherland has protected us from fascists. We live among brothers." And so on.

We were burning with a desire to run somewhere, to find those Jews, to spit in their servile faces, to prove our point to somebody. But what was the use? Everyone has a right to his own point of view and, if they were compelled to sign those articles, what can you do with people who are afraid? Whatever the number of signatures on those articles, we knew the number of applications for exit visas to Israel was incomparably larger. Some of the Jews wrote open individual or collective letters to *Pravda.* We read and reread them. They were open only to us Jews who thought differently and to the world as they reached it. In the Soviet Union there was no reaction to them.

OPEN LETTER

To: L. Berenshtein and M. Fridel—authors of the article, "To Whose Tune Do The Zionists Dance" (Izvestia–No. 292, December 14, 1969).

Lately, in the newspapers Pravda *and* Izvestia *there have appeared articles devoted to the attitude of Jews living in the USSR toward the State of Israel. The authors of these articles—G. Plotkin, L. Berenshtein, and M. Fridel—are Jews, and they have evidently taken upon themselves the mission of speaking in the name of the entire Jewish population of the USSR.*

As we, the signatories to this letter, are also Jews living in the USSR, the questions mentioned in the articles directly concern each of us—and this is why we consider it necessary to answer the authors of the article, "To Whose Tune Do The Zionists Dance."

And so you, L. Berenshtein and M. Fridel, write that the Parliament of Israel has adopted a resolution in which it demands "respect" for the indubitable right of every Jew to live on the soil of his historical motherland—that is to say, Israel.

It is here to the point to ask: do you know of any other historical motherland of the Jews that is not "so-called"? Perhaps you wish to say that the Jews—unlike other peoples—have no historical motherland, or, at least, should not have one? Or, as you are trying to convince the reader, that the Jewish national question can be solved only in the field of class struggle? What it comes to is that it is not historical continuity, not the ancestral spiritual heritage, not the history of the country and its people, that shape the soul of a person, but the class struggle and only the class struggle. Moreover, you consider that the Jewish problem can be only political, social, and even religious, but by no means national (in the sense of their own statehood).

But how much more human, after your awkward lines, appear to us other words about the Fatherland, patriotism, and internationalism, expressed by I. Vuzylev and A. Kraminov in this same Izvestia *(December 15, 1969), in the article, "Love and a Ring": ". . . We feel ourselves citizens and workers of the huge, proudly expansive, global territory that is called the Union of the Soviet Socialist Republics. And we feel that it is our Fatherland. . . . This is a personal attitude as well. And it is precisely this that, sooner or later, had to impel us and did impel us to visit that corner of the earth, small in comparison with the vast areas of the country, that is situated to the north of Moscow and is called 'Rus,' around which Russian statehood was constructed, around which the Russian people confirmed itself and felt itself to be one. All of us are children of our parents. Our existence, everything that we are, we owe to them first and foremost. And this gratitude toward an endless number of generations surely makes up part of the lofty concept of patriotism. And another part of it is the consciousness of the fact that each of us is a link in this chain of generations and bears full responsibility toward those that follow us. After all, it is doubtful whether true internationalism is within the reach of a person who lacks the feeling of national dignity. Because how can the soul and the beauty of another nation be understood by one who is capable of scorning his own spiritual heritage?"*

Do you hear, L. Berenshtein and M. Fridel? What can you say to this? What source nourishes your feelings of national dignity? To what endless row of generations are you grateful? You who come out in the name of the "Jewish population of our country," will you be able to read P. Markish, S. Halkin, L. Kvitko, I. Fefer, and Bergelson in your own, Jewish, language? Do you know even one Jewish letter? Are you proud of the spiritual heritage of your people—even of the Bible, if only in its literary and historical aspect? Do you, your children, and your grandchildren know about the heroic national uprisings of the Maccabees and of Bar Kochba against foreign rulers? What do such names as Yehuda Halevi, Maimonides, Moses Mendelssohn, Ch. N. Bialik, and S. Frug say to you? Or is all this not your history, not your spiritual heritage? If so, then what is yours? And where is it? Is it only the "field" . . . the bare field of class struggle? And on the basis of what national spiritual heritage do you dress up as internationalists?

On April 1, 1964, in the newspaper Izvestia *it was written: "The constant striving for unity, for life on the land of the ancestors has preserved the Armenian nation." Then why don't you see that it is precisely these forces—the striving for unity and for life on the land of the ancestors—which have preserved the Jewish nation as well through centuries of even greater trials? By what right do you—the pathetic product of assimilation!—come out in the name of the "Jewish population"? And don't try to convince the readers that the decision of the Israel Knesset demanding respect for "the indubitable right of each Jew to live on the soil of his historical motherland," is an anti-Soviet campaign. Don't follow the path of blackmail, don't hark back to those times when violation of laws was a habitual matter. And don't hasten to stick the label of "traitors" and "betrayers of the Homeland" on the Soviet Jews who have so far only expressed their desire to unite with their kin on the land of Israel.*

Neither the French, nor the English, nor the Russian peoples had to prove to the entire world their right to a national existence. The history of the Jews was different. The Jewish people had to prove this right. And it was proved in 1947. And the world recognized this right. And the Soviet Union was one of the first to recognize the State of Israel. Doesn't this mean that from now on every Jew HAS THE RIGHT to take part in the building of HIS STATE and in the formation of a JEWISH national culture on the land of HIS ancestors? And you, the so-called "representatives of the Jewish nationality," are not ashamed to make police threats and describe this right and the open expression of the will of the people to return to the land of its ancestors as "treachery" and "betrayal"!

As for the class struggle, it is successfully carried out by the Communist Party of Israel (even two of them!), which is, incidentally, the only legal Communist Party in the entire Near East, the representatives of which even sit in the same Knesset whose resolution inspired you with the idea for your article.

It is clear that your aim is to prove to readers both in the Soviet Union and abroad that the idea of settling in the "land of the ancestors" in Israel is alien to the Jews of the Soviet Union. You should take a look into the Visas and Registration Section attached to the Ministry of Interior of the USSR and ask, how many tens of thousands of Jews come there in the vain hope of getting a permit to leave the USSR and to reunite with their relatives in Israel? Although the lawfulness of their strivings is not refuted, these people are nevertheless deprived of the possibility of achieving their lawful aim. This open violation of human rights becomes more and more obvious and acquires greater and greater publicity before public opinion.

And this is in spite of the fact that, under the Universal Declaration of the Rights of Man, "all of whose provisions"—according to Izvestia *no. 289—"have long since become a habitual norm of life," states, in article 13: "Every person has the right to leave any country, including his own, and to return to his country."*

Try to understand, L. Berenshtein and M. Fridel, that the right to leave any country is the lawful right of every person and is nowhere in the world regarded as "treachery" and "betrayal of the Fatherland."

Therefore the recent appeal to the UN on the part of the eighteen Jewish families from Georgia, complaining against the

Soviet organs that arbitrarily impede their departure, is also fully understandable. It was precisely this appeal that was the basis for the resolution of the Israel Parliament, something that you have preferred not to mention in your article.

Persons who desire to go to Israel do exist. There are thousands and thousands of them. This is not "a fabrication on the part of bourgeois slanderers." These people exist and openly protest against the infringement of their human rights.

And we add our voices to this protest.

As for you, L. Berenshtein and M. Fridel, like every one "who knows the laws of social development," you must be aware that the wheels of history cannot only not be turned back, they cannot be stopped either. And today, when the Jewish State has been revived and has existed for twenty-two years, "the striving for unity, for life in the land of the ancestors," is natural and incontestable.

Therefore all the Soviet Jews who wish to reunite with their people in the land of Israel would certainly welcome respect for their indubitable right "to live in the land of their historical motherland."

And to the great Power which gave shelter to many generations of Jews, we repeat the words of our distant ancestors who demanded the right of Exodus from Egypt: "LET MY PEOPLE GO!"

Vitaly Svechinsky
Dora Kolyaditskaya
Mark Elbaum
Tina Brodetskaya
Lev Freidin
Bliuma Diskina

Moscow, December 1969

OPEN LETTER

To: The Editorial Office of the newspaper Pravda

In Pravda *of 13/1/70 were published letters to the editorial office under the general heading "Exposure of the Provocateurs."*

All the letters are founded on your paper's assertion, which does not correspond with fact, that the appeal of the Government of Israel had been directed to all the Jews of the USSR. In fact the call for emigration was addressed only to those Jews who wish to emigrate to Israel within the framework of family reunification or for other reasons.

I do not doubt for a minute the genuineness of the published letters and the sincerity of their authors. But, with some variations in the answers published (from coarse, foul insults to the Government of Israel in the letters of persons that do not contain the authors' social position, to the restrained expression in the letters of the more intellectual economists and the librarian), all these letters have one thing in common: they are written by citizens of Jewish origin, who do not wish to regard themselves as Jews.

This idea is expressed in all the letters, but it is particularly frankly stated in the letter of G. Tsypin. This, so to say Jew, writes: "I don't know what has remained in me of Jewishness, perhaps only the nationality paragraph in my passport, but as long as I am considered (!) a Jew. . . ."

Here it is, the fruit of assimilation, when a man lacks national pride and national dignity, he turns into a person without kin and without a tribe.

As long as the writer does not consider himself a Jew, the question arises whether he and others like him have the right to appear publicly in the name of the Jews on a matter that concerns Jews exclusively (Jews not only by origin) and no one else.

The editorial office of Pravda *has made an obvious miscalculation in publishing letters like the one quoted, because it follows from them that there is no national life for Jews in the USSR. Not a single one of the authors mentions (and they have no grounds for it) any national, cultural, or spiritual life of the Jews in the USSR, a life without which the normal existence of any nation is unthinkable.*

Can you find among the Russians, Ukrainians, Bielorussians, Georgians, Armenians, and other peoples of the USSR any persons asserting that all that has remained in them of their nationality is but a paragraph in the passport? Such a statement on the part of the Jews testifies to the pitiful situation of their national culture and their national life! There are no Jewish schools, newspapers, magazines, theaters, or textbooks for learning the Jewish language!

A policy that is directed toward assimilation does bear some fruit, but as a whole it is doomed to failure. Nobody has yet succeeded in assimilating the Jews throughout the 2,000 years of their homeless history, when there was no Jewish State. This will still less succeed now, when the Jewish State exists and is a center of attraction for all Jews who have kept their national pride and dignity.

V. Polsky

In April the authorities surpassed themselves. They organized a press conference for foreign journalists with prominent

Jews—one minister, military general, scientists, actors, government officials. The press conference was broadcast on television and then repeated three times during the week. The newspapers gave the full text of the conference.

Of course, the press conference was not announced beforehand as the organizers had feared that other Jews would come "to greet their compatriots," so we could only grind our teeth ex post facto watching the television, the mocking faces of the American correspondents, and the pale faces with nervous tics of the speaking Jews.

And the whole of Russia was splitting its sides with laughter over the "new performance of the Soviet Circus with tame Jews." "It serves them right," the anti-Semites said. More intelligent people would shrug their shoulders with disgust. And only the gray Soviet masses, the basis of power, would believe, agree, and approve.

"Other" Jews answered the press conference with a letter which became known to the world as "the letter of the 39" and was to become one of the first great rallying points of the now open struggle of Soviet Jewry for exodus. Only since then, we have added to our appeals the awkward phrase, "for those who want it."

To USSR Ministry of Foreign Affairs
The Chief of the Press Department
L. M. Zamyatin

We are those Jews who insist on their desire to leave for Israel and who are being constantly refused by the Soviet authorities.

We are those Jews who have more than once addressed open statements to the Soviet press but whose letters were never published.

We are those Jews who were not invited to the press conference on the 4th of March and were not invited to express their point of view.

We suppose that you must feel uneasy about the one-sidedness of the press conference organized by you, more so, that you certainly know, at least from the press, that since 1968 when the Soviet authorities began accepting applications of Jews who want to leave for Israel, till November 1969 more than 80,000 applications were handed in. (See the well-known Soviet press weekly Newsweek, *November 24, 1969.) And this happened in the atmosphere when the desire of a Soviet Jew to live in the land of his forefathers is not encouraged, to put it mildly.*

If we suppose that every application was handed in by a family even if not large, even if of three persons, this already means that more than 240,000 Jews in the Soviet Union are unsuccessfully seeking permission to leave.

Proceeding from the elementary understanding of justice formulated already in ancient Rome as "Let the other side be also heard!" you, of course, will like to remedy that disappointing situation which was created by the one-sidedness of the press conference organized by you on the 4th of March.

That is why we Jews, unlike "the citizens of Jewish origin," we, who are ready any moment, leaving everything behind, as we are, even to make our way on foot to the State of Israel, request you to give us also the opportunity to appear at a news conference before Soviet and foreign journalists and to make a declaration.

Please inform us through the press on the place and time of this news conference.

The text of our open declaration is as follows.

DECLARATION

The Anti-Israel campaign in the Soviet press has reached its culmination in the recent press conference of a number of prominent persons of Jewish origin.

The participants of the press conference expressed the opinion of only a certain, even if numerous, part of Soviet Jewry. We do not belong to that part and think that our opinion is characteristic of many of our fellow Jews, although we admit that indecision is preventing many of them from openly expressing their views.

We declare:

The military events in the Middle East have once more been used for anti-Israeli propaganda. This is shameful propaganda, for war is a great disaster and, if Arabs perish in this war, this does not please Jews.

The emotional heat of anti-Israel propaganda is now very great, and we consider it necessary to clarify that the myth of the imperialist character of Israel is nothing more [than] a method of political propaganda. The accusations that Israel desires to move all the Jews to its territory irrespective of their will are unfounded. Only the help in moving those who want it is Israel's humane task.

The idea of Jewish statehood has nothing to do with preach-

ing of racism and national exclusiveness. Internationalism is peculiar to the Jewish national character and is consecrated by Jewish law. It is said: "Seventy bullocks were offered up by Israel for the seventy nations of the world." (*Tanhuma* 88, 3)

The attempt to criticize the idea of Jewish statehood from the "class" point of view, to substitute the class problem for the national one is groundless. Unification of people according to the national principles does not and is not supposed to exclude various contradictions among them, including the so-called "class" ones. In any case this is the internal affair of a nation.

The essential task of the press conference was to show that its participants had reached prominent positions in society, in spite of their Jewish origin. But this was all they could show, for their Jewish origins do not mean that they have preserved their spiritual link with the national Jewish culture. Every Jew has of course a right to any degree of assimilation. We, however, do not want to forfeit our national identity and our spiritual link with our people.

We worship those sons of the Jewish people who accepted torture and death to preserve their national identity, for, thanks to them, the Jewish nation was preserved. We are proud of our people who have carried their religion, language, culture and national traits through thousands of years of suffering and are proud that this people has now found in itself the will to revive the State of Israel and to defend it.

And it is the very preservation of the national identity of Jews that is the problem in the Soviet Union. No references to completely equal and joyful labor with Russians and no examples of a brilliant military or social career can divert our attention from the problem, for in this, Russians remain Russians, and Jews cease to be Jews. Forcible assimilation in this case does not mean, for example, prohibition of reading Jewish books. It means that young Jews do not know how to read Jewish books as there are no schools in the Soviet Union where the Jewish language is taught.

But we are in our right to remain Jews and to educate our children in the spirit of Jewish culture, and we believe that those who prefer or will be compelled to remain in this country can defend their right to be Jews not only by origin.

One of the basic issues of the Jewish question in the USSR is a guarantee of the right of repatriation. The Soviet Union does not recognize that right, and many thousands of Soviet Jews who want to leave for Israel are being refused. The reasons for this anti-repatriation policy given at the press conference do not even deserve to be argued against.

We shall insist on our right to decide our own destiny, including the choice of citizenship and country of living. We are able ourselves to estimate all the possible difficulties awaiting us concerning military events, change of climate, or of social order.

The present state of our citizenship includes the right for the State to demand from us no more than obeying the laws, and our claims to freedom of repatriation are based on Soviet laws and guarantees of international law.

The Jewish people has undergone many persecutions and suffering, many malicious or well-intentioned assimilation campaigns and has succeeded in maintaining its identity.

We believe that now also Jews will respond to the anti-Israel campaign not by abdicating, but that on the contrary, their pride in their people will grow stronger and that they will declare: "Next year in Jerusalem!"

Moscow, March 8, 1970

No press conference for "other" Jews followed, but all those who signed the letter were called for individual talks by the local Party committees. The talks, with a representative from the KGB present, were as usual and no repressions followed them. But those who were members of the Communist Party were expelled from the membership. However, that had long ago stopped being a punishment. It had become one of the honorary awards on the heroic road to Israel.

* * *

On the 22nd of April, the Soviet Union and "the whole of the progressive world" celebrated the 100th anniversary of Lenin's birth. We knew of its approach by the appearance of more and more red color in the streets and a general fuss in our places of work and Institutes. On the "Great Day" there was a meeting in the Palace of Congresses with the representatives of all Communist and Working Class Parties of the world as guests of honor. We had heard before that Meir Vilner, the leader of one of the two Communist groups in Israel, would be present. It didn't bother us, for we had long ago understood what Meir Vilner was and felt he had no more to do with Israel than did a Chinese peasant.

But in the afternoon, when we were at Natasha's place, her grandfather suddenly decided to switch on the television to watch the meeting, all the while wearing the sarcastic smile of a former Communist. We immediately saw a good-looking, middle-aged man with gray hair approaching the speakers' platform, while the whole Palace resounded with applause. Before we could recognize him, he began his speech:

"*Haverim Yakarim!* Dear comrades!" and he followed with the usual Communist nonsense in brilliant Russian.

The fact that this fellow had used "our Hebrew" even for the greeting had irritated us terribly. We left the house and went to the synagogue. It was the third day of Passover and two nights of the "dark" Jewish holiday were over, but we still found a small group of young Jews there. We spent that evening in teaching them simple Hebrew songs on the staircase of the synagogue with red banners swinging threateningly over our heads.

I was on my way home late at night when I was suddenly terrified by a frightening sight in the sky. A huge portrait of Lenin was hanging high up against the stars and was lit by giant searchlights. When I came to myself after the first fright, I thought with disgust that they were already surpassing their Chinese brother-enemies in idolatry.

I stopped looking at it and began to think instead that there were only eight days left till Tallinn.

17

In April the time for our visit to Tallinn was quickly approaching. How long it had been! But the waiting was over, the eternity had passed, and we had to pack and think about tickets. Our fancy clothes were already finished and we filled our suitcases almost entirely with the new things. Natasha and I had dared to have pants suits made, which were still unheard of in Moscow but which we hoped would be accepted in Tallinn and Riga and appreciated by our boys.

The problem of tickets proved to be difficult. Many students and working people traveled dring the vacation period beginning with the first of May. There were no tickets. At last, having paid off somebody, we got tickets for a very strange train which went to Tallinn in fifteen hours.

We boarded the train and easily found places for ourselves. The carriage was almost empty. The seats were hard and we began to arrange our bags under our heads. Everyone was in good spirits and, soon exhausted, we fell asleep.

In our dreams the hard benches seemed to penetrate into our bones and some hard object in the bag turned into a Turkish execution device for the head, but our sleep was too sound and, without awakening, we simply changed sides. In the middle of the night, we all suddenly awoke and could not find each other. Other people were sitting on our benches, blocking us from the world; others were sitting on the floor; children were sleeping on sacks. They were all wearing quilted jackets, warm worn kerchiefs, or fur caps. The air was filled with the smell of Russian sweat, stale straw, and everything that means a Russian village.

After the first shudder, looking out through the fringe of legs in tarpaulin boots from the upper benches, we began to call each other weakly:

"Alla!"

"Natalik!"

"Basja!"

"Sanja, Olja?"

"Where are we? Who are they?"

"Just people."

The people were sleeping soundly or sitting still looking steadily in front of them. As if they had been traveling like that for an eternity, they didn't notice us or each other. No one was talking.

We soon understood that they were not traveling for long. At a certain moment, they began to waken their children and got off at the next stop. At one of the stops, the carriage was filled with soldiers. We shrank into dark corners, trying to hide ourselves. They were all huge and silent, with gloomy, exhausted faces. Without words, they lay down quickly on the benches or on the floor and fell asleep. Two soldiers sat down on our bench and offered their coats to us. Not wanting to offend them, we accepted and answered their simple questions.

The soldiers on the next benches suddenly became drunk and, before we knew it, they began violently beating each other. The carriage began to shake. Basja stretched out her plump white little hand with pearl nails as if trying to defend herself from the heap of bodies that was ready to come down on us.

Suddenly Natasha began to laugh. I also couldn't stand the tension anymore and began to giggle. Then Natasha began to recite some stupid childrens' poem, swinging her arms, and overturned a bottle of milk on the people who lay on the floor. She began to giggle and said:

"It is only milk, don't worry!"

A woman with milk running down her head looked at Natasha as if she were mad and didn't utter a word. They were all dumb.

The people kept coming and going, coming and going. They were all alike and yet different. The smells depended on which village they came from. The whole of Russia seemed to be moving, the real Russia, which was concealed from the rest of the world.

This was not the first time we had seen these people. All of us had gone through the Komsomol work in kolkhozy (collective farms) and had seen and experienced that life. But on our way to Tallinn, this meeting with Russia seemed to be a terrible mistake.

As we approached Estonian territory, the people began to leave and soon we found ourselves alone in the carriage. We fell on the benches and were asleep immediately, having forgotten their hardness and the absence of pillows.

We awoke in the afternoon as the train was approaching Tallinn. The terrible night seemed to be a bad dream. We quickly put ourselves in order.

The boys were standing on the platform in the gray Tallinn rain. When the train stopped, they entered the carriage to help us with our suitcases. Again I felt shy and didn't dare come up to Yosif for a kiss. The moment of which we had dreamed all these 116 days and nights had come. Yosif and Lev immediately took their places near me and Natasha like guards, and Tsvisha took Basja, Olja, and Sanja under his care. Laughing and interrupting each other, we told them about our night. But on approaching the city, we decided to forget about everything that didn't concern Tallinn and entered it in silence.

On the way I asked Yosif not to separate us from the rest, but he interrupted me with anger and despair:

"I have had enough of Moscow's New Year's holiday. Now I want to have only you and don't care about the rest. If anybody dares to interfere with us, I shall be direct and frank with him."

His despair came from his already being aware of my stubborn and independent character, and he feared my resistance. His anger was at the whole world that parted us for such long periods and at such long distances. He squeezed my arm above the elbow as if trying to keep me from going away, but he needn't have done it. I didn't want to be strong and independent any more. I belonged to him.

We crossed some unseen border and found ourselves in the medieval city. This was the sixteenth century in Western Europe. Two- and three-storied buildings with high red-tiled roofs and small windows with iron shutters were bent over narrow cobbles. Tall gray churches and towers pierced the sky with their spires like bony old Don Quixotes with spears. Everything was unnaturally clean and there was not a single man in the street or a single face in the windows. On a corner we saw a huge clock hanging over the road. I shuddered. It had two large hands and no figures at all. I looked around, fearing that a horse with a coffin would appear from behind the corner or a faceless man in black would fall down and disappear.

"This is the world of Ingmar Bergman," Yosif said, as if reading my thoughts.

In the central square we found at last some people who passed us with stony faces. They were almost all pale of complexion, with gray hair, thin, and dried-up. All the men were neatly dressed and the women wore all kinds of elegant little hats—something you rarely see in other republics.

To celebrate the First of May, the square was decorated with a huge portrait of Lenin and Soviet slogans on stripes of red material. But here it didn't irritate us. Lenin looked not like a guest or an invader, but more like a stranger who suddenly found himself in the wrong place. The famous turn of his head now made him look like a man who moves his head left and right to find out how to escape. The slogans looked like ribbons that someone had dropped by accident. Time had stopped here in the sixteenth century and the spears that hung over entrance doors and pierced the street reminded us that the unseen knights of Estonia were on guard and ready to repulse any invasion by the modern world.

But this was only scenery. And the "dropped ribbons" and "frightened" stranger enveloped half of a big building in the square on every Soviet holiday.

The German Teutonic style of Tallinn didn't appeal to me, but I admired the national pride and bright identity of the Estonians. Our walks in the city passed under a melodic fugue by Bach descending from a violin played by a little musician in black sitting on one of the clouds. His music was sometimes penetrated by the warning sounds of the Mendelssohn First Concerto.

We had four days to spend in Tallinn and more than ten famous restaurants to visit. Sleeping in a big room in a student's dormitory that we had rented, we tried to get up early to be ready for a short tour of the city and at least five visits to restaurants or small bars. In the morning, after a whole night of laughter, jokes, singing, and dancing in our room, we shouted through a thin wall to awaken each other.

The new world delighted us and the boys introduced us to it with the pride and confidence of habitués. They were not habitués in this world, but they had been born and brought up for it. The life which they lived working in factories with drunkards and immoral people, living in communal apartments with the same people for neighbors and all this after years of exile to distant regions of Russia—this life they considered temporary and strange and the world they lived in foreign.

We sat in semi-dark restaurants and the delicate sparkling crystal was reflected in lights in our burning eyes. The boys treated us to the tastiest food and most interesting cocktails.

In one of the restaurants we watched a variety show—one of the few existing in the Soviet Union. Young beautiful singers shook the room with the passion of their singing. Slender, half-naked girls danced among the tables. We clapped our hands with childish delight and couldn't tear our eyes from the play of the muscles of the strong and handsome male dancers. This small world with colored lights and beautiful music in the round hall of the restaurant filled us with passion and joy. It reflected our hidden inner feelings and encouraged us to live and feel.

After one such visit, Natasha and I went out into the street completely drunk, half with the strong cocktail, half with pleasure and happiness. We walked in the streets and couldn't stop laughing loudly. We uttered some indistinct sounds, trying to say something to each other, but immediately split our sides in laughter. Yosif and Lev looked at each other seriously and said:

"What a shame! Let's walk at a distance as if we don't know them."

And they ostentatiously stepped back with stony faces, but with laughter in their eyes. We laughed all over the street, took each other by the hands, and ran forward. Suddenly Natasha stopped and put her finger to her mouth. "Sh-h-h." Then she minced on her tiptoes after a passing sailor. I ran after her and grabbed her.

"But I want to pull him by the ribbons on his cap," she protested.

We laughed and began to hold each other, having forgotten who wanted to run and who didn't.

"O.K.," she said at last seriously. "Then I want to kiss this militia man. Don't stop me."

We both walked decisively toward the man and suddenly were grabbed by our boys. They had been running after us, having guessed what we were up to, and had decided to separate us. We waved to each other laughing and clung to our lords.

At the entrance to our room, I whispered to Natasha not to tell the others anything about our state. She winked at me and we entered the room with serious indifferent faces.

"I am terribly drunk," announced Natasha in a loud voice.

* * *

"I found you and I am not going to lose you. You are mine and I want to defend you from all the evil of this life. I want you to forget all the troubles that were, all the disappointments and all the people who have ever done you any harm. I just forbid you to remember. Do you understand? Do you promise me? Now I shall stand between you and all of them so that you can never meet them again. Because . . . I love you. I mean it. I have never in my life said these words and didn't want to say them to you before. I wanted to feel it to the full. And now I say: I love you. . . . And it means for me that you are the only, the closest, and the best in this world. My beloved . . . I love you."

Thus my bad dancer, my awful pen pal, and poor speaker, but the best human being in the world, brought to me our Song of Songs.

* * *

On the 4th of May we all left for Riga to spend a week enjoying the city and the cold sea. Natasha and I came to be introduced to the families.

On our way to Yosif's house I stumbled about ten times, not seeing the way from fear. When we entered the doorway, I was ready to faint when Yossi said, "Not yet. This is not our entrance."

We crossed through the house and found ourselves in a backyard. At their doorway it was already no longer original to faint and I stood green with fear and dumb with shyness.

Yossi opened the door with his own key and I appeared before his mother.

* * *

A week later I left Riga for Moscow with Yossi's love to support and defend me and with a heavy weight of uncertainty lying on my heart. We couldn't make any plans. We were both not yet twenty-one, with our studies unfinished, without means of support, without a place to live, both under the threat of arrest, and in the middle of struggling for an exit visa. We were both reasonable enough to realize all of this and not to decide anything.

Natasha arrived in Moscow three days later, fat, pink, and laughing with happiness all the time. She brought with her a full suitcase with presents for the whole family, the announcement of her engagement, and plans for the wedding in July.

But Moscow met her with the first shock of the many that were to come—the beginning of "the great thing" that I had predicted and that now became a reality.

The permission to leave for Israel that was granted to Natasha's family was so unexpected that it brought neither joy nor the feeling of victory. They were the only family to receive this permission and they were leaving all their friends behind. Natasha was leaving everything.

At the moment she heard the news she looked at everybody around her with big astonished eyes. She understood all it meant immediately. She began to cry, became weak, and could not regain control during the three weeks before their departure.

Lev immediately came to Moscow. He was like a nurse with a seriously ill patient and was full of love, caresses, and reason. During this time Natasha was gripped by a wild idea—to stay with him. But she knew that the family would not leave without her. She was torn between two loves, with no way out. The struggle broke her heart and her mind.

Only one thing would help a little, she thought. She begged to be married to Lev and to be able to leave the Soviet Union with the knowledge that they belonged to each other and were bound by something more than their love. Under those conditions and in such a short time, they could be married only in a religious ceremony. Most of their adult friends did not approve of this step, having already forgotten what love was or never having known it at all. But nobody could refuse her.

The wedding took place on the 24th of May, Lag b'Omer, in Sanja's apartment, and in the presence of only the closest friends, the rabbi of Malakhovka (a little settlement near Moscow), and ten witnesses.

The days passed agonizingly slowly, sinking in Natasha's tears. On the 24th of May, we dressed the bride in clothes that we had gathered from all over Moscow. With the most important representatives of the Jewish Zionist movement holding a big bedspread over their heads as a *chuppah*, the rabbi read his prayers, the young couple exchanged rings, and Lev broke the traditional glass with his foot. "*Mazel tov*!" And from under the *chuppah*, Natasha gave us her first smile in weeks, holding tightly a small piece of paper in her hand—a *k'tuba* (a Jewish religious marriage certificate).

On the 10th of June, the family left the Soviet Union.

* * *

Inna gave a last glance around her room, which was hard to recognize now. But the walls were still the same, her own dear walls with the traces of their life over the years. The corner near the window was covered with inkspots—there Natasha did her homework. There was another dark spot left by the back of her father's bald head. The big window and Hertzen Street down there and the Kremlin just down the street. . . .

But stop! There was no time for this. She looked over her family and took her sick mother by the hand. Natasha was supported by her friends as everyone went down the stairs.

Inna's three Russian friends, the young women with whom she studied in the Institute, came to say good-by.

The group went out into the street. Immediately about a dozen civilians in black surrounded them. They didn't interfere, but just stood and stared with their hands behind their backs and their legs apart. Inna felt her heart beating in her throat, but not a muscle moved on her face. Natasha saw nothing.

The family stood on the pavement waiting for a taxi. Half a minute hadn't passed when a black Volga came up. The driver looked out of the window and asked, "Who is for Sheremetyevo (the airport)?" Anxious to be on their way, Inna did not think a moment and ordered everyone into the car.

The black "guards" were left standing behind. "Scoundrels, scoundrels," the Russian women were exclaiming in whispers, seeing the real Soviet "freedom" for the first time. Inna hurriedly kissed her friends and said loudly, "Girls, stop being afraid!" And she entered the KGB black car where the whole family was already sitting.

The guards hurried to their cars and the column started on its way. The old Bolshevik and his romantic daughter were leaving Moscow with an escort of black governmental cars.

Inna leaned her head on the back of the seat and suddenly understood. The truth struck her like a flash of electric current. It came as soon as she tried to think over what had just happened, with the first glance at the driver's face. How could she fail to understand at once? A black Volga comes up in the center of the city and the driver asks for passengers just for Sheremetyevo. There was no doubt that a provocation was being arranged. Inna grew cold with terror, but knew what to do.

"Stop the car!" she ordered the driver. He did, suspecting nothing. "Everybody out of the car!" Inna said to the rest. Old Abram had also probably understood everything, but he was ready to fight. "No, we shall stay here. We shall go to the airport," he insisted. Inna was on the brink of hysterics. "Papa, go out immediately," she said quietly, but in an unnatural voice.

"Citizen! What happened?" they heard the driver's bawdy voice. "You said you wanted to go to Sheremetyevo!" he shouted threateningly.

"I have changed my plans. Here you are!" Inna said, handing out two rubles.

"Take your money back, you, mamochka," he roared, beginning to slip out of his role.

The "black" people were watching the scene from their cars with surprise, but did not move.

In three minutes the family was riding in a city taxi, not daring to discuss the situation in front of a strange man. The escort was still following the taxi.

They reached the airport after all their friends had arrived. They were all silent and cautious. A few days before, the KGB had called one of the happy Jews who had received permission after the Slepyans and told him to leave in silence without any noisy "Going-away party." The warning was serious and unambiguous and Jews didn't dare ignore it. Still, all the friends were there, though silent, with songs and cries of hope stuck in their throats. They all came to see off the first big family from Moscow to leave—to rejoice, to envy, to guess at the future.

Not knowing what to say, everyone tried to help with the numerous bags or sat silently or talked in whispers. Foreign tourists arriving in the capital of the Communist world cast curious glances at the silent but very uneasy crowd.

Natasha did nothing. She stood near her husband, holding his hand. They didn't talk. Her face was red and tears kept rolling down her cheeks. Some of the young people came up to her to say something and the corners of her lips twitched in a semblance of a smile. Everyone felt uneasy. Lev stood straight and tall with a stony face, not wanting to show his suffering. The ceremony with the tickets was soon over and it was time to say good-by and pass through the door in the glass wall, the wall that would separate them from the world they were leaving. The wall was thoroughly covered with thick curtains to prevent farewell looks; the curtains had appeared not long before, when the Jews began to leave.

Inna began hastily to kiss everyone around her. Later she wrote from Israel that she felt horrified that she might have kissed a KGB man in this crowd. Then we all came up to say good-by to the old people and Natasha. She was kissing everybody, leaving her tears on their cheeks and lips, looking for someone she had missed, trying to prolong the ceremony and delay the dreadful moment. At last she stopped, for no one was left, but Lev standing behind her. She stood for a moment, then turned around and walked toward him, swaying, ready to fall into his arms. But his stony eyes stopped her. "Don't do it!" they said. "Don't show!" And she understood. He kissed her cheeks as if she was his child and pushed her slightly toward the door. "Go, dear." And she went.

By that time the Jewish movement in the Soviet Union had not only grown in quantity, but it had acquired some special forms.

Our own theoreticians were writing: "Now we can call these Jewish activities in the Soviet Union a national liberation movement. It has its own special aims, but its scale and methods are similar to those of well-known liberation movements in world history."

The main purpose of this movement was emigration to Israel by means of a legal, open struggle for an exit visa. But everyone who took part in the movement remembered how he had come to this idea and saw as his own important task the bringing of this idea to those who were ready to accept it. It was brought to them through information about Israel, distribution of articles on Jewish history and religion, political and philosophical essays on the problem of Jewish revival, slides of historical places in Israel with accompanying explanations, Hebrew textbooks, and everything that could possibly give people knowledge and understanding of what Judaism and Israel meant.

Those who had at one time or another asked themselves these questions: "What does Judaism mean? What is Israel?" understood their unnatural and humiliating position in the Soviet Union and sought a solution. They greatly appreciated the information we brought, longed for it, imbibed it, and soon joined in the struggle for emigration. But there were still masses of people whom the little Jewish "Samizdat," the circulation of prohibited manuscript, could not reach, and this fact stimulated its growth. The Jewish "Samizdat" had appeared in two forms. One was a collection of articles on Israel, political and philosophical essays on the Jewish problem, and was duplicated by photographic methods and had the name, *Iton* (the Hebrew word for newspaper). The same and other articles also circulated separately in many copies.

The second was a periodical under the name of *Exodus* and reflected the struggle of the Soviet Jews for emigration. It was a collection of individual letters and collective petitions of Jews to the authorities and to the world organizations, as well as information about the trials, searches, and any other acts of the KGB against Jews. This publication was of great importance for those who had just begun the struggle for an exit visa and for world opinion.

We didn't know the sources of these publications, but we did our best to duplicate them and to distribute them among our circle of acquaintances.

Fully understanding the legal character of their struggle, the Jews made themselves acquainted with the numerous laws that concerned their problem. Twenty-year-old young people bombarded the officials of the OVIR and the Ministry of the Interior with juridical formulas and references to the laws.

At the end of May, Moscow was filled with red flags and placards and slogans. The country was preparing for the Sixteenth Congress of the Young Communist League of the USSR, which was going to take place on May 26 in the Kremlin Palace of Congresses.

I suddenly remembered that I had had something to do with this organization in the past and I decided to make some trouble for myself and the authorities. At that time we felt that we should be as bothersome as flies in summer and write as many letters to various organizations as we could. The record was held by one young person who wrote over one hundred letters in a few months. I was rather lazy in this regard and hated to write just for the sake of writing, but this opportunity seemed to me too good to miss and I wrote the following letter:

To the Presidium of the Sixteenth Congress of the Komsomol

I, Milkina Alla Tsalevna, born in 1949, former member of the USSR Young Communist League, ask for my appeal to the delegates of the Congress to be read out.

APPEAL

To the delegates of the Sixteenth Congress of the Komsomol and the representatives of progressive youth organizations of the whole world.

My whole life has been indissolubly linked with the Komsomol. The Komsomol was for me a symbol of justice and humanity, the personification of democracy, breadth of outlook and service to the ideals of internationalism.

The Komsomol appeared to be an organization capable of bringing us up as consistent and faithful soldiers in the struggle for freedom, equality, and brotherhood. This is why all my most intimate dreams and aspirations were always linked with the Komsomol. I felt that my actual work in the Komsomol organization formed precisely that meaning of life to which it is worth giving oneself fully.

These ideals are still dear to me and this gives me the right to appeal to the delegates of the Sixteenth Congress of the Komsomol.

In 1969 I lost my parents. As an orphan, I decided to reunite with my relatives who live in the State of Israel and who sent me an authorization to enter the country. My desire to go to Israel is explained not only by my wish for reunion with my relatives but also my long-standing aspiration to return to the country of my people.

I felt that my desire did not contradict the constitution of the Soviet Union or the statutes of the Komsomol, as I thought that the struggle for high ideals proclaimed by the Komsomol did not have any geographical frontiers.

But my request to Soviet organizations to grant me permission to leave for Israel provoked a tempest of indignation. I found myself surrounded by an atmosphere of hatred, of calumny, of blackmail, and of shadowings. Every minute somebody called me "traitor" to my face. The First Secretary of the Krasnaya Presnya Regional Committee of the Komsomol, L. L. Baidakov, stated openly that the Jewish people had always betrayed the Soviet Union and were still betraying it.

I was expelled from the Komsomol. All doors were closed to me. But this does not worry me now, I ask for only one door to be opened to me—the door to Israel.

I am twenty-one. I am a Jewess. Today I choose my path in

life. And today I understand that my fate is indissolubly linked with the fate of my people. I am desperate because I do not know my own language and the history and the culture of my people. Every participant of this Congress who lives on the territory of his home country, amongst his own people, must understand me. I envy you, I envy you your fate and your possibilities, because a person deprived of his national identity, a person torn away from his homeland cannot have the feeling of being a fully valid personality.

I cannot imagine my future without returning home. But the answer I receive is always the same: YOUR APPLICATION IS REFUSED. The Assistant Head of the Moscow Department of Visas and Registration of Foreigners tells me cynically: "Not even in a year, not even in two years . . . not even in five years. . . ." This is the present-day policy of the Soviet Union and the government is not interested in the fact that for me these are years during which a person's character is formed and defined. The years when one acquires one's basic training, the years when one's direction and tasks in life are defined, will prove for me to be years of unending suffering, of extreme solitude far from my country and from the people who are close to me. They will be years of insecurity, of painful waiting and despair. Fighting against the terror that seizes my mind, I think: "If only I can survive. . . ."

Young people of the world, I appeal to you, my contemporaries! I appeal to you and to all those who retain feelings of justice and humanity, to raise your voice against a gross violation of international law and elementary humanity.

Milkina Alla Tsalevna

25 May 1970

On the 26th of May at nine o'clock in the morning, I was at the Borovitsky Gate of the Kremlin—the main entrance to the Palace of Congresses—waiting for the delegates to arrive. There were a number of young civilians and middle-aged men loitering about and I had to keep my eye on them. I didn't expect to return home that day and I had asked Sanja to come and stand not too far from the palace to watch what happened to me.

I sent the first copy of the letter in through the reception room and I then waited for the foreign delegates to arrive. It was rather a long time before I noticed a French-looking young man and gave him my letter in an envelope. The second attempt failed. I had accosted a foreign-looking man in English, but he didn't understand and asked in pure Russian, "What? What?" I left him without answering, swearing to myself at the damned Komsomol boys at the beck and call of the KGB who were so successful in looking westernized.

Suddenly a black car approached the gate. Sleek, blond young men jumped out of the back seat and rushed to open the front door of the car. A smiling American Negro got out and started for the entrance, accompanied by the fussy young men. I blocked his way and handed out my last envelope. He jumped back as if I held a grenade.

"It is a letter of solidarity," one of his guards explained and obligingly stretched out his hand. "Give me the letter!"

"Take your hands away! It is not for you!" I muttered through my clenched teeth in disgust and addressed the Negro in English, "It is a letter to you personally. Please, read it."

He accepted the letter with trembling hands and thanked me, and I stepped out of his way.

There were no other copies left, so I looked around and slowly walked away. I was exhausted with tension. Several blocks away from the gate, I met Sanja. He had not noticed anyone following me and nobody seemed to be paying any attention to me, but he himself had gotten into a very stupid situation.

He had been standing among those "ordinary looking" young men whom I feared most of all, when he suddenly realized that they were looking steadily at the lapel of his jacket. He looked down and grew cold with terror. He had forgotten to take off a badge which he had recently received from some American Jewish tourists. On a blue circle, there was written in white: "Israel needs peace."

When he raised his eyes, one of the men was approaching him. His blood had already curdled with horror when he heard, "Got a cigarette?"

Nothing happened. The men probably did not understand English, but we decided not to tell anyone about the incident, lest they consider us complete fools.

On my way home I began to think that the Soviet devil was

not as black as he had been painted. Our Jewish *chutzpa* (impudence) had already gone beyond all limits and we were still unmolested. Maybe there was no need for fear and caution, and we should understand that we could not only write letters, but openly demand and demonstrate. Perhaps the whole population of the country was afraid to lift its voices because of this imaginary fear and perhaps the authorities were supported by a terror which had been created before they came to power.

I remembered my first interview at the synagogue with an American correspondent. One of his questions had been, "Why are you all not afraid to be here, to sing these songs?" I couldn't answer then, but now I understood that the courage of thousands of people came only out of a feeling of impunity and that the fear had been gradually overcome because nobody had been punished for coming to the synagogue. Probably only particular individuals possessed the other kind of courage which would be tested if the authorities decided to punish.

A week later I was called for an interview at the Ministry of the Interior. The note was signed by Ovchinnikov, Chief of one of the departments of the Ministry. "Oho," I thought. "People wait for months to get an appointment with him and here he himself is calling me. I must have struck home."

I took some books with me, having decided to go after the interview to the library to read for my exams at the Institute. I didn't want to place any special significance on this talk and spent the day as usual. However impressive it might be, there might be many of them and I decided not to let them disturb the course of my everyday life.

The Chief made me wait for a while in his reception room, for which I forgave him—for once. At last I was invited to come in. A middle-aged, balding man in a military uniform greeted me without standing up. He was not short and had a slender, well-cared-for figure. He seemed to have no face because all his features and hair were the same pale blond color. Instead of eyes, he had a thin pince-nez with two sharp lights. I could easily imagine two well-polished boots under the table. "How banal," I thought. "They even look like the Gestapo." I sat down opposite him across the table, which was empty except for my personal card which he held constantly in his hand.

"You wrote to us, didn't you?"

"No."

"No?"

"I wrote to the Presidium of the Young Communist League. The address is a little different."

"Well . . . The Komsomol authorized us to answer you."

"So what is your answer?"

"Your request to leave for Israel is refused."

"Why?"

"Because Israel is waging an aggressive war against progressive Arab countries."

"Perhaps you think so, but I don't."

"Well, ours is an objective opinion. Yours is subjective."

"Again, that is what you think. In my opinion, my belief is objective."

"We shall not discuss it now. You are not allowed to leave. Is that clear?"

"No. I don't belong to you. You do not own me. I am a free person."

"It only seems that way to you."

"Well, then I shall have to struggle for my freedom."

"Ha-ha-ha-ha-ha."

I gave him time to finish his laughing performance which lasted for at least two minutes.

"Did you call me just to say this?"

"Yes."

"Then you have wasted my time." And I left the room without saying good-by. I had learned how to be impolite. When I came out into the street, I breathed in the fresh air, looked at the blue summer sky and the sun, and went on my way to the library.

In the summer my sister and brother-in-law rented a country house. Since they were both working, I spent the days practically alone, looking after my brother-in-law's twelve-year-old daughter, typing, and working at the album about Israel, which was almost ready.

Once a week I went to town to pick up some new portion of work and to get paper. Once when I had come to Moscow to pass along the typed materials and couldn't find anyone at home, I found myself far from home, late at night, with a storm about to break. I thought there was no use wasting time waiting for the storm to be over and stepped out into the street. Next day the papers were to write that it was the worst storm in many years, but that night I was on an empty street with rain pounding down. The heavy shower was especially unpleasant because I was wearing a woolen sweater and it was soon full of water. I walked in water up to my ankles. The wind swung the street lamps, and the shadows of the trees and telegraph poles danced a wild dance around me. My ears were deafened by thunder and my eyes began to ache at the bright lightning.

I did not react like King Lear, but accepted the terrible situation with some sense of humor. I considered the storm quite natural for my way of life and began to analyze the absence of fear in me.

First, I imagined what my feelings and thoughts would be if I were afraid of the storm. I immediately thought, what if a person was waiting for me, knowing I was out in this storm. Then I would probably feel uneasy. And, since there was nobody to wait for me and worry if I didn't come home that night, I was not afraid. It occurred to me that usually the greatest part of the fear that we experience in dangerous situations is the fear for those who are waiting and worrying. Having understood this, I smiled at the next flash of lightning and invited it to rage still more. There was not a single person waiting for me now and there was something comforting in feeling lonely.

That night I did not, as usual, connect the great storm with my "great" prediction.

On the 15th of June, I came to Moscow to pick up some things I needed for the country house. In the evening I packed them very awkwardly, having taken too much, and left my apartment. I planned on my way to drop in at my friend's place for a little chat and then take the bus to the village. I had two huge net bags with me and a big can, which I had filled with thirty eggs. I had put several pairs of shabby shoes to wear in the country in one net bag, and clean writing paper, carbon paper, and a lot of material from the "Samizdat" to read and to retype in the other.

The bags were terribly heavy and I stopped with relief on the third floor in front of my friend's apartment and rang the bell. The door was opened by some strange people and I saw that the apartment was full of men. "Oho," I thought, "the Jews have got together. I shall have a nice time now." But their strange silence and the expressions on their faces put me on guard. They were too tall for Jews, too blond, too ordinary looking.

"Search!!!" the thought pierced my mind. I saw my friend's desperate face in the back room. He had always been kind to me and didn't want me to get into trouble.

The men had already stretched out their hands. "Come in, you are welcome. Can I help you?" One took my bags away from me, the other took me into one of the rooms where women were sitting. My eggs, shabby shoes, and the papers were put carefully in the corner and I was politely warned. "Please, don't touch anything. Don't move. Sit quiet."

There were five people from the KGB, four men and one girl, whose role I understood later. We, the Jews, were three women and three men. The "visit" had struck pay dirt. The people who came to the house that evening were really important and had brought a lot of material with them, but I was not aware of this yet and thought my visit to be the most compromising for the host.

Fear, dreadful paralyzing fear, filled me. This was the first time in my life that I had felt real fear, fear for my life. Fear turned out to be red with yellow flaring candles. It blocked the whole world for me. I didn't see, didn't hear anything. I couldn't sit and stood leaning against the wall as if it were easier to meet the danger standing. A big hammer seemed to be striking me on the head, but I was numb and couldn't resist anything. It was bodily fear without understanding of what or why.

At last something deep in my mind began to function and told me I was terrified. I tried to shame myself out of it, but nothing helped. Fear was stronger, more vital, than any other feeling. I called to mind the image of Yossi and told myself he would be ashamed of me if he knew how I was reacting, but that didn't help either. On the contrary, it gave me more reason to fear. Yossi would suffer greatly if I disappeared that night. The thought almost made me cry, but I would not let them see me crying.

The man who was obviously the chief had finished with the materials of the others and turned to mine. He was working like a surgeon, taking every piece of paper carefully, examining it, and putting it to this or that side.

"Well, what is your name?" the man behind the red shroud asked.

"Why should I tell you my name when you didn't introduce yourself?" I stammered. Somewhere I had read that courageous people behaved like that.

He smiled and showed me his red identity card. Perhaps he had also read the same thing. There was nothing else to do but to give him my name, since he had my documents in front of him. Then he continued to examine my baggage.

"What is this?" he asked, pointing to the can.

"Eggs," I answered.

He lifted up the lid and looked into the can. I wished the eggs could explode out of there.

"And what is this?" he pointed to the first net bag.

"Shoes." This time he didn't open the bag.

"And this?"

"Paper. . . ."

He took the whole bag and put it on the table. His face lit up as one by one he began to put the typed sheets on one side and the clean paper on the other.

I looked at the table and images of the KGB headquarters, its chambers and tortures passed before my eyes. I thought, "If they go with me to the country house, they will find the typewriter and then I'm finished. How can I stand all this?"

The man stacked every sheet, dictating the name of it to his assistant.

"I typed translation from English, 'Modern Literature in Israel,' 52 pages; a typed translation from English, 'Education for the New Generation,' 48 pages; a typed translation from English, 'Massada,'; a typed collection of letters from Israel, 8 pages; and what is this?" he showed the sheets of paper to his assistant.

"It is Hebrew. Some poems, I think."

"Can you read it?"

"Not yet."

"Oh," I thought, "they prepare their own specialists in Hebrew. Idiot! He couldn't learn enough for such translation. But it really sounds respectable: a Department of Special Importance, Operative Group for Searches and Arrests, Preparatory Course in Hebrew for the staff."

"I am sorry, but we shall have to ask for your help," the man turned to me.

"You are welcome."

"Can you translate it?"

"Certainly." I began to recite in Russian without looking at the paper.

> *"When returns to me from the battlefield*
> *The man whom I love*
> *All the soldiers will embrace each other*
> *And the cannons become silent."*

"O.K. That's enough. And this one?"

"The air of mountains makes me drunk like wine
And the smell of pine trees,
And the wind in the twilight
Is full of ringing of bells.
My Jerusalem of gold
And of copper and of light
I am your violin to sing
Songs to you."

My voice quavered.

"Enough, thank you." And he put the song into the pile of Special Importance.

"Now, Alla Tsalevna Milkina, what an unfortunate visit for you," he began, with the smile of a boa constrictor. "Don't you have any sense of self-preservation?"

"No, you see, I was born only in 1949. If I had been born in 1937, I might have such a sense."

"No, Alla, it didn't help me either," said one of our women who had been born in 1937, the year of the Stalin purges.

"Then you would have had to be born in 1905," one of the KGB men said. That was the year of the first Bolshevik Revolution.

"Oh, that would not help me in all cases."

"If I were in your place now, I would not talk like that."

I shut up.

The man started to read my letters. I had two, one to my sister and one to my uncle that I had intended to mail the next day. And one letter was the last loving letter from Yossi. The man took a penknife and opened the two closed envelopes as if he were opening a living thing. He read all the letters thoroughly and then handed them to his assistant for a second reading.

"Now, you have a wonderful writing style."

"I don't need your compliments," I said, irritated especially by his reading Yossi's short letter.

"O.K.! Now, you begin, please, Tanja," he nodded to the girl and left the room.

Tanja came up to me, shy and confused, and asked me to

take off my clothes. I laughed. The length of the ceremony and all the talking had blown away the red shroud of fear and I had come to myself. This new act reminded me of a detective film and I unbuttoned my dress with a smile. The girl, following some strict instructions, looked into what seemed a dozen hidden places, thanked me, and turned to the other two women.

They looked at her with disgust.

"I am not going to show you what I have in my underpants."

"Neither am I."

The girl stepped back. By that time, the rest of the group had finished the same ceremonies with the men and brought their findings into our room, which had been turned into the headquarters. The table was piled with heaps of typed material, photocopies of Hebrew textbooks, films, and dozens of individual and collective letters from Jews to the General Secretary of the United Nations, U Thant, who was due to arrive in Moscow the next morning.

I realized that my papers were not the worst and didn't add much to the troubles of the family, at least. The whole procedure tired me and I lay down unceremoniously on the sofa. The whole KGB group began to examine the walls, the bedding, the cupboards, and so on.

Suddenly the doorbell rang. The KGB men looked at each other and one went to open the door. It was 12 o'clock at night.

"*Shalom, haverim*!" we heard the familiar voice of one of our friends and the cold answer, "How do you do! How do you do!"

They took him into our room and we saw with relief that he was without a single bag or book. We looked at his perplexed face and didn't show a sign of knowing him. Maybe some day we would have to prove that we were strangers and had met by accident.

They immediately searched him and took a small piece of paper from his jacket pocket. The little note said: "Grandma Ronja has unpleasant guests whom she did not expect." It meant that Sanja's apartment was being searched also. But our guests were also good readers and understood what it meant. The poor man who had brought the note was for a long time after called "*Shalom, haverim*" or "Grandma Ronja."

The search continued until three o'clock in the morning. At the end we were all sitting in a group discussing with our guests different items of the Criminal Code. They were polite and participated with frankness. At that time the KGB had put on a new mask. They assured us that they were only doing their job. They didn't have anything against us personally and treated us like common Soviet people. They acted only by order of the Prosecutor of Leningrad, who gave the orders to make the search in connection with an act of high treason committed that very morning in Leningrad.

We were at a loss and did not understand.

At three o'clock, the KGB left the house, leaving us behind in the apartment. We all had a cup of tea.

"Comrades!" one of the men exclaimed. "We are all witnesses of the greatest liberalization that Soviet Russia has ever known."

"You're crazy! What are you saying?" we all protested.

"Yes. If we are all sitting here and drinking tea after a night search, it means a real and great liberalization."

We all laughed and agreed.

21

The summer passed after the shock of June 15. Two more searches were made in other Jewish homes in Moscow and we all exchanged guesses and impressions of what they meant.

Both other homes had their own anecdotes about the terrible night. Sanja's father, in the full swing of the search, suddenly fell asleep sitting on a chair and began snoring terribly. His friends had often laughed at him for his snoring, but this time everybody envied him his unruffled calm. During the search, the

KGB men asked him, showing him the portrait of Theodor Herzl in his bookcase, "Who is this?"

"Grandfather," he answered.

He watched them writing down: "So-and-so claims that it is his grandfather."

"No, no!" he protested. "I didn't say 'my.' Just 'grandfather.' "

They crossed out the word "his" and "the portrait of a man with a black beard with his hands crossed on his chest" was registered as a portrait of "the grandfather." In each case it was perfectly true.

In the other Jewish home the KGB found a Hebrew lesson in full swing. The host, a man with a great deal of experience in dealing with the authorities, invited them in with a hospitable gesture and suggested to his pupils that the lesson go on. Somehow the pupils could not compose their thoughts after the coming of the "guests." The KGB men went about their search and the family cat watched, sitting on a small table in the room. Hours passed and the cat didn't move. After the search was over, the hostess picked the cat up and found under it their pocketbook with the names and addresses of all their friends. Just what the KGB wanted! Moved by the loyalty of the cat, the mother of the home treated it to a big steak and promised to take it to Israel.

But the whole business was not funny. We soon learned that fifty searches had been made all over the Soviet Union—in Leningrad, Riga, Kharkov, Kishinev, Sukhumi. Little by little we found out the reason for this campaign—or, to be more correct, the pretext.

On the 15th of June, in the morning, twelve young people (ten Jews and two Russians) had attempted to hijack a plane in a Leningrad airport to cross the border. The Jews who took part in this plot wanted to go to Israel. I was terrified when I learned their names: Israel Zalmanson and his brother and sister and her husband; Leib Khnokh and his young pregnant wife, Mary; Joseph Mendelevitch. I had met them all in Riga the previous year. Driven to despair, they had decided to challenge the Soviets and break through the tortuous bureaucracy by this courageous act.

Better such a risk than years of fruitless waiting. How I understood them and how I envied them their courage! Still. . . .

Most of them were leaving their parents behind and everyone knew that if you crossed the border you exposed your family to persecution. Could they have thought only of themselves at that moment? Maybe they wanted to be caught and draw the attention of the whole world to the plight of Soviet Jewry by their trial. But how could they take women—and one of them pregnant? And was the whole affair worth the breakup of all Jewish activities in the Soviet Union, mass searches, and arrests of many other people? Hadn't we already drawn the attention of the world by our open letters and legal activities? And besides, why choose this form of crossing the border at the very moment when our country, Israel, was suffering more than any other state from hijacking and world opinion was decisively against it?

No, they couldn't have failed to realize all this. We found it hard to believe the story because it was just unbelievable. And the events that followed it seemed typical and planned—all the searches carried out on the same day, the 15th of June, and all over the country. A short announcement of the attempt appeared in a Leningrad newspaper for that day. The KGB undoubtedly knew about the plan beforehand. Had it perhaps not only known, but instigated it? Was it a frame-up to find a pretext to search all important Jewish places, to arrest people, and to put an end to this Zionist "infection" inside their healthy body?

But these twelve people in fact went to the airport; they did plan to hijack the plane. They were arrested in the act of approaching the plane. The KGB sadists had been playing with them like a cat with a mouse. So what was it? A voluntary involvement in a provocation? Nonsense! There is no use in trying to guess. The future will show the truth.

In the meantime, we all curtailed our activities and I sat in my country house like a fool, waiting for the invitation from the KGB.

(Once a wife said to her husband: "Look here, Ivan. Guests will be coming soon. Go and wash your neck." Ivan sighed heavily and went to the washstand, but suddenly stopped on the way. "And if they don't come," he said, "I shall sit like a fool with a clean neck, hey?")

Such a fool was I, as I cleared my apartment of all compromising material and sat waiting.

* * *

In June I received a parcel through an English firm, Dinnerman and Company. These parcels came to Jews who had once signed a collective letter and we assumed that unknown friends or organizations wanted to help us. They themselves might not have realized what kind of help that was. These parcels often found us on the brink of starvation and despair. But even in such cases we sometimes could not help saving some of the things—so beautiful were they. Jewish wives, exhausted with economic problems at home, enjoyed wearing luxurious nylon fur coats over worn old dresses.

At that time I had left my job and was sitting in the country house as if in prison, dependent upon my sister's money. The decision to leave my job had come in April. I felt I could no longer stand the calls to the Special Department, the constant following, and the atmosphere of complete silence around me. I had to admit their success in making the place too "hot" for me to stay. The salary which I had been receiving could no longer save me from starvation anyway. I was leaving without sorrow and with confidence. The Chief, who had long before taken the other side, considered it his duty to warn me about the consequences.

"The authorities would not like you to be without a job."

"But why? According to the law, I have the right not to work as long as I am studying."

"I am not talking about the law. Your classes are only in the evenings and you will have a lot of spare time. Authorities do not like it when people have spare time."

"Why?"

"Because people begin to think, to read a lot, to ask themselves questions, meet many other people."

"A-ah, now it is clear."

It was a revelation. A lot about Soviet laws and ways of thinking became clear to me. But I was to make many more discoveries, which were no longer painful.

The Dinnerman parcel which arrived at the end of June saved me from the loneliness which had been choking me. I left my foolish country house and went by train to Riga, to Yossi.

At that moment, which was dangerous for both of us and full of unexpected visits and calls, I wanted to spend a few days with him. No letters or telephone calls could substitute for his single kiss, for a single look of his dark eyes. I rushed to Riga in spite of all the devils in the world.

I arrived in the morning, ran to his house, and rang the bell. Yossi opened the door and stood there dumfounded.

"You?"

"Me!"

"How?"

"So!"

He seized me without further questions and began to kiss my face and smell my hair, laughing with joy.

We spent three days just being together. Wherever we had to go, we were just two of us together, becoming irretrievably involved in a state where you feel you can't live your life without the other person, where you exist, move, think, create, only when he exists, moves, thinks, and creates somewhere near you—the feeling which is called love.

I returned to Moscow and sank back into emptiness. I entered the empty country house and sat heavily on a chair, looking at the paint on the wall without seeing anything or thinking. I sat like that for a long time until my emotion burst out. I lay on the bed, screaming, biting the pillow, and sinking in a flood of tears. This time reason didn't stop me or shame me. I understood myself and, deep in my heart, was glad that I had become a healthy person again. Yes, I was screaming and sobbing, but who wouldn't when she is in love and scores of obstacles stand in her way to marriage? To marry? No, even to be together. I shuddered at the thought of marriage. Marriage meant for us a terrible new obstacle on our way to exodus. How could we get ourselves involved in marriage when all of us were struggling for an exit? Both of our cases were a contribution to the general struggle and, if we stopped in the middle, wouldn't it be betrayal? But we could apply together! No, all these marriages had to wait until the border was crossed. Here—nothing, until we got out! But I wanted to be with him, I didn't want to lose him here or there! But he hadn't yet proposed. . . .

This train of thought went on and on, over and over, and no amount of reasoning could help me. I thought I would go crazy. I called Yossi and said, "I am dying."

"So am I," he said in a terrible voice.

"I can't live like this," I said evasively.

"I can't live without you. We must think of something. Maybe I shall come soon."

In a few days he came to spend a day in Moscow. We lay on the grass in the garden.

"I want you to be my wife," he said.

"So do I. When?" I knew what to ask.

"You know, with all these troubles around us and it is so difficult to find jobs and places to live, I think it is better to do it in a . . . year."

"O.K.," I said carelessly, jumping to my feet. "Then we shall talk about it again in a year."

I was not offended. I understood him perfectly, but at the same time I decided to find a new job in Moscow, to continue my studies, my regular life, and to cut off my head if it dared to think too much. I had again to be a good, reasonable girl, if there was a year to wait. But what kind of a period is a year? How long is it? I couldn't imagine.

* * *

I still had half a year before I could again apply for an exit visa. Six endless months. It would be too easy for the OVIR if I left them in peace for this period. I had to do something, to go to someone to make a scandal, to write to someone somewhere. The third was the easiest for me. By that time the Israeli radio had announced the formation of the new Committee of Solidarity with the Jews of the Soviet Union. We felt that Israel had definitely heard our call and was trying to help. It had begun the previous year when Golda Meir for the first time put the Soviet Jewish question on the agenda of a Knesset meeting. Now we could feel that the second front was open. And the new committee was a new address to which we could send our letters and feel certain that someone would act on our behalf.

It was difficult for me to ask for something from anyone in Israel, but I knew that my letter, if received, would be read by different people all over the world and it would add to the general noise which we wanted to make about our problem. And I wrote this letter:

To the Israeli Public Committee of Solidarity with the Jews of the Soviet Union

From: Milkina Alla Tsalevna

Dear Sirs:

It is only extreme despair and a hopeless situation that force me, in this difficult moment for our Homeland, to appeal to the Israeli Government for help.

The establishment of the Israeli Public Committee of Solidarity with the Jews of the Soviet Union gives me hope and permits me to apply directly to you and to ask you to transmit my letter to those who can help me in any way to emigrate to the State of Israel.

I am twenty-one years old. I have no parents. My close relatives live in Israel. In 1969 I applied to the Soviet Government with the request to give me permission for emigration to Israel. However, all my appeals and complaints have been categorically denied.

From the time that I submitted documents for emigration to Israel, my life here has stopped. All the doors are closed to me, but I ask that only one be opened to me—the one to Israel. It is my Homeland, the land of my people, and I cannot imagine my life without my return to the land of my Homeland.

From my earliest childhood, I was isolated from any manifestations of the Jewish culture, even in those forms that are possible here in the Soviet Union. The Soviet educational system has done everything that it could to deprive me of my national face, to tear me away from Jewish culture and traditions, to force me to forget everything relating to my people. I heard the word "Jew" only as an insult, thrown about by those surrounding me. And, after leaving school and entering life, I found out that I had a "bad fifth point" in my form. But this was not the main thing.

There is in a human being something higher, something that is stronger than any educational systems and state apparatuses. And I have returned to my people. I am happy that I have acquired a Homeland and, together with it, a sense to my life. Everything that has now opened before me: the heroic history of my people, the literature, traditions, its great unbreakable spirit —all this has allowed me to say: "I am happy that I have been born a Jewess!" And the sense of my new life is in my return to my Homeland and in my service to my people, the people of Israel.

But even my first attempts to make use of my lawful rights, guaranteed to me by the Constitution of the USSR, have shown themselves unfruitful. The rights are not for me—because I am a Jewess, and a "traitress" to boot! I applied to the Ministry of the Interior of the USSR, to the Council of Ministers of the USSR, and to the Supreme Soviet of the USSR. The answer was the same: "No! Never!"

Finally, as a former Komsomol member, I appealed to the delegates of the Sixteenth Congress of the Leninist Young Communist League of the Soviet Union. An officer of the Committee of the State Security answered me in the name of the Leninist Komsomol. He invited me to the Ministry of the Interior and confirmed the refusal to my request. When I protested that I was a free person, he answered: "That's what it seems to you!"

Yes, I have already understood this. I am not a free person because I live in the Soviet Union and I am a Jewess. But—I want to be free. I want to return to my own country and, hand in hand with my brothers and sisters, to build it and to defend it.

Every new day that I spend far away from my Homeland brings me despair. Because each such day is a day lost in my life.

I beg you to do everything that is possible and to help me to get permission to emigrate to Israel—permission to live.

Respectfully yours,
Milkina

There was now the problem of smuggling the letter abroad. No special efficient ways were available then after the catastrophe of June 15. I had to do something myself.

So I went to the Sheremetyevo International Airport to hunt for foreign tourists. There were scores of them, for it was the summer tourist season. Singles, couples, and groups—they were all so bright, noisy, laughing. I could only choose one of them, so

I sat looking and listening. A terrible shyness and fear prevented me from acting quickly. I examined people around me. Was anyone watching me? No, but I couldn't move.

Suddenly an episode made me feel better. I saw a young French woman saying "good-by" to a man and crying bitterly. They must have been lovers and recent ones, and she didn't want to leave him. I looked at her with a smile. These beautiful, bright, noisy people from the other side also had sorrow and grief. They also could cry. At that particular moment I was happier than she was because I was not crying. I felt stronger. If there is sorrow all over the world, then we shall attack it together, so that there need no longer be partings or fear of parting anymore.

I looked around once more and saw the right one. He was a member of a French tourist group and spoke fluent Russian. I approached him quickly.

"Can you do me a favor and mail this letter from Paris?"

He looked at the letter. "I am sorry, but I can't. I am really very sorry. Please, excuse me," he said with a shy smile.

"It's O.K. Excuse yourself," I blurted out with disgust and turned away, ready to rush out of the terminal. But suddenly the failure made me stubborn. I had spent three hours in the terminal and I would not leave like that. "They are more afraid than we are," I thought bitterly about the Frenchman.

The right one proved to be a young French girl who looked at me with surprise and said, "Why not? Of course, I can take it. Give it to me. I shall put it deep in my pocketbook." Soon she was already in the plane.

I waved "good-by" and "thank you" to her and jumped gaily out of the terminal, sending my last smile at all suspicious-looking people in the hall. My letter was on its way.

* * *

On the 8th of August, Yossi and I went to Leningrad. Yes, just like that. I took a train from Moscow; he, a plane from Riga. We met in Leningrad, took each other by the hand, and ran along the streets, boulevards, and embankments of the city. It was a strange choice for a tour then, but Leningrad was not only the place of the hijacking plot and the "cradle of the Great October Revolution," it was also the most beautiful Russian city of the eighteenth and nineteenth centuries, the city built by Peter the Great, who had done his best to make it no less beautiful than the best capitals of Europe. Here Russian czars competed with each other in luxury and magnificence. They were neither intelligent nor liberal, but they loved to build. The masterpieces of Petersburg are a monument to this.

We walked our feet off through the numerous and the best picture galleries in the world, twisted our necks looking to the right or to the left, up and down, at the huge cathedrals and palaces. It was for all this that we came to Leningrad, to spend ten days away from our world and together.

On the 9th of August, we went to a restaurant to celebrate Yossi's twenty-first birthday. Before we left my uncle's apartment where we were staying, Yossi pulled me to him and said: "Tallinn is Tallinn, Leningrad is Leningrad, but there always comes an end."

"So what can be done?"

"I want to marry you."

"You told me that once. But when?"

"Whenever you want."

"Oh, you want me to decide?"

He stared at me with a desperate look. He wanted to get an answer from me, but what answer did he want? And I decided to be frank. This was no time to be shy or proud. My answer now might decide my future.

"You know, with all that is going on around us, there is so much danger that we can lose each other. I think we must marry as soon as possible, so if anything happens, we will be together and nobody can separate us. I understand that we don't know each other very well, but, as for me, judging by what I do know about you, I can expect only the best. And if I am running any risk, I do it with confidence." Of course, I had to sound reasonable and clever, but the meaning of all this long speech was, "I love you. I terribly want to marry you."

His face brightened and he smiled happily. "You know, I think so also."

"So when?"

"Now."

"How do you do!"

"No, I mean that after Leningrad we should go to Riga and register ourselves for marriage."

"Do you really mean this?"

"Why not?"

I was going to explode from the happiness that filled me and I began to laugh. I had never known before that happiness can be expressed in laughter. And he looked at me smiling.

In the restaurant we plunged into semi-darkness, low music, and the light clatter of crockery. We were certainly going to spend a huge sum of money there, but we didn't care. From that evening on, we would do everything together—saving, wasting—so nothing mattered then.

I looked at the handsome man opposite me who seemed so big across the small table. I could hardly believe that his beautiful hands with their long, straight fingers now also belonged to me. I could touch his shoulders whenever I wanted, put my fingers into his black curly hair. He is mine now. He is responsible for me and I for him, but the first is more important. From now on, I would not decide any large problem for myself. I would just stop thinking. My head would serve as a holder for face and hair, and I would be all body and nothing else. The silence bothered me. I wanted to shout, to jump, to beat the crystal, and I could hardly suppress wild sounds that were ready to escape me.

Yossi looked at me with his quiet smile. There were no more questions in his eyes. At last he was calm. He had achieved what he had wanted. He was taking me from that mad Moscow and, if I were to do stupid things or go crazy, at least I would do it under his care. He was like a parent watching his child playing with toys, but constantly on guard lest the child hurt herself.

We visited all the palaces of Petersburg with their luxurious halls—gold, silk, jewelry, silver, velvet, lace looked at us from under the glass covers. Now I felt stronger than all the czars. They had been overthrown and I was alive and happy; I was enthroned by my love. I jumped on the pedestals, overthrew the metal statues of the ex-emperors, and stood in their places. We stood silently in the house-museum of Pushkin over his deathbed and I felt pity for the greatest love poet of Russia, for he had not been as happy in love as I. I stuck out my tongue at the stony sphinxes on the bridges of the Neva. They stood opposite one another and would never be able to approach each other and they could not apply for exit visas. I was happy.

* * *

On the eve of our leaving Leningrad for Riga, we came home late. My uncle and aunt were preparing to go to bed when suddenly the telephone rang at that late hour. I heard my uncle talking to someone, "Yes, Milkina, yes Alla—my niece." We looked at each other, surprised. My uncle finished his conversation and came into the room very pale.

"Switch on Kol Israel."

We did, but the program was already over and we heard only a phrase from "The News in Brief." "A letter of a young Jewish girl from Moscow to the Israel Committee of Solidarity with the Soviet Jews."

My uncle, an old Communist, who didn't know much about my plans, was angry and frightened. After several angry remarks, he left us alone, not being able to say much. Besides all the rest, he also felt sad because he was a good Jew.

I felt triumphant. I walked to and fro, feeling strong and impatient to act. Suddenly I felt irritated at being there far from Moscow, wasting time.

"You are so proud," Yossi said, looking at me with alarm.

"Yes, I am," I said shamelessly and rudely, and looked at him with challenge. I was not going to conceal my vanity from him. "Yes, I am very proud. I feel that it is my great victory."

"Yes, I congratulate you, but it is not your victory. You didn't do anything more than others in this case. It just worked out."

"Maybe you are right," but I could not stop. "But, you know, I want to be frank. I don't know what leads me in my way, real love for Israel or just a desire for anti-activities, heroism. There are certain kinds of people who can't live without idealism and struggling for something. Israel is just a dream for me, just my imagination. This dream hasn't the foundation it has for you. I created it myself and I don't know whether I did it for the sake of going to Israel or just for the sake of my own vanity."

Yossi looked at me with pain. "You, too, Brutus?"

"What do you mean?"

"I mean what I say. There are so many of this kind among us, but I didn't know you also belonged to them."

Everything I had said was not true. I knew I was not like that and had used this theory to check myself sometimes. I had said all this aloud, but I had not shown Yossi that it was my game with myself. But the fact that he had become so quickly disappointed in me and believed all this nonsense irritated and offended me terribly.

He found me late at night in the street and it was only his great love for me that helped us to overcome this misunderstanding. He accepted me with all that I was. Next day we left for Riga to announce our engagement and to discuss with the family the plans for our wedding.

That wonderful new feeling of becoming a wife! In the Leningrad-Riga train I felt for the first time a new capacity. Moving about our sleeper with unknown people around me, arranging our bags, or just sitting and looking out of the window at the passing forests, I had a very strange and pleasant sensation in my entire body which now seemed to become stronger and more elastic. In my entire being I felt the look of the man beside me and I knew that the look in those eyes would be with me all my life whatever I did and wherever I was. And all my acts would now take into account those eyes and their owner, his wishes and his needs. I would never more exist as a single human being—I was a half. And a half of something that was many times more than I ever was alone. If a few days ago I had felt myself in the middle of life, I was now at the very beginning.

I moved more quickly and more gracefully. I enjoyed my movements and that new sensation. What a wonderful new feeling it was to become a wife!

The night passed and we approached Riga. I felt confident in my future, yet I was very nervous. I did not know what the parents' reaction would be, but I was certain they would not be delighted and the thought of the impending serious talk made me tense. I hoped that the slow walk from the railway station to the Rusineks' home would calm me down.

Then—there was Ezra Rusinek approaching us . . . with a bunch of flowers. "Congratulations!" he said and smiled, looking into our startled frightened faces. "Go home, have breakfast and a rest. Mother is waiting for you. I'll be back home after two."

We ran home excited. Yossi's mother really was waiting for us with eggs in silver nests, cheese, and coffee ready on the table. We had a merry breakfast, a nice chat about Leningrad, and a short rest. When his father came home, we all became silent; his mother cleaned the table and they both sat down opposite us. The empty table between us seemed like a field of battle.

"Nu?" said father. "What do you have to tell us?"

My eyes fell and began to bore through the table.

"We want . . . uh—nu . . . uh this—I mean to marry," Yossi said.

"That is good," his father said. "Have you thought about everything? I mean, a place for living, your studies, work, a means of living?"

"I want to go home," I thought to myself.

"Oh yes, of course," Yossi hurried to assure the parents and began to set forth our plans. The thing did not prove to be too awful and the parents took a lively part in the discussion, but still when it was all over, I felt much relieved. And then, why should they not be happy with me? I am a fine girl and they would soon come to know me.

We did not have any problems with a means of living with both of us working and studying. On moving to Riga, I could change to the correspondence department and finish my fifth year of the Institute in Riga. The real problem was a place to live, which we did not have.

The Rusinek family lived in two rooms of a three-room apartment, with a young Russian couple for neighbors in the third room. Ilana, with her husband and little Hadassah, lived in one room, and the parents slept in the second room. Both rooms were very nice, although poorly furnished and sometimes reminding one of a railroad station with all the inhabitants running about. Those inhabitants also included all the friends who never missed an evening to come for "a chat with Ezra," to sign a new collective letter, or just to sit and read a newspaper. With all of them gathered in the evening, the Rusineks' apartment could compete with the Moscow subway at rush hour.

Yossi, with his long legs, was out of place here in the full sense of the words. So, when by the age of seventeen, he had shamelessly reached six feet and the folding bed could no longer hold him, his parents had had to rent from their neighbors a closet adjacent to the kitchen and the bathroom. The closet was two square meters and in it they managed to put a small bed. Yossi was triumphant and in his letters to me he liked to mention: "I have retired to my room to write this letter to you." This delighted me and proved to me that he was a perfect match, but the real delight came when I became acquainted with "the room" personally.

Of course my room of eight square meters was a palace compared to the closet. There Yossi could at least stretch out his legs and rest them on the opposite wall, but the idea of his coming to live in Moscow had only arisen when we began to discuss the problem of applying for visas.

And then moving to Moscow turned out to be a wonderful way out. For the last two years, the Rusineks had not been able to apply, for the Riga Department of Visas (OVIR) began to ask for a reference from the school of a young applicant. This was in order to prove to them that the applicant was not due to be drafted. Thus an applicant had to inform his university about his wish and the authorities at the university then immediately expelled the student "for the desire to leave for Israel" or more evasively "for behavior unfitting a Soviet student." This trick of OVIR worked. Dozens of Jewish families were stymied by this and could not apply for years.

For a young man, being expelled from the university meant immediate draft into the army—two years of service and then five years prohibition from leaving the country for military reasons. Nobody had dared to risk this except Lev, who now was due to be drafted in November. He is quiet and strong, but poor Natasha! How she would suffer for him.

The Moscow OVIR did not do this and we could safely apply in Moscow. In this way was our living problem solved.

When all the problems had been discussed, we went to the City Registry office and registered our marriage for October 15, 1970. We could have been married in a month according to Soviet law, but we needed time for all the arrangements and so set it for the middle of October. In order to avoid a lot of gossip in Jewish circles, we decided that nobody should know about our plans.

That same day Lev came to visit us. We looked at him mysteriously, "You know, Lev, we want to keep it a secret, but you are our closest friend and so we are telling only you—we are getting married."

He looked at us with a complete lack of surprise and said, "If you think that it is not written on your happy faces, you're deeply mistaken." Then he smiled warmly and added: "Congratulations! Let it be happier with you than with me."

Next day we went to the seashore to soak up the last summer rays of the sun.

The Riga seashore . . . it is a whole world. If, in summer, you want to find some of your friends, go to the shore—it is a meeting place for the Jewish population of Riga, who own or rent country houses all along the shore. For us Russian-speaking Jews, the Latvian names of the railway stations always sounded strange and pleasant, reminding us of past times spent there: "Boulduri, Dzintari, Meluzhi. . . ." The Riga seashore is a special page in the life of Latvian Jews. Pictures: Mïriam, Ezra, Hadassah on the shore; young Ilana and little Yossja, bespectacled Lev, and fat little Yehoshua, and finally little Hadaska, playing in the sand.

And now the whole Jewish seashore population seemed to be passing especially to see "the bride," the girl who had caught young Rusinek. We did not know whether our happy faces had given us away or rumor, which is stronger than all secrets.

One boy came up to me and politely invited me to come to Riga the following year. The whole shore resounded with laughter. He looked around confused, then understood, and grumbled in his bass voice: "Nu, what are you laughing at? I never know anything. No one tells me."

In a week I left for Moscow. Yossi's mother saw me off at the airport. In the terminal we ran into one of their acquaintances. Mother greeted him and introduced me: "Our daughter-in-law."

Daughter-in-law? Is it all real? I suddenly felt that I had a definite role in life. I was no longer a faceless actor in mass scenes, but had an important place in the performances of life. I felt very proud and entered the plane thinking of myself as a grown-up, independent woman.

When I reached Moscow, I found excitement among Zionist circles. People were being granted exit visas one after another. I went to the Department of Visas. At the entrance a young Jew, running out of the door, seized me in his arms, kissed me on the nose, and ran away shouting: "Permission, permission!"

With a rapidly beating heart, I entered the office. To my relief, the officer answered my inquiry to the effect that my refusal remained in force. Yet my nervousness did not leave me and when I learned that Basja was leaving I became panic-stricken. All kinds of feelings were mixed in me. I felt as if I were a small child and could do nothing alone. I was afraid I would be separated from Yossi; and I was ashamed of my feelings. I envied everyone who was leaving and I was afraid I would myself be given permission. And all these feelings were so jumbled together that I could do nothing but cry. When Yossi called from Riga, I couldn't utter a word and just sobbed into the receiver. Yossi kept shouting: "What has happened? Why are you crying? At least say something."

"Ba-a-sja is leaving," I sobbed into the receiver at last.

He sighed with relief. "So why are you crying? You must be happy for her."

"I am happy."

"So why are you crying?"

"I am afraid," and I started to cry again.

"Nu, stop it, please. Compose yourself. Everything will be all right," he assured me, but I felt he himself was not so sure.

He hung up the receiver and I was left crying, unable to do anything or to come to any decision. Next day Yossi suddenly called me again: "The registration will be on the 1st of October. I went to the registry office and this was the earliest that they could make the registration."

Oh, that Rusinek character. Why couldn't he have told me he was planning to do this? I would have hoped together with him, but to get a word out of a Rusinek is impossible.

The one month that I had to wait now until I went to Riga was a mere nothing compared to the month and a half. I discovered that I had to do so many things that I would hardly have enough time. And what a wonderful occupation it was to prepare one's own dowry.

We took out our huge old trunk, a dozen old bundles, and soon our room turned into a sea of *shmattes* (rags), which reached to our knees. Our Aunt Musja, who came to help us and to watch that justice be observed, stood in the middle of that sea like a general among defeated enemies. I screamed and begged them to throw all that away and Myra fell onto the bundles in convulsions of laughter.

But our general didn't pay any attention to us. She considered every *shmatte* with her experienced eye and expressed her thoughts aloud, "You can take this. This material you will divide in two. This dress hasn't served its time yet. It will do for a little longer. This to the bundle . . . this to the bundle . . . and this. . . ."

Soon all the *shmattes* were again packed into bundles and put into everlasting storage. I took some of the old pieces of fabric for sheets and tablecloths, the remains of father's practical mind and better times. And an old jacket of mother's, flannel, red with white spots. She had worn it when she was pregnant and when we grew up she put it on us when we had the flu. I washed and ironed it and put it deep among my things.

My aunt helped me sell some of the old furniture and bought for me a table and a double sofa. When the sofa was opened at night, it occupied the whole room from wall to wall. So we would have a real bedroom.

Then the day came when I waved everyone in Moscow my last maidenly good-by, invited the whole family for the wedding on the 17th of October, and went by train to Riga.

The day after I arrived in Riga, Yossi was urgently called to Moscow to meet one of our most active Zionists, at whose apartment I had visited on the 15th of June. The fellow had been called for interrogations several times and he felt he had to warn Yossi about the course of the questioning.

We were getting married during a terrible period. Person after person was being called for interrogation. Searches continued. Moscow and Riga, Leningrad and Charkov were in the clutches of the KGB, which tortured people with promises of exit and threats of prison. Everyone was torn between hope and fear. All Samizdat work was curtailed. As much as possible had to be concealed. Now the only way of struggle was caution.

And I was getting married. Father Rusinek constantly warned that if he were arrested, we should remain calm. And I wondered which one of the three of us would be arrested first or whether we should succeed in registering our marriage first.

I had brought from Moscow a pair of white shoes. And the wedding dress was supposed to come from Israel, from Miriam. Would it come in time? A wedding dress from Israel!

Newly married couples are given a pass to special shops for brides and bridegrooms. We decided to use the opportunity to buy gloves for Yossi. In the shop we ran into Ruth. She was also a bride and her wedding was set for the same day, October 17. We exchanged greetings, but I had little to say to her. She was so pale and tired. Every day there were hours of interrogations, threats of imprisonment—and all this before the wedding. The KGB kept their promise to give her a wedding gift. On the 7th of October, she was arrested and was not allowed to marry. Her fiancé, although he was granted an exit visa, remained to wait for her in Russia for the whole of her term of imprisonment—a year in a hard labor camp.

Nothing happened to us up to the day of our registration except that we overslept that morning. At 9:30 I jumped out of Yossi's bed closet and ran into a family friend with a camera, following me. I covered my face and ran into the bathroom.

The office was near the house and at five minutes to ten, a solemn procession of the Rusinek family directed its steps to this holy Soviet office, with the family friend's camera recording our every movement. We had asked for the registration at the earliest possible hour to avoid the music and the handshake of a deputy of the City Soviet, decorated with orders. We came very simply dressed, to the astonishment of the whole office staff. But there was one facility in the office I could not resist using—the photographer. And we were suitably punished: the picture was terrible.

The only thing we wanted to get from them was a seal and a notice in our passports saying we were married, meaning that we belonged to each other and no one could separate us.

The entire ceremony consisted of filling out forms and signing them. All was done in complete silence with the entire family standing around holding its collective breath and the family friend running around with his camera recording the historic moment for future generations. When the woman filling out the forms left the room for a moment, the friend passed his camera to Ezra, sat at her table shaking his head over the documents, looked through them and then shook our hands with a wide smile to the camera, and hastened to get away when the woman returned. That scene was the most impressive in the historic film.

At last the woman raised the seal and pressed it, first on Yossi's and then on my passport. The family let out a sigh of relief. Yossi and I winked at each other. *Mazel tov*!

The return trip passed in the same solemn manner. At home we all drank "*L'chayim*" and everyone returned to his usual occupation. Ezra, Yossi, and Ilana went to work. Mother and I sat at home chatting, discussing the wedding problems and waiting for our husbands.

The problems were usual. There were many close friends who could not be invited. By silent agreement, Jews avoided showing their acquaintance with each other in order not to reveal community ties. And at the same time a large party would not be expected at such a moment, especially one to which Jews from other towns would be invited.

But still about seventy guests had been invited, which was too many for the two rooms, even including the closet. So the parents had to rent a hall in the nearby Teachers' House.

Days passed. I was getting used to the family life, listening to stories, looking through the photograph albums, watching the home life of men with all their shirts, socks, jackets, and trousers, for my youth had been lived in feminine surroundings.

In consideration of the situation, we began our married life on the day of our civil registration without waiting for the religious ceremony. Our honeymoon began in the notorious bed closet.

Since it was adjacent to the bathroom, our sleep was accompanied by all the sound effects of such a neighborhood, which gave us rather romantic dreams of waterfalls, seas, rivers. Morning greeted us with the crash of pots and pans and the sizzling of frying eggs. Although the bed was very narrow, we were not concerned with falling out, for the walls on either side left us no room to fall. We awakened with the first visitor to the bathroom and listened with rage to the sounds of the waking house. The flushing of the toilet every fifteen minutes struck like a hammer on our heads. We both involuntarily became early birds, something we had never been.

When the last person left the bathroom, we put our heads out of our "bedroom" like partisans out of bushes and listened to hear whether anyone was approaching. When we had made certain the way was clear, we jumped directly out of bed into the kitchen and rushed into the bathroom.

We both looked terrible, but the parents surrendered first. They talked to some friends who immediately offered us a room in their apartment. In 1949 they had shared a room with Ezra, Roza, and baby Yossi. Now they were more than happy to invite Yossi and his wife to use one of their three rooms. The lady of the family, Frau Kil, liked to remember the times "when Yossi was not yet born," her good friend Frau Rusinek ("How is she there in Israel? She must be very old now."), and the years they had spent together in Siberia. She made us delicious cakes, "teiglach," and dreamed about our wedding party for which she would make a special kind of "teiglach."

On the 7th of October, Yossi as usual was leaving with his parents for his job after breakfast when the interurban interrupted telephone ring delayed him. Myra was calling from Moscow. I took the receiver.

"Alla?"

"Yes."

"Look here, I shall kill you." She always began with something pleasant. I tried to remember whether I had left a hot iron on the table or a teapot on the stove when I left, but then remembered that many days had already passed. And in her voice I heard that nervous smile that was so typical of her.

"What's happened?"

"There's a postcard for you here, from OVIR."

"What does it say?" I tried my best to keep my voice indifferent.

"It says: 'Please call us urgently. Telephone so-and-so.' "

"Urgently?" I raised my eyes to Yossi. He understood everything.

"O.K. Myra, thank you."

"What are you going to do?"

"I don't know. We shall see. I'll call you." The conversation was over.

It had happened. I went up to Yossi, put my hands on his chest, stroked him and said, "Don't worry. Everything will be all right. Go to work, dear. We'll call father. Don't be late for dinner."

When Ilana learned about the postcard, she ran home from her clinic and we went to father's place of work. The trolley-bus we took was as slow as if nothing had happened and I hated it for giving me time to think. I didn't want to think. I knew there were other people to think for me now and I was willing to leave it all to them. At last the trolley-bus came to our stop. Father was already standing there, quiet, but pale and tense. We walked silently to a nearby park. None of us doubted that it was the permission. Our long experience in dealing with the OVIR had taught us to understand every little thing in their behavior. And the word "urgently" meant a lot. We sat down on a cold bench. Father was silent. Ilana and I looked at him and waited. There was not a single thought in my mind. I was just waiting to be told what to do.

All my life I had really wanted someone to guide me. I had always thought there was someone stronger, cleverer, higher than I—the Party, the Komsomol, the school—and I was happy to serve them. In spite of the great change in my way of life, I was still ready to let my destiny rest in someone else's hands. But this time no one was willing to make a decision.

"You'll have to decide for yourself now," said father at last. "Only you and no one else."

Me decide? How could I? I didn't know what to decide. Yes, I really wanted to go to Israel. I wanted very much to go. But how could I leave Yossi and all of them behind? Would I be happy doing so? And it seemed to me a crime to leave one's husband and save oneself. Of course, I want to stay. But maybe they want me to go—to go and help him from Israel. It is a strong reason—to apply for an exit visa to rejoin your wife. No, it's nonsense. I'm just trying to justify my desire to go to Israel. Yes, at least let me be honest with myself. How will I feel if I lose this chance to leave for Israel? I have dreamed so much about it and now it is a reality. Israel . . . a dream . . . happiness. And Yossi . . . here in Russia, in danger. Doesn't he also want to go? A thousand times more than I. And what happiness could there be without him? The thought of him left behind in Russia. . . . No, I want to stay, I am sure. To be with him, to wait together, to struggle together. And if they want me to go? I am ready. It will be hard for me, but I shall go. The thought that I was doing it for them would help me.

Nu, say something. But father was silent. Oh, that Rusinek silence. But I saw now that the silence was deliberate. We all went to the chemical factory where Yossi worked. He came out and father and Ilana left us alone, my eyes following them with irritation. I was certain they would talk to each other. I looked at Yossi. This was the first time I had seen him in his overalls and I saw that he was sorry that I had. He had on a cotton suit, black with dust and chemicals, holes all over it, a white cap, and high rubber boots. And his divine pale face of a prophet looked out of all this. I felt ill and avoided looking at him. All of my irritation was turned on him.

"Are you going to tell me to decide for myself?"

"Don't be angry! If I knew what to do, I would have told you immediately. Calm yourself and let's think together."

I felt ashamed. Wasn't it harder for him than for me? If I go to Israel and he stays here without me? And if I stay, he will feel guilty.

We were standing in a wooden entrance gate with an indifferent man sitting behind a small window. I began to think aloud. "It is not yet certain that this is a permission," I said, hardly believing myself. "And if it is a permission, when they learn that I am already married, they will certainly annul it. But let's suppose they do allow me to go. Then I can leave only on one condition. You must be registered through the Moscow OVIR and apply there as we planned it before. Then, even if I leave, you will be able to apply safely and the rest of the family can then apply separately in Riga. I don't even want to go to call the OVIR before we get you registered as an inhabitant of Moscow. I am sure they will refuse me when they discover I'm married. I've heard about such cases. They think that such marriages are Jewish Zionist tricks, so they try to punish those who dare to make them. If they refuse, I'll be glad. But, to be on the safe side, we must register you in Moscow. Then, if they still tell me to leave, I shall go. I think it will be better if I am there. I feel you all think the same, but just don't want to say it."

Father and Ilana returned. Yossi kissed me on the forehead and we went home. In the evening we all discussed the plan and decided to put it into effect as soon as possible.

Next morning Yossi went to a doctor to get a certificate of sick-leave. He was successful. Any doctor would have believed his complaints, he looked so broken. That same afternoon we got tickets for an evening flight to Moscow.

Our plan was to spend one day in Moscow and take care of everything. If we didn't succeed, then I would stay in Moscow and Yossi would go back to Riga. On Saturday he had to go to the doctor again to reaffirm his sick-leave certificate. That Soviet red tape which had to be observed even at such a moment made me furious, but we were still living there and couldn't afford to make more trouble for ourselves.

At 12 P.M. on October 8, we arrived in Moscow. Next morning at eight o'clock, we left our house to begin our operation. Our plan involved several definite steps: militia, military registration and enlistment office, house-management office. The procedure of being discharged from the Riga military and house offices had been effected in one minute and I hoped that we could manage the Moscow business in one day. We were determined to try. It usually took people months, but I refused to consider failure and felt that if we didn't manage it, I would not be able to stand it.

All my nerves were taut. I felt as if I were walking on ice. I thought, "If the ice doesn't break, I shall be happy," and my hope grew as we approached the first step, but then there would be another step and another, each one to be taken in hope and fear.

The ice began to break immediately. We went to the militia and were informed that we must first go to the housing office. We took a bus back and ran into the office. The passport office is open after four o'clock and the secretary is not there. Can anybody give us the necessary form? No, her room is closed and she must fill it in herself. But try to go to the military office. She must be there now.

We took the subway and in half an hour were there. The woman had just left and gone to the militia. Can you enlist a newcomer now? No, a form from the passport office is needed and a document from the Institute. My God! We don't have one. O.K., we shall see about that later. Now to the militia.

We took the subway back and rushed into the militia. She was there. It's so wonderful we found you! You see, we are here only for a day, we must get him registered in my apartment. Can you give us the necessary form?—I work after four o'clock in the passport office.—But please, it is only noon now. We shall waste the whole day.—Leave me alone. I don't bother you at your work, so don't bother me. After four. She barked at us and left.

I could stand it no longer. Why did this have to happen at my happiest time? Why did I have to beg these people and run about to these dirty places? Why had I come back to this hateful Moscow? I was choking and sobbing on Yossi's chest and he didn't know what to do with me.

"Are you crazy? Stop immediately. People are staring at us. Pull yourself together. We still have time. Stop it. Where is your handkerchief? Here, take mine. And, Alochka, please, stop it."

We went out into the street. Stuffy, dusty. Where should we go? We had four hours of enforced idleness.

We took the subway to the airport terminal. Half an hour. There we bought Yossi a ticket back to Riga for the next morning. An hour, the line had not been so long. It was not the season for interurban flights. Only people on business and crazy people like us flew back and forth. Then we had dinner in the terminal restaurant. An hour. Only an hour and a half more. But let's not wait in the office. Better to be far from it, here in the terminal. No one must see me, no one must know I'm in Moscow. It might reach the OVIR. Better to be cautious, on the safe side. We could not even talk. Everything hung by a thread, and we were powerless to help each other. Better not to talk. How many people came to the airport even at such a season? Why are there always millions moving? Is there ever a single moment when everyone is at home, sleeping, resting, and no one is in terminals, on trains, planes, ships? Why do they go? They all have their reasons, but our reason is so special and so rare. Not many people can have such special reasons. And why are they sitting here? I always come just in time for a flight. I never sit in terminals. There are a lot of thieves in terminals. What a terrible thing is the militia. All together. Thieves, teen-agers getting their first passports, prostitutes. Like in the registry office.

When we had gone with Myra to register mother's death, we had been in line together with young parents registering their newborn baby. Myra began to cry when she turned in mother's passport. When we were children, we had liked to play with it. It was all torn. You can always tell a person's age by the look of his passport. Shall I turn in my passport when I get a visa? Certainly. Then it will be as though I have died and am turning in my own passport. Yossi's passport is quite different. There the writing is both in Lettish and Russian. Like in our marriage certificate. Could I ever have imagined my marriage certificate would be in Lettish? When she had registered us, Yossi couldn't find any place to put his legs; the chair was too small for him. He is sitting so motionless now. What is he thinking about?

"Alla, what are you thinking about?"

"Nothing."

"Really?"

"Yes. I don't remember."

Why was I thinking about our registration. Ah, yes. Our matriculation certificate—Lettish—passport—my death—mother—registration office—militia—thieves. Ah, yes. The terminal. What is the time? Half past three. We can go now.

Exactly at four o'clock, we were in the housing office. Slowly and indifferently, the woman took out the necessary form and began to fill it in. I couldn't sit, out of impatience. At last she finished. Militia works until five o'clock. We took a taxi to militia. Yossi rushed into the office and I stayed in the taxi in order not to waste time. I was jittery with nervousness. Suddenly Yossi ran out shouting, "My military document!" I rushed to him with it, he seized it, and disappeared again. In two minutes he reappeared, plunged into the taxi, and the car started on—"To the military office!"

"Made it," Yossi breathed out. "Idiot! He began to ask me all kinds of stupid questions. Why do I want to live in Moscow? Why doesn't my wife go to live with me in Riga? I gritted my teeth in order not to shout at him. Nudnik. He couldn't do anything. There is a law that a wife can register her husband in her apartment even in Moscow. But he wanted to get on my nerves. Can you imagine—short, fat, blond with tiny pig's eyes, filled with his own importance. Holds your papers in his hooves and asks you in a nasal twang all sorts of nonsense. Are we in time?"

"Don't know. Now it depends on the military office. If everything is O.K. there, we shall try to catch that woman in the housing office and hand in all the papers."

In the military office we rushed to the window and pushed in the form.

"And a reference from your Institute?"

"Er, you see, I don't have it with me. Maybe. . . ."

"O.K. It is not important. You can send it later. I'll register you without it now. Just don't forget to send it."

I nearly fainted with joy. Twenty-five minutes to six. We rushed to the subway. I was all out of breath, I'm not such a good runner. Yossi held me by the hand. At five minutes to six, we fell into the passport office.

"Oho," she raised her eyebrows at us, looked through all the papers and said: "Everything is correct. Next week you'll receive your passport with the seal of registration."

I was ready to kiss her. I loved this passport woman and her office, the militia and military office. We had made it!

"And you cried, silly little girl!"

Dead beat, we climbed the steps of my house and dragged ourselves to my apartment. It was nearly six. The OVIR worked until six o'clock. It would not be dangerous to call them then. They would not be able to tell me to come immediately. No, better not do it. Yossi would think I was very anxious to leave and would be upset.

"Yossi, let's call the OVIR."

"What for, it's already late."

"Just for fun."

"O.K."

I dialed the number.

"Good evening. This is Alla Milkina's sister calling. I have received a post card for her, but she is not in Moscow. What does the post card mean?"

"Yes, yes. This is very urgent. She is allowed to leave for Israel. Her visa is valid up until the 13th of this month (My eyes met over the bridge of my nose—four days!) Where is she? Can you find her immediately?"

"No, I don't know where she is exactly. She is traveling somewhere in the Baltic."

"That's bad. Please, tell her to come immediately when she appears."

"Certainly. Thank you. Good-by."

I put down the receiver and repeated the conversation to Yossi. I didn't give him time to react but hurried to add: "Like hell! If they are so anxious to throw me out, they can wait. I'm not going to leave now. Our wedding is planned for the 17th and on the 17th it will be. After that, we'll arrive at the OVIR as if nothing were the matter and announce that we are married. And then we'll see what they do. A week earlier, a week later doesn't matter. The important thing is that you are registered here. Ah, isn't it great? Don't you think I'm a wonderful girl?"

"You? Have you forgotten your hysterics in the militia? Weren't you ready to give up and lie down? If it weren't for me, you'd have sat there crying until now."

"Never. That was just for a moment."

"O.K., we're both great kids. I love you crying or not crying, but better not cry. You're not beautiful when you cry."

"Really? I shall try."

"By the way, now that everything is finished, why should you stay here? Myra can bring the passport when she comes to the wedding."

"You mean it? You really want me to come with you? Wonderful. Then why do we wait until morning? Let's fly tonight and get out of this hateful Moscow."

"O.K., it's a great idea."

In the central terminal we returned Yossi's ticket and bought two tickets for the midnight flight to Riga. We took a taxi to the distant Vnukovo airport and waited for the flight. Two sandwiches for me, a newspaper for Yossi, and the time passed quickly. But at 11:30, the flight had not been announced. We asked at the Information Desk. "Wait for the announcement," they said. In half an hour we heard: "The 12:00 o'clock flight to Riga is delayed eight hours because of bad weather."

We looked at each other with horror.

Then it struck us both simultaneously: this day had been the day of Yom Kippur of the new Jewish year of 5731.

I looked at a clock. Eight hours. The short hand had to move along more than half of the clock face. There was no question of returning to town. The return trip takes two hours and buses had already stopped running. Only taxis. No money for a taxi. Eight hours in the terminal. No place to sit. Hundreds of people sitting everywhere, lying on the floor with their bundles under their heads. Stink, stuffy air. And this—the central airport of the Soviet Union.

Eight hours. How can one endure it? Better not look at the clock. How badly I want to sit down—or at least to lean against a wall. But there doesn't seem to be a single piece of free wall. Better to walk, then the knees don't feel so tired. And if I try to look at the clock to watch every single move of the long hand in order to feel that time is passing—No, it doesn't help.

People couldn't stand the stuffy air and went out of the terminal to breathe. Then we grabbed a seat. I put my head in

Yossi's lap and tried to fall asleep. My legs were too heavy hanging down on the floor. I managed to put them on the bench. Dropped off for a minute. My whole body was aching. Yossi was groaning.

"Let's go out. There's no air here at all."

We went out and walked back and forth in front of the building. It was cold. We went back to our seat. It was occupied. The same cycle of ordeal was repeated. Within four hours, I completely lost all sense of myself. Time passed without my awareness. I walked, stood, sat—all unconsciously.

In the gray dawn of the next day, we stood for half an hour in the rain near the plane and at last boarded it. The shaking of the plane didn't allow me to fall asleep. I felt terribly ill and kept running to the toilet every half hour with fits of vomiting.

Two hours later, we entered our home in Riga. We couldn't even talk to tell the parents about our adventures. They put us in Ilana's room on two separate beds, covered us with warm blankets, and we fell into the abyss of deep sleep.

Several hours later, I awoke completely recovered and hungry and began to laugh at our night's adventure. Yossi was still sleeping and I felt bored. I wanted to awake him and ask, "How did you like it?" I went and sat down on his bed. Mother noticed my intention and hurried to stop me.

"Don't! Don't ever do it. He is always so angry when someone awakens him. They are such sleepyheads, these Rusinek men. Better not to touch them."

But I did want to wake him. He was sleeping on his stomach with his thick lips stretched out. I scratched his ear. He didn't move. Father came in to watch the reaction and to come to my help if trouble broke out. I scratched Yossi's nose. He frowned in his sleep, then opened his heavy eyelids, saw me, and smiled happily.

What a wonderful feeling to be a wife!

The last week before the wedding passed very quickly. No one had noticed our absence on the 9th of October and we decided to keep what had happened secret. The news would have disturbed everyone and spoiled the joy of the wedding.

All the friends of the family helped to prepare the wedding. Lev's and Yehoshua's mother, sweet Aunt* Milja, helped Roza to make *gefilte fish* and *gepeklte fleysh* (boiled spiced meat) beforehand. Ilana ran all over town to get the bedding and towels for our future married life (near or far future—all the same!). Others got together large tablecloths and plates and dishes for the wedding tables. All ran their feet off, using all sorts of influence to get good wedding gifts for us. The bearded family friend arranged to have a special *k'tuba* (marriage certificate) made for us. A month before I had gone to the Moscow synagogue to buy a *k'tuba*. One of the hunchbacks took five rubles from me and handed me a photocopy of something very indistinct with angels holding torches and not a single *Mogen David* on it. I threw it away as soon as I left the place. That Moscow synagogue is an embodiment of insult to all Russian Jews.

Two days before the wedding, the family friend brought and solemnly handed over the *k'tuba*. We all looked at it with delight. The usual handwritten text with blank spaces for names and dates was surrounded by a frame made with devotion and love. Rachel's tomb, David's tower, the monument of Trumpeldor, the emblem of Jerusalem, the scroll of the Torah, two Israelites carrying a huge bunch of grapes, a *Mogen David* at the bottom, and a transparent, hardly seen *menorah* as a background through the letters of the text. What could be a better symbol of our love and our union!

* In Russia grown-up women of close acquaintance, even if they are not relations, are called "Aunt" by younger people.

Lev sweated over a big placard with two words: "Mazel tov!" This reserved man said to us, "It is such a pleasure and comfort for me to do something for your wedding."

The long-awaited wedding dress and bridal veil arrived just in time, a week before the wedding. I had never seen anything so beautiful and at the same time so modest. A long, narrow dress with long, narrow sleeves—all made of white guipure. And an airy, light veil with two parts, one for covering the face. Everything for a Jewish bride.

We decided we would not let either Yossi or father see the dress and veil before the wedding, so their delight would be greater. October 17th came and we both forgot about the ill-timed permission. There were so many more important things to think about at the moment.

All the women began their busy day at a hairdresser. I went too, which was a stupid thing to do. To make my long hair curly, I would have had to wear curling pins for no less than all the hundred and twenty years of my life. But I had only one day at my disposal and for all of that day I looked like a Martian.

The rest of the time, I was occupied in making my own wedding cake. We had bought several round cakes, all of a different size. Then I began to decorate this tower with whipped cream, sweet butter cream, and all sorts of little sweet treats. When I had done this at home, Myra usually came along to make me nervous and to laugh at every crooked line of cream. This time Yossi came "to help me spiritually," but I threw him out of the kitchen and continued my work with my mouth open in zeal.

At four o'clock in the afternoon, the telephone rang and the whole family froze at the words: "Tel Aviv is calling." Miriam and grandmother were calling to congratulate the parents and Yossi, whom grandmother had last seen at the age of twelve and whom Miriam had never seen. By the way Father looked at me I knew he intended to pass the receiver to me. I ran away, but the family found me and dragged me to the telephone. I resisted and protested, "I don't want to, I don't know what to say, I'm afraid!" But the receiver was put into my hand and I heard the distant voice of an English-speaking lady. She spoke very warm words of congratulation without waiting for me to answer, so my function was limited to saying, "Yes, thank you . . . thank you . . . yes." For this I found enough English words in my vocabulary. The whole family was standing around me with tears in their eyes. Then I passed the receiver again to Ezra and Miriam at the other end handed it to eighty-nine-year-old grandmother. "Mama!" Ezra cried out. We all looked away.

The telephone talk was over and everyone in silence returned to his occupation. Father, mother, and Yossi to carrying the last plates and dishes to the hall, Ilana to drying her hair in the oven, and I to my "Tower of Pisa," thinking, "How much a part of this family I am, how much I feel all their griefs and joys. How wonderful that this time my ability to give myself completely to someone has not led me into trouble."

The time to get dressed came. The hairdresser came to arrange my curls. She assured me that they would certainly fall at my first movement. I accepted her verdict and retired to the second room to array myself in the wedding costume. I forgot all about the cooking and arrangement problems. Subconsciously putting a solemn expression on my face, I began to move slowly and carefully. I can't remember how I slipped into the cool, heavy dress, put on new elegant shoes, and arranged the veil on my hair. When the procedure was over, I looked in the mirror and sighed in pleasure. I looked very pretty even to me. Ilana came to make the last adjustments and opened the door. . . . Yossi began to blink helplessly, father hummed, and Ilana's imperturbable husband pronounced, "Not bad."

I stood in the doorway with my arms down along my sides and the ends of my lips trembling in a shy smile. It is nice to feel beautiful!

The whole family went to the synagogue. Myra, Yossi, and I took a taxi, stopped off at a photographer, and then went on to the synagogue.

On narrow, medieval Riga Street where the taxi stopped, a large crowd was already waiting for us. I trembled with cold and excitement. We all entered the synagogue and Yossi was immediately separated from me. I stood in the cold entrance hall in a circle of my sister, cousins, and girl friends. All the men gathered in the main hall—father, Yossi, and witnesses discussing with the men of the synagogue the filling in of the *k'tuba.* Lev and another good friend of Yossi's, Elijahu, signed the *k'tuba* as witnesses. At last when all that procedure was finished, I was led to a distant corner of the hall and seated on a chair. Aunt Musja, Uncle Misha, and his wife stood at my side ("If only poor Polina could have seen all this" was in their eyes).

Suddenly I saw Yossi with two friends, a young couple, and the parents beside him, approaching me. He came up and put the veil down over my face. His solemn face nearly made me laugh, but I controlled myself. I made my face as motionless as his. I would allow no such mundane expression as laughter. Neither would I cry, although my nerves and deep emotions had me on the brink of tears when I was told to stand up. I began to move slowly to the music of a violin. The sounds of the violin—mournful, complaining, sobbing, compelling—were touching my soul. But I would not weep. Such music had always made me cry, just as sad movies did, but this time I was the object of that music, of that living movie, and I would not cry.

The silence in the synagogue seemed tangible. Everyone had gathered near the *chuppah.* I moved past the empty rows of synagogue seats, which would never more be filled with praying men.

I reached the *chuppah* and began walking seven circles around Yossi. I did not know their formal meaning, but for me they were full of meaning. Those seven rounds were binding us forever. They were giving me up to him at his full disposal, rule, and responsibility. I was winding him seven times into my love and care. Every round meant something new and something indispensable for our union: loyalty, care, tenderness, understanding, selflessness, passion—love. I was willing to go around more and more.

Then we all stood under the *chuppah*, Yossi and I together. There was no rabbi in the Riga synagogue, so the ceremony was performed by the *gabbai* (manager) of the synagogue. He did not look nice, but we did not notice him. In this ceremony there were only Yossi and I.

"*Baruch atah adonai eloheinu, melech haolam. . . .*" We drank of the wine, we exchanged rings, the *gabbai* read the *k'tuba* and handed it to me. We drank of the wine again. "*Baruch atah adonai eloheinu. . . .*" A glass was put on the floor in front of Yossi. Everyone held his breath. Yossi raised his foot. . . . . Crash!

Mazel tov! Mazel tov! Mazel tov!

I started and came back to the world, so unexpected and loud was this cry of good luck by everyone. And the violin awoke also. Now it began to dance, jump, sing, transported by joy. I did not notice how the boys and girls formed a big circle and began to whirl in a *hora* around us: Lev, Yehoshua, Olja, Elijahu, Tsvisha.

The corners of my lips stretched wide and almost reached my ears. I could not make them return to a solemn position. Joy swept over me. Relatives, friends, even unknown people who happened to be in the synagogue, came up to congratulate us. I recognized no one and answered automatically: "Thank you, thank you. . . ." I did not notice when a huge bunch of flowers was thrust into my hands. I looked at Yossi and we both could not help laughing from joy.

On our way to the hall, we again took a taxi, made a circular route through the center of the town, and then went to the building. When we arrived, there was some fuss; we were asked to wait for awhile downstairs and at last the doors were opened. We climbed the stairs between two rows of people—women on the right and men on the left—to the music of the "*Hassene* song" sung by the Barry sisters. I nearly exploded with delight and self-importance.

In the big hall were two long rows of beautifully decorated tables. I thought with disappointment that again I would lose an opportunity to eat delicious food. I can never eat at a holiday table. And indeed everything, including the rare caviar, remained untouched on our table.

The two families sat down at the main table connecting the

two rows; all the rest of the guests found their places at other tables.

Father opened the evening celebration with the first toast. Other older people followed him in Russian, Yiddish, Hebrew: "*Kol hatan vekol kalah, kol Yosef vekol Alla*!" The whole table burst into laughter and applause every time some one included a Yiddish joke in his toast. Each time I nudged Yossi and demanded a translation, but he didn't have time to tell me between laughing and listening to the next joke. "And you know it is impossible to translate it into Russian." Toasts were given in the form of a joke or an anecdote, a poem, or a song. One man began to tell the whole story of how he had to marry his wife because he owed her parents forty rubles. His wife turned away from him with a smile which meant: "Talk, talk, talk—no one believes you." "But," he added, "according to the new regulations of the OVIR, I now owe them four hundred rubles."

The whole hall was filled with laughter and hand clapping. The point was that formerly a Jew had to pay forty rubles to get an exit visa if allowed to leave. But only a week before the entire Jewish Zionist population had been thrown into a panic by a new regulation. Everyone who was leaving for capitalist countries either as an emigrant or tourist had to pay four hundred rubles instead of forty. Since the Soviet Union is not a country which sends forth a lot of tourists or emigrants, the regulation was understood as a blow at the Jews. After the first shock, the Jews considered the situation, decided they would pay the fee whatever it was, and even began to be optimistic that it meant the government had decided to let them go and make money on them.

When I had heard about it, I also had gripped my head in despair. But then I thought of the last parcel from abroad which I had just received from an unknown source through Dinnerman and Co. in London. It was good to feel that we might manage even this with the help of Jews from all over the world.

Yes, Soviet Jews received news of the regulation with readiness and good humor, and the laughter at our wedding was the best proof of it.

Then our young friends followed the older generation. When their turn came, they bounded from their seats and ran to the far end of the hall where there was a piano. Gana sat at the piano and Elijahu, Yehoshua, Lev, Aviva, Tsvisha stood near her. Everybody in the hall began to smile in pleasant expectation.

The "kids" began with a well-known "*Hassene* song" in which they changed the words "*hatan vekalah*" (groom and bride) to Yosif and Alla.

And then came the words in Yiddish, "Even if this is a dream, it is a wonderful dream and we wish for the young couple that it become a reality as soon as possible."

Then the Yiddish song, "*Zol zain,*"

> *Let it be that I just build castles in the air*
> *And my God exists only in fairy tales.*
> *This helps me in grief and makes my dreams lighter.*
> *In dreams even the blue sky is more blue.*

And from a poem by Jabotinsky:

> *White as snow in this land of sorrow*
> *Blue as you, distant heaven attracting me*
> *Yellow as our shame. . . .*

Then the young people said: "But now we have only two colors —the blue and the white. *Kahol velavan.*"

With the first words of the new favorite song, everyone smiled. Then they began to demand that I join them and I could not sit any longer. I loved this song and sang it better than any other, always being completely carried away by the melody and the words: "Like a song, like a dream." This time I flew to my friends in delight.

When the song was finished, Elijahu added in Hebrew in continuation of the last line of the song: "These are my colors forever. And forever since now the groom and the bride will be together. And this all began this way."

They began to sing in broken Hebrew:

> *Once a boy went to a party*
> *And met there a beautiful girl*
> *And this happened on the Baltic seashore.*

The second time the boy went to Moscow
And the girl was waiting for him there
And this was in the capital on the river of Moscow.

So the two came together in good luck
And we wish them liberation
May it come soon
And this will be happiness!

Next a joke was told by Lev: "Yesterday a citizen named Yosif Rusinek was arrested on Trolley-bus No. 5 for trying to get off through a closed door. He explained his strange wish by saying he felt sick in the trolley-bus and in general he felt bad there. The driver answered that if he felt bad he could open a window and that it was very easy to sit (here there was a play in Russian on the words "to sit down" and "to sit in prison") and that everyone in the trolley-bus was comfortable and had his own seat; and everyone was happy to go together to the stop of the Happy Future.

" 'But I don't want to go in the trolley-bus,' said citizen Rusinek. 'I want to get out. My grandmother is waiting for me.' He began again to try to force the closed door. The disturber was arrested and brought to this Teacher's House and you must decide what to do with him."

"Let him out! To grandmother!" Everybody cried.

Father laughed until he cried. Then there followed the reading of telegrams from Riga, Moscow, Jerusalem, and Tel Aviv.

What can be better for a Jew in the Diaspora than a dance! A strong, free *hora* or a merry *freilachs.* Everyone moved to the second part of the hall to join in or just to watch the dancing. *Freilachs* was for us and I pulled Yossi, who was resisting, into the circle and compelled him to dance with me. Fortunately, the strong old building stood the test. Yossi was embarrassed at the dance, sure that everybody was screaming in laughter watching his awkwardness. When the young people's *hora* ended, our elders formed a big circle for their *hora.*

After midnight, I put my veil on Olja's head as a sign for her to be married next. The serious ones remained at the tables and began their discussions, the merry ones continued dancing, and the most emotional sang. No one noticed when dawn came, but one by one guests began to take their leave.

And then we remembered. Tension filled our hearts. We had already decided that the evening after the wedding we should leave for Moscow. There was no use in delaying telling our friends about my permission.

We went up to each one separately and told them our story. Watching their shocked reactions, we were glad we had kept it secret until after the wedding. In the gray dawn we went slowly to our wonderful room to have our last quiet rest.

Next afternoon, the entire family was busy looking through and packing the wedding gifts and other useful things we would need for our life in Moscow. I was happy looking at these beautiful new plates and dishes and bedding that were now my own and that were for me a symbol of our new home. I remembered the broken dishes and torn bedding in my Moscow home.

In the evening a slow procession of the closest friends and the family saw us off at the station. It seemed as if all of us were just taking a walk in the city. We were all talking to each other, discussing everything except our departure. In this slow fashion we reached the railway station. Everybody stood silently by our train car. Mother began to cry. I suddenly realized for the first time that I was taking a son out of a large, united family. We entered the car and looked at them all through the window. They stood in the darkness of the night and only their black eyes sparkled in their pale faces. I could divine the message the eyes of Lev and his parents were sending to me: "How is Natasha? Stay near her." Others had in them envy that I might be leaving, but I was ready to exchange places with any of them.

24

On the morning of October 19, six days after my exit visa had expired, we arrived in Moscow. I had been able to play the game of indifference to the OVIR until after the wedding when, in fact, both of us could stand it no longer and rushed to Moscow. When we arrived in the city, I gathered all my resources to pull myself together and hold back that indecent impatience. We went to our Moscow apartment, put all our things in their places, sat for awhile, had breakfast, and then went quickly to the OVIR. I expected and hoped for a refusal.

"Good morning! I've just arrived from Riga and found this post card waiting for me."

"Milkina? At last you've turned up. You've had permission to leave long ago. You can get your visa now."

"Yes, thank you. But the fact is that I have married meanwhile."

"I don't think it is of any importance, but better go talk to Zolotukhin, the Deputy Chief of the Department."

Zolotukhin? What will he tell me now? Every time I had come to him during the past year, the purebred, neatly dressed official had talked to me lazily, hardly looking at me with his sleepy colorless eyes. His tone had seemed to say, "I don't want to waste my time on you, you mere nothingness." And each time he repeated monotonously, playing carelessly with a sharpened pencil. "Not in a year, not in two . . . not even in five years, probably never." I did not know how to talk to him. Not that I was afraid of him, but I felt that arguing with him would be like roaring at a dog sitting at a closed gate.

Others, however, didn't mind roaring at him. Basja used to stand in front of his table, strike her plump little fist on it, and shout, "You've fired all of us from our jobs! Who is going to feed my family? You?" Another Jew spoke more generally, "You must remember that fascism is not excusable. German fascism is being severely punished and your turn will come."

But really Zolotukhin was nothing—just a dog sitting at a gate. But as Jews could not see real guards of the gate, they poured out all their feelings on him. And when the first Moscow Jews began to leave, they laughed and said they would send him an invitation to come to Israel.

Only three months had passed since I had last visited him and listened to his monotonous prophecy about the chances of my getting exit permission. What would he tell me now?

Sleepy as usual, he looked through a list of names on his table (what Jews would not have given to be able to look through that list) and said with a drawl: "Yes, Milkina Alla Tsalevna, you are allowed to leave for Israel for permanent residence."

"Thank you. I have already heard this. I came to inform you that I have married meanwhile."

"So what? It does not matter." (Had I really expected anything else?)

"What about my husband?"

"I repeat: you, Milkina Alla Tsalevna, are allowed to leave—only you. Is that clear?"

"Clear." I stood up and left. There was no use talking to him, so I returned to the official handling my documents. "Zolotukhin has confirmed the permission, but you must take into consideration that I am now a member of a family. I shall expect my husband to be allowed to leave also."

"You had better leave now and your husband can apply for an exit permit on your invitation. Then we shall see."

"What about my passport? I was going to change it to my new surname."

"Please, don't do it. We've prepared your visa in your maiden name and it would take time to change it."

"All right. It really does not matter." I remembered the seal of marriage in my passport and that was the important thing. I went back to Yossi.

I didn't have to ask. Everything had already been decided. I was leaving.

"When shall I get the visa?" I had asked the official.

"It will be delayed a few days until a new regulation is issued. Meanwhile you can prepare all your documents and nine hundred rubles."

"Nine hundred rubles? Why?"

"That is the new regulation. Those who leave for capitalist countries pay four hundred rubles and those who leave for Greece, Spain, and Israel pay five hundred rubles more for denunciation of Soviet citizenship."

My God! Nine hundred rubles . . . What a sum! It was difficult even to imagine it. My mother, who had saved money all her life, had never managed to save a sum near this. It amounted to my yearly salary.

But Yossi comforted me, "If we had only this problem, you could consider that we had none. We'll sell some of your things and father will think of something."

And what a combination—Greece, Spain, Israel—the three countries which Soviet propaganda calls fascist. But why should we care what they call us? In fact, they lay their own fault at another's door.

And so I was leaving. What did I feel? Nothing. And it was better so. If I began to feel, I would feel too much.

We called the parents the same day and told them about my final permission. The news was received with sad acceptance.

That same evening I occupied myself with the most urgent task—looking through my goods and chattels and choosing the least torn and old clothes to take to the capitalist world. As it turned out, I could take nothing, or Yossi threw aside everything I was going to pack. "Shame on you," he kept exclaiming. "You'll never put it on there. Throw it away immediately." I did pack some of the things that were dear to me as a memory of our home: a large brown silk shawl and an embroidered Russian folk costume which were lying in our old trunk and which would probably continue to lie there even in the capitalist world.

I chose a few books which could be of use and interest to me in Israel. Four of them had been published before 1945 and so, according to a regulation, I had to get special permission from the State-Lenin Library to take them and had to pay for them.

The largest part of my luggage would be wedding gifts, which it was decided I should take with me to Israel. I also took records of Russian classical music and some elk's horns which my father had brought from an expedition to the North, and a few other souvenirs. And my mother's red and white jacket. There was really nothing to pack in a big trunk.

Next morning we began our rush. First to my Institute to get my matriculation certificate and a document on my studies for four years at the Institute—two different offices in different parts of the city. It took us a week to get it. I trembled in impatience and fury as I stood in lines, meeting with the usual procrastination and indifference.

We gave the list of those "valuable" four books to the library, but permission could only be given on showing them the exit visa. We had to leave it until the visa arrived.

Our *k'tuba* had to be copied, for I might need it in Israel. We found a good Jewish photographer who agreed to do it in two days. But the longest and most exhausting process was the copying and legalization of all the documents: my matrics, studies certificates, service record from my place of work, and our marriage certificate. All the documents had to be photocopied or retyped and then attested to first in the Central Moscow Notary office, then in the Supreme Court of Russia, then in the Foreign Ministry, and finally in the Dutch Embassy, which represented Israeli interests in the Soviet Union.

At last, on the 26th of October, I got the visa. I went for the last time to the Moscow OVIR. Never before had the procedure there been so businesslike and respectful. I was already a foreigner. At the door to the office, I took solemn leave of Yossi as a Soviet citizen, for on returning I would be a free person. I entered the room and sat down at a table. An official took my Soviet documents and stretched out her hand for something else.

I looked at her in wonder. "What else?" "A receipt from the bank." I grew cold. How could it have happened that we had forgotten to pay the money? I stood up and moved toward the door. "I'm sorry. I'll bring it now." She looked at me with a smile.

"Yossi," I rushed to my husband. "We're both big fools. Do you realize we forgot to pay the money?" He gripped his head in despair over our ability to forget everything even in such moments of our life.

Fortunately the bank was only two minutes walk from the office and in fifteen minutes I was again sitting at the official's table, having handed her a receipt for nine hundred rubles. Slowly and accurately, she began to fill in a long pink form with the magic words: to Israel for permanent residence.

At last with the long-awaited visa in my hand and no Soviet passport in my pocket, I left the room. Yossi smiled at me and shook my hand. I smiled back, but I was sad. The visa was valid until the 2nd of November. We had five more days.

The getting of the visa was followed by a new race—to the Dutch Embassy, the Austrian Embassy, Airflot booking office, again the library, the Foreign Currency Bank to get my hundred dollars which was the only money I was allowed to take out of the country, and finally to the custom house to send my luggage to Vienna.

All the days turned into a continuous chain of subways, buses, lines, running, sitting in offices. We were like hound dogs running about the city, hardly talking to each other.

Only at night did we turn to each other. We lay on our huge new sofa in the strong white light of the moon which looked directly in at us through our window. And we forgot about everything. Our bed was a magic carpet carrying us away from the earth into the quiet night of heaven. I wanted to become pregnant and we did our best, but failed. And when I realized that, I lost heart for the first time during all those days of pretending coolness.

We both avoided talking about our parting and only my careless stupid joke interrupted that mutually agreed-upon silence. "Nu, Yossi," I asked him once, meaning it as a joke, "Will you be true to me?"

He looked at me suddenly very seriously. There was again a question and pain in his eyes. "You know that you don't have to ask me that. It is I who should ask you."

Any other time I would have been offended by the emphasis of the difference in our natures. But this time there was no room for offense. I went up to him, raised my head, looked straight into his eyes, and said: "Look here, I think it is better if we don't promise anything to each other. The future will tell. Isn't it better if I don't promise but do wait for you, than vice versa? But just try to believe in me."

I don't think he was relieved by my words, but at least he was thankful for my frankness. And I was frank. I couldn't even promise myself anything. How could I know what was awaiting me in the future? But neither could I imagine that I wouldn't wait for him.

One evening we went to the Bolshoi Theater to hear *Eugene Onegin* by Tschaikovsky. It was one of the best productions of the theater, with its best cast. Sitting in one of the boxes, looking at the red velvet and gold bulwark of the great Russian culture, listening to Tschaikovsky's music in its true home, for the first time and the last time, I felt sorry and humbly ashamed that I was leaving.

In the afternoon of the 2nd of November, we took two taxis and went to the International Airport. Several times had I passed through that beautiful Russian suburb and had always tried to imagine my feelings, on my last trip, at the sight of those slender white birches standing along the road. This time I forgot to look at them. Nor did I look at the people around me. I just felt Yossi near me. I looked straight ahead all the way, seeing nothing. I didn't know how to behave, what to feel. And I felt nothing; I acted automatically. There were many friends, relatives, acquaintances, and unknown Jews who came to see me off and a second family which was also leaving. I did not notice who had come.

Two days before, even more had come to my place for the

usual going away party. I hardly remembered them. They sang, danced, talked loudly, gave me their names and addresses to send them invitations. I gave them sandwiches and coffee, and sometimes joined in the singing. But who they were, I hardly remembered.

And again they came to the airport. Newly reborn Jews with their aspirations, and readiness to struggle. And I was leaving. I was leaving my husband. What emptiness in my head. How many bags do I have? Where is the ticket? That woman going with me is with her sixteen-year-old son. I hardly know them. Her husband died a year ago and she is taking his ashes with her in a suitcase. Is it an analogy? No. Nonsense. How much time is left?

Yossi and I were walking hand in hand to and fro in the hall in silence. Nobody bothered us. Sometimes I thought they were casting glances at us waiting for the scene. But the scene would not be. I was not going to cry or tear my hair. I was determined not to. I doubt if I really wanted to.

I held his hand. He looked embarrassed, but I did not feel sorry for him. With his strength, he didn't need it. Nor did I deserve pity. So what was there to cry about? My head was empty. It was such heavy emptiness, and I tried my best to preserve it. I could not collapse then. I had a long way ahead. There was one person in that crowd who could make me cry—my sister. I avoided thinking about our parting. We talked very carelessly, pretending to be busy with the luggage, the ticket, and the like.

Suddenly Ezra came up to us: "It is time." My heart sank and at the same time the blood rushed to my head. I think I shook hands with everyone, kissed the relatives. And then there was Myra. My whole life, my broken family, my reproachful mother looked at me through her. My only sister, in her shabby fur coat, seemed so small there, standing alone and waiting for me to come to her. And I went and felt that my feelings would break me. I felt a choking lump in my throat and tears ready to flood. I knew that if I came closer to her, kissed her, said something, or even heard a word from her, I would collapse. I pressed her fur-coated sleeve. She turned away her eyes, clouded with tears, and I stepped away from her. She did not utter a sound.

I crossed the entrance through the glass wall. Yossi came with me to help me with the suitcases. We put them near one of the counters of the customs officials for a search. I had to show someone my ticket, to fill out some form. I moved very quickly, not looking at him, but holding him tightly by the sleeve.

"You are not allowed to be here," I suddenly heard someone addressing Yossi. It was a girl in the airport uniform.

"He must help me," I flung casually and held Yossi more tightly.

"It is not allowed." She did not leave us alone.

I felt a terrible fury rising in me. "Don't you see that I cannot manage all these bags alone?"

"My wife is leaving, can't you understand?" Yossi suddenly begged.

"But it is forbidden. You must go out, do you hear?" She began to be nervous.

I began to tremble with fury. "Yossi, don't talk to her. And you leave him alone," I was already shouting. "He will be with me here until I leave."

Yossi seized me and I turned away from her. She went away, but in a minute she returned with a woman official.

"It is not allowed that he be here. If you do not obey, you won't leave either."

I did not give her a glance, but I felt that more arguing would be useless and dangerous. "All right, Yossi. This is the end."

"Allochka," he said suddenly and his voice quavered.

"Don't you dare," I cried in despair and terror. "Go." He went away quickly.

I turned away and stood by the customs official. The last search in my life. The last Soviet official in my life. I stood and thought that I should never forgive myself for such a parting with Yossi. The man was not really interested in my things and looked only through the tops of the suitcases. When he took the four books, I handed him the permission. He told me to pay the twenty-nine rubles for them to the cashier and I suddenly remembered that I had no more Soviet money with me. I called for Yossi. He was again with me. We paid for the books, the woman official watching us fixedly.

I put my head on Yossi's chest. "Good-by, Yossi."

"Good-by, dear." He embraced me gently. I pressed my forehead against his chin, rubbed it against his prickly cheek. He kissed me softly, slowly turned around, and went away. I followed him with my eyes until he disappeared behind the curtained glass wall.

The customs official began the search again, feeling the clothes, boxes, pockets. At last he came across a package with letters. That was it! He began to look through them attentively, taking every single letter out of its envelope. Why do they like letters so much? Written material—the ideological arm. The man saw that all the letters were only love or everyday letters and began to just feel the envelopes. One of them, the thickest, attracted his attention. He opened it and took out many small pieces of paper covered with writing and folded in two. I glanced at them and blushed. It was a part of my diary which I had torn out of its notebook and put into one of the envelopes. The man settled down to reading. He seemed very interested. It was the part in which I had written about my being expelled from Komsomol and the way I had come to it. After he had read two pages, he understood that he needed nothing more from me.

"You can pack your things and shall leave this with us."

I felt very relieved. There was really nothing compromising for anyone in that part—only my feelings and thoughts. Were they afraid that I would show it to someone? I didn't need that, I remembered it by heart. Let them take it. Let them read it. Perhaps it would be enlightening for them. So in answer to his statement I just shrugged my shoulders and did not say anything. I went on to the last control pass post. On my way I passed the door in the glass wall. It was open. Yossi, Myra, Ezra, Ilana, and someone else all stood tightly pressed in the opening, looking at me.

"They took my diary," I cried to them.

"Scoundrels," Myra exclaimed loudly. She had come to herself and was aggressive as usual. I noticed Yossi's and Ezra's worried looks. "Don't worry. There is nothing important there."

I hurried to the control pass post. I was late. I stopped by a window in a glass box. A man in a military uniform checked all my documents, returned them, pressed a button, and an iron barrier separating me from a restricted area was moved aside. I took the first step and stood hesitating, not knowing where to go. There was a staircase in front of me. It must be there. I ran quickly up the stairs. Up, up, up! Suddenly I felt a sense of joy which gave me wings, and I flew up the stairs.

"Hello! What are you doing here? Where are you going?"

I looked in the direction of the voice. It was a girl who probably worked there. Her face seemed familiar to me, but I could not remember where I knew her from. Perhaps she was from the same Institute or I had worked together with her. A colorless face, one such as I can never remember. What does she want from me?

"I am going away from this country. Forever! Forever! Forever!"

I ran on, leaving the girl standing on the staircase dumfounded. I passed some large hall, then a glass corridor, then a small round hall. And here was the frontier guard and behind him—fresh air, a staircase down to the airfield, to the bus that would take me to the plane. From there, I knew I would see them all again, standing up on a big terrace for those who come to see their friends off. I ran down the stairs and looked up. There was no one there. The terrace was completely empty, all covered with thick snow. And far away there was the closed glass door with barely visible people pressing themselves against it. I waved my hand, just in case. . . .

In two minutes I was on board the airplane which was to take me to Vienna. "Only three hours of flight and there is my Homeland, my home," we used to sing.

What a terrible plane. It made much noise and trembled terribly.

It will be the last straw if I begin to feel sick, as I always do in planes. Just look at them. They serve caviar on foreign flights. I had better not look out of the window. I become dizzy. It is beautiful there. I am flying abroad? How does it sound? No, I am returning from abroad. I am making an *aliyah* to Israel. Doesn't that sound better? I must think this over. I must impress it on my mind in some way. No, I can't. What are *they* all doing now? Going home. By bus. Yossi is very quiet, I know. Are they talking about me?

By the end of the flight, I could not think at all. I was ill and dizzy and completely out of my senses. The plane landed safely and I went to the exit. There was a dark opening in front of me. I began to feel nervous as I approached that entrance to the world. I bent down, stepped out, and straightened up. A surge of feeling swept through me. A wild cry of joy, victory, and liberation escaped me. I breathed in the air. It was so rich, so warm. I felt I could swim in it. What was it? Was it true that the air of freedom had its special taste and smell? Or was the weather just warmer and milder in Vienna? Whatever it was, I felt happy. I had to feel happy. Whatever my fate might be, I was obliged to feel happy for the sake of the struggle behind me, for the sake of those who were left behind.

I ran happily down the steps. A bus took us to the terminal. I ran to the glass door and when I was half a meter from it it opened itself. I stood puzzled. Then stepped back. It closed. I stepped forward again. It opened again. What is this? Doors open themselves? Strange! Ah, this is one of the tricks of capitalism. I laughed, jumped back and forth on the black rubber spot, and at last ran into the hall looking around. Two curly-haired men immediately came up to me and said:

"*Shalom!* We are from the Jewish Agency."

"*Shalom!*"

In the Soviet Union As Seen By Ezra Rusinek

It happened nine days after Alla left. By no means a surprise, but quite unpleasant.

On November 11, at 11 A.M., when I was as usual working in my watch department, I was suddenly called to the management office. At the entrance to the office, a young man with a pleasant appearance greeted me with a wide smile, as if he were an old friend: "I am from the KGB. We shall have to disturb you today. You won't work anymore today. Please go and turn your work over to someone else. I shall wait for you here."

He had no written order. That was not according to law, but there was no point in arguing. I used the opportunity to call home. Yossi had better disappear. Our number did not answer. I told a young Jew with whom I had been working that I was being taken to the KGB and asked him to keep calling our apartment and tell Yossi to leave immediately.

I checked my pockets, took out everything "unnecessary," and put on my coat. Then I dialed our number once more, but there was still no connection. The Chief was hurrying me, "You are being awaited. Don't delay."

I left the building with the young man. We got into a blue Volga. I was silent, but the young man began immediately, "Aren't you surprised that we trouble you?" What politeness! I answered, "No, I am not the first." Then he asked: "Did your daughter-in-law leave?"

"Yes, on the 2nd of November."

"And how is it with Yosif?"

"He will get an invitation from his wife and will leave also." I tensely waited for his answer.

"That will depend on you, on how you behave today."

I had been afraid of this all the time. For the last few months we had been waiting with tension for this call. I had expected it to come much earlier. So why had they not come to me until now? I had been watching the course of the investigation very attentively and there were not many people who knew as much about it as I did. I knew everything or almost everything about the activities in Riga concerned with the publishing of Samizdat. From the persons called to the KGB and the questions they had been asked, I knew what the KGB had already found out and what they had not, who of those called had confessed or confirmed facts and who had refused to give evidence or confirm the accusations. And I knew that the course of the investigation must lead them to me and that I would be called, but the question was at what stage of the investigation it would happen.

I was ready. For a long time I had hesitated in deciding how to behave at the interrogation—to say "no" to every accusation or to refuse to give evidence. Little by little, I had come to the conclusion that there was only one good way—to refuse to give evidence.

I was well aware that such a refusal was in itself a violation of the law. A witness was obliged to give evidence. And I realized also that at any moment I might myself be accused—I could not avoid that. Nevertheless, my decision was made not only from the point of view of expediency, but also on principle.

The blow the KGB struck at the Jewish movement in 1970 was aimed at intimidating the Jews. They were acting again according to Stalin's principles, although their methods had changed and had assumed a cloak of legality. But they had not succeeded in intimidating us, and the proof was in the following: In the summer of 1970, it was difficult to collect signatures to a letter and many Jews simply refused to sign. In autumn the situation changed completely. Despite the KGB pressure, Jews ceased to be afraid and exerted counterpressure through their collective letters.

Such conditions gave me the opportunity to behave as I had decided—to refuse to give evidence and not to talk to the interrogators at all. I knew I would have to give reasons for my refusal. They might be unfounded from a juridical point of view, but not from a moral one. I had them. The KGB had given the process of Samizdat the name "The Case of Anti-Soviet Activities." But what was anti-Soviet about it? Our activities were pro-Jewish, pro-Israel, pro-Zionist, if you like, but in no case anti-Soviet. Did we intend to overthrow the Soviet social order, to change something in the USSR? Nonsense! We wanted only one thing—reunification with our people in Israel, to share in its joys and difficulties, the whole of its fate. And no one was trying to settle scores with the Soviet Union, although we had enough reasons for that.

Only the abnormal imaginations of the KGB people, brought up by the "Father of Peoples," and thinking according to his logic, could bring them to the idea of "anti-Soviet activities." The old slogan, "He who is not with us is against us" was again being used.

My second reason for refusing to give evidence was Ilana's fate. It was already seven years since she had been expelled from the fifth year of the Riga Medical Institute. What had she done? Nothing. Together with us, she had applied for an exit visa to Israel. She did this in December 1963, and at the end of January, two young Jews who were in the same course, members of the Komsomol Committee, came to our house and told us—begging us not to tell anyone—that the KGB had called the Party Committee of the Institute and had ordered it to expel Ilana. At the same time the KGB had said the entire family had been refused exit visas.

And soon they convened a students' meeting, prepared several Russian students to condemn Ilana, and shut up those who wanted to express their incredulity. In a short time Ilana received an official notice of expulsion. She continued to attend lectures, but soon one of the lecturers ordered her to leave the auditorium and refused to continue in her presence.

How many letters had I written! How many times had I personally applied to ministers, prosecutors, and other high officials. Each time the same thing happened. The first reaction: "It is impossible. No one can be expelled for applying for an exit visa. If they did this, it was against the law." This would be the beginning. Then the minister or other official would call the rector of the Institute and as soon as he learned who had ordered them to expel Ilana, his attitude changed. He would spread his hands and say: "Nothing can be done."

And so in this way the KGB was following the tactics of the former General Prosecutor of the USSR, the theoretician of Stalin's legislation, Andrei Vishinsky: "For the sake of expediency, even the law can be ignored." This was his famous saying and though Vishinsky himself had been forgotten for a long time, his spirit and teachings were still alive.

Ilana's expulsion had a very simple purpose. The fact became immediately clear to the whole of Jewish Riga and frightened Jewish students from applying for exit visas. Nor could their parents apply.

All my complaints and protests brought no result. Each time Ilana heard, "Give up the idea of going to Israel and you will be studying again." To renounce Israel meant to spit in one's own face. Ilana would not agree to it. I suffered from the fact that she could not continue her studies, but I was and I am proud of my daughter. Not once did she reproach me. But my pain remained and now, facing the KGB, I was expected to tell them what they wanted to know. Like hell!

All this flashed through my mind during those minutes the blue Volga went along the streets of Riga in the direction of the center. So they are not satisfied with Ilana's spoiled life. Now they want to blackmail me with Yossi's destiny. And slowly, but persistently, the thought came to my mind, which had first occurred to me when Alla came and told me that she had been called to the OVIR. Then it struck me that her permission was not accidental, but the blackmail was being prepared. They had already decided to play upon the feelings of a father who wished for the happiness of his son and was ready to part with him so that he could go to his wife in Israel. For the sake of this, the father would also give the evidence which would be so useful for the investigation and the success of the process of intimidation.

Their reckoning was insidious and they had already created the necessary situation. I began to feel fury mounting in me, something that had seldom happened to me.

We approached the KGB building. There is a gloomy joke in Riga. They say that this building is the highest in the city. Why? There are a lot taller than this one. The answer is because even from its basement you can see Siberia. Now all the floors were busy with the Jewish question as though the KGB had nothing more to do. There were four of our friends already sitting in the basement now. What could the conditions there be?

Suddenly the young man said, "Wait in the car." I waited. In two minutes he returned with two more men and they all sat in the car. One of them had a long box and a probe. I wondered what it could be. Then the young man said, "You've probably understood that we are going to search your apartment, haven't you?"

Of course, how could I not have understood immediately? This box with the probe was a mine detector. But what were they expecting to find? My apartment had long been "kosher." Even for Passover, Jews do not clean their homes as well as they did in the summer after all the searches that had started in June. So what did they hope to find now in November?

We arrived at my house. The two new men went to find two witnesses and the young man and I entered the apartment. Roza met me at the door. I immediately warned her: "The comrades have come to see what we have in our house." She understood immediately.

But, oh God, what did I see! My Yossi was only just pulling on his trousers! He probably had slept late as usual and the call from my place of work, as I learned, had come through only a minute ago. Of course, they switched on the connection only as we left the KGB building for my place. They themselves would need the telephone during the search. So what could be done now? Yossi had been caught and the KGB had thought he was in Moscow.

The other two entered with two witnesses. Everything according to the law. They showed me an order for the search "for the purpose of finding typewriters, subjects, and typed materials that have relation to the case of anti-Soviet activities." All signatures were in their proper places and the order was confirmed by the Prosecutor of the Latvian Republic.

But one thing was very strange. This was the 11th of November and the order was signed and confirmed on the 28th of October. Almost two weeks had passed. Instead of coming on October 29, they were waiting—for what?

On October 28th I had left for Moscow to see Alla off, so they had been waiting for her to leave.

They began to search, but before they did, they suggested that I give them all the anti-Soviet materials I had, especially typewriters. Then they would cancel the search. So this was what they needed the mine detector for! I said I did not keep typewriters and offered them a Hebrew book that had just arrived that morning. But they didn't want it. Letters from Israel were not interesting to them. That was progress! A year before they had confiscated not only books and letters, but post cards, stamps, anything. Something had changed in their tactics.

The search was conducted very carefully. Nothing was spoiled, or torn; everything was handled carefully to avoid complaints of a violation of law. How times had changed!

The investigator looked for a long time at an engraving on the wall by the Riga Jewish painter Kuzkovsky, "The Stepmother." It shows an old termagant, who strokes a Jewish boy with one hand and with the other pinches him on the back. "And whom do you think this old woman symbolizes?" A provocative question.

"Decide for yourself," I answered.

All the books were thumbed through. All the old letters from Israel were looked at. Suddenly one showed the other a telegram from Miriam from Jerusalem in December of 1966. Neither could understand English. I took the telegram and read deliberately and distinctly: "In connection with Mr. Kosygin's statement that the Soviet Government will not prevent Jewish families from reuniting in Israel, I have sent such and such letters. . . ." They looked at each other and were obviously confused.

Then they looked through a file of typed applications for exit visas and took some of them. They obviously wanted to compare the type with that of Samizdat, but I was not disturbed. The Samizdat typewriters were never used for official letters.

Then our telephone notebook was put aside, but I still was not disturbed. The old notebook with important telephone numbers and addresses had been burned long ago.

One of the men opened the drawers of the table and looked through the old films. Suddenly a closed casket was in his hands, a metal one, and it wouldn't open. My polite Yossi took it and managed to remove the stained lid. Film fell out of the casket. The man took it and looked at it against the light. Yossi and I also looked at the film and then at each other. "What is this?" we asked each other with our eyes. "Samizdat? We are caught!"

The man happily showed the film to the witnesses. "Do you see? Film with a text," and he put it aside.

Suddenly there was a ring at the door. The interrogator went to the door and Mendel came in. Of course, he was supposed to come with a list of lawyers who could be approached in connection with the defense of the arrested. This was the third time he had walked in on a search.

"Who are you looking for?" the interrogator asked.

"The neighbor." Brilliant logic.

"What is his name?"

"Aljosha." (The neighbor's name was Volodja. At a previous time Mendel had said he came to see a Katja Ivanova.)

"His surname?"

"I don't know."

"His age?"

"I don't know."

"Your documents, please. . . . Ah, Mendel Gordin, how do you do? A familiar name." Mendel was searched and ordered to sit down on a chair and not to move.

It was already afternoon and the second room had not yet been searched. They sealed it up and left for the dinner hour interval. They seemed to realize that they would not find anything interesting. A car remained in the yard and the several men sitting in it did not take their eyes off our door.

At 4 P.M. the investigators came back with the Chief. The latter sat down at the table and looked through the confiscated material. He was obviously displeased.

"You will have to go with us," he said to me, although the search was not yet over.

The Chief, the young investigator, and I left for the KGB. We went to the investigation department on the sixth floor. A simple room, a telephone, a typewriter.

The Chief left. The young investigator, whose name was Amelkovitch, was to interrogate me. I took off my coat and lit a cigarette. The moment had come. Did they have an order for my arrest or not? I didn't know and they wouldn't tell me until the end of the interrogation. It depended on how many of the arrested had given evidence against me—one or two. If only one, it would not be enough for an arrest. If two, it would be quite another situation. I noticed that Amelkovitch was not hurrying, he was looking through some papers. He must be getting prepared for our talk. He would begin as though he were talking not for the record. His job was to bring the witness to a state of mind where he would answer the recorded questions in the way the interrogator wanted him to.

I knew what kind of an interrogator Amelkovitch was. Not the Stalinist who shouts, curses, and threatens. This man would talk with me as a friend, a well-wisher. He would offer me a cigarette, he would ask if I was hungry or wouldn't I like a drink or perhaps I was tired. He would not raise his voice. And occasionally he would say, "I understand you perfectly, believe me" or "I sympathize with you" or "I am very sorry," but at the same time he would persistently try to achieve his purpose. One of his most effective weapons was flattery. I knew of how two weeks before he had made a very clever man open his mouth with the help of flattery and patience.

Of course, to deal with such an interrogator is much less pleasant than dealing with a boor, and much more dangerous.

He began his talk with the heaviest weapon: "I must warn you that a lot for you depends upon this talk. You son has a chance to get an exit visa and you can hope to see your motherland in a few years. But if you don't behave properly, you will have to learn that no one gets an exit visa without our permission. Your son will not see his wife very soon and you cannot imagine what the consequences for you will be."

Again I felt fury rising in me and together with the fury, contempt. That was good. It would help me to remain composed. I didn't answer him but just looked straight into his eyes.

He continued: "Believe me, many of our people have considered whether to call you or not. Young people come to you, listen to you, and then they are ready to commit any crime, as for example, hijacking."

At that I could not be silent, and I interrupted him: "If I had known about that hijacking plan. . . ."

Amelkovitch tried to catch me: "Wouldn't you have come to us then?"

"No, of course not. But I would have done my best to talk them out of this step, which I consider very wrong. I would have tried to prove to them that it was the wrong way and that we must follow the more difficult but right way of a mass struggle for exit, an open and legal struggle, by appealing to world opinion, so that the entire world can know there are not just a dozen but many Jews (I admit, not all of them) in the Soviet Union who wish to leave, who feel their national ties with Israel, and who are ready to demand persistently their right to live where they wish.

"If I failed to persuade them, I would have found some other way to prevent them from doing this. Because of this, they have given you the opportunity to disrupt our activities by searches and arrests.

"Your press conference with prominent Soviet Jews on March 4 was aimed at intimidating Jews. You were already planning this new attack, but just waited for a good pretext, for a mistake on our part. And if there had not been 'the hijacker's plot,' there would have been something else."

At this point Amelkovitch suddenly spoke with a strange intonation: "Yes, there would have been something else." I understood that I had hit the mark.

But Amelkovitch was just an interrogator. His task was to get information out of me, so he stopped "the general talk" and got down to business. For three hours he read me evidence in which my name was mentioned, for the entire three hours he tried to convince me that all the facts had been proved, tried to trap me in my own words, using all kinds of methods, such as "I shall ask you only about the typewriters, although we understand that you know much more. But I shan't ask you about everything."

The baby! Didn't I know that if in the KGB you confessed to one fact the tangle would keep unrolling and unrolling. At last at 8 P.M. he told me in a shrill voice that never had he had such an unpleasant interview and put a list of questions for the record into the typewriter.

The decisive moment had come. Everything so far had not been important. The important thing was what would be written on the record.

Always the threat of harm and suffering. In 1939 we had not managed to leave Russia. The certificate was delayed. The Second World War broke out. Then came the Siberian exile, returning to Riga, again exile and wandering all over Russia, returning to Riga in 1963 and beginning the struggle for exit. Then Ilana's expulsion. And now Yossi and Alla! Their happiness depended upon me. But all I was being offered was a KGB promise. Could I believe them? Could I believe the enemy? No, I shall believe only my children and care only for what they think about me. And the most important thing for me is that they not lose respect for me, their father. If I confess, I can hope for no respect from them. I knew my daughter and son and Alla. It was painful to think about their destroyed young lives, but nothing could be done. There was no other way.

I had taken leave of Roza long ago. I was delighted with her selflessness. Never once had I heard a word of reproach from her. I was sorry only for mother and Miriam. Still there was only one way—to refuse to give evidence and whatever would be, would be.

Amelkovitch was typing the first question: "Are you acquainted with the accused Shpilberg? Where and when did you become acquainted?" He looked at me and waited for the answer.

"I shall write the answer myself."

He took the list out of the typewriter and handed it to me. I wrote: "I refuse to give evidence." Amelkovitch had not expected this. All through our long discussion, I had not even given a hint of my refusal. He looked at me furiously: "When did you make this decision?"

"Just now, during our talk."

"You must give a motivation for the refusal."

"Just a minute." I took the record again and wrote: "because I am not involved in any anti-Soviet activities of any kind," and put my signature under it. He again put the list into the typewriter and repeated the question again about others of the accused. And each time I wrote the same.

And suddenly all my inner tension wore away and I became perfectly composed and cool. And it gave me great pleasure that Amelkovitch was evidently very nervous.

The telephone rang. I heard only Amelkovitch's desperate answer: "But can you understand that he just refuses to give evidence?" Aha, the Chief wanted to know if their labors had had results. Amelkovitch completed the interrogation, asked me to stand up, and took me into a tiny room at the other end of the corridor. I had to wait.

This room was familiar to me, for I had heard many stories about it. It serves as a place where a witness is taken "to think again." The room is rather gloomy—an old sofa with broken springs, a table, an ashtray. That is all. A lot of people had been taken here "to think again." It was not yet prison, just an "agitpunkt"—an agitation station.* The door was not closed, but

* "Agitpunkt" is a very important permanent agitation center in every district, village, settlement which serves for Party propaganda—especially before elections. Ezra uses this word ironically.

to try to leave would be useless. No one would let you out without a pass. Only the barred window reminded me of prison.

There are many funny anecdotes about this room. Many of our boys have been left here for "thinking," and sometimes the oppressive loneliness and feeling of doom and no way out led to a success for the KGB. But there were other cases which made the KGB shrug their shoulders and finally made them understand that they could not manage the Jews.

For example, Sasha was left there for quite a long time after an exhausting interrogation. The boy was tired, so he just fell into a peaceful sleep. *Chutzpa.* No pacing back and forth, three steps there, three steps here, wringing his hands in despair. Just sleep.

There was another case. Elijahu was left in this room many, many times. He had become religious, studied Hebrew, read prayers, and practiced it all very seriously. One day when he was left there, he remembered that the time of *Minchah* (the afternoon prayer) had come and he began to pray. When he was reading the eighteen benedictions (the *Shemoneh Esreh*), Amelkovitch entered the room, saw Elijahu standing and praying, swaying a little, and said, "Let's go!" Elijahu didn't pay any attention. He continued praying and just turned a little to the interrogator and mumbled "m-m-m-" which meant that it was forbidden to interrupt the *Shemoneh Esreh* prayer. Amelkovitch retreated, quietly closing the door behind him, and returned only minutes later, when Elijahu had finished the prayer.

So now it was my turn to sit there for half an hour while the chiefs were consulting. At last Amelkovitch came in and the first thing I saw in his hand was a summons to come the next day at 9 A.M. for a second interrogation. Together with it, Amelkovitch handed me a pass for leaving the building and then slowly, watching my reaction, handed me a second summons for Yossi, also for the following day at the same hour. So he was also to be involved. I didn't say a word and left.

It took only ten minutes to walk to our place, so there was no use calling the family. I entered the apartment and saw not only my folks, but several friends also. Everyone stared at me with a silent question in their eyes, but I asked first for a cup of tea.

I handed the summons to Yossi and he was silent. I told them about the interrogation, all the while watching Yossi's reaction. But both his and Ilana's reactions were the same, as I had expected. And when later I hinted that perhaps I should change my behavior the next day they all became indignant.

I wondered what was awaiting me tomorrow. Amelkovitch had promised me a confrontation with the arrested man. But would he really do it? I thought not. Though it is forbidden to talk during a confrontation to one arrested, Amelkovitch knew that I would do it anyway and this would spoil the course of their investigation.

And I was not mistaken. The confrontation did not take place. In the morning the two of us entered the building and were taken to different rooms. Amelkovitch warned me immediately: "Today the interrogation will take place in the presence of the Deputy Prosecutor of the Latvian SSR." Of course he meant the Deputy Prosecutor for supervision of the KGB, Chibisov. I had heard a lot about him already. His work was to provide the legal procedure during investigations, but I had heard from previous cases that he often interfered directly with the investigations and tried to pressure the accused.

Chibisov came in and sat down. "You have refused to give evidence. It is my duty to warn you of the consequences of your refusal. Comrade Amelkovitch, read to Rusinek the statute of the Criminal Code."

Amelkovitch took the Soviet *Talmud* and read ". . . six months of forced labor." I knew it without their reminding me.

"I've considered the matter," I answered and again became silent.

Chibisov tried again to explain to me that they were not going to accuse me, they just wanted to find out some facts. The search? Well, they wanted to locate the materials that had a connection with the criminal case. I might have in my house such materials even though I myself was not involved in anything. Wasn't it possible? I answered quietly, "Perhaps in your house it is, yes, possible. But there is not and never has been anything anti-Soviet in my house. And you have no right to demand that I observe the law. Laws are made not only to punish citizens, but to protect their rights also. If you divide citizens into two categories, one that has all rights and another without rights, then how can you ask me, whom your law does not protect, to observe the law?

"You, the prosecutors, did nothing when my daughter was expelled from her Institute against all Soviet law and against the UNESCO convention on the struggle against discrimination in education, which was ratified by the Soviet Union. Then you did nothing to restore law. Why do you expect me to respect the law? Let my daughter study, condemn those officials who expelled her, and then you may have the right to demand from me respect for your laws. But since you spit on Soviet law, I do the same."

I watched Chibisov growing red in fury and his lower jaw moving from side to side. As soon as I finished, he bellowed at me; "Israel is a hostile, capitalist, aggressive state and we are not going to train cadres for it."

"That happened in 1964 when the Soviet Union had normal diplomatic relations with Israel," I answered. "If you consider an application for an exit visa a violation of the law, then you should close all the OVIR's. And, by the way, your answer has nothing to do with the law."

Chibisov turned to Amelkovitch: "Begin the interrogation!" The latter began to type the questions from the day before as well as some new ones, and to each I answered in the same way I had before. This went on for a long time. Amelkovitch had not lied; they really asked only a small part of what I really knew. Perhaps they had understood any other way would be useless.

At last Chibisov stood up and said, "I will myself personally take care that you get the punishment you deserve." He left without saying good-by.

In accordance with ritual, Amelkovitch took me to the small

room, but returned very soon with the pass. "We shall call you again and more than once." The expression on his face was not very pleasant.

I stopped by my house and then went on to my job. Yossi came to me later. His interrogation had been longer—two hours. His summons had said that he was called to the Chief of the Investigation Department, Brovadsky, which had made Yossi nervous. Brovadsky was a Stalinist type of boor and Yossi hates to have anyone shout at him. But when he reached the KGB, he was taken to another investigator, one who had made the search in our home, a dull official. The man automatically asked him questions and automatically put the answers down on paper. Yossi chose the tactic of "no." To every question, he gave a negative answer: "I don't know," "I am not acquainted," "I did not give," and so on.

The first test had been passed, but the real fight was still ahead.

* * *

Meanwhile the Jewish struggle continued, a struggle with still only one weapon—collective letters. But this weapon was a strong one, and once we were able to make certain of this.

One day in the beginning of July 1970, an acquaintance of mine, a sympathetic Jew, came and told me a story in secret. He said: "The other day I went to Moscow on a business trip and met in the Ministry an old friend of mine, Semyon by name. He is far from Jewish activities, but his heart is very Jewish. In his more favored times he was a 'court Jew' of one of the ministers of the Government. The Minister was later promoted and became Chairman of one of the State Committees. Semyon was on friendly relations with the Minister and helped him deal with his personal affairs, which he could not do himself because of his post. In other words the Minister used Semyon's 'Jewish head.'

"One day at the end of June 1970, the former Minister called Semyon at his place of work and said, 'Come immediately to Café Shokoladnitsa.' 'What has happened?' 'Come immediately!'

"Semyon left his work and rushed to the café. He saw his Minister in quite a gloomy state of mind.

" 'Semyon,' he said, 'We are old friends and I want to beg you for God's sake, if only in your dreams you think of Israel, throw it out of your head. If you want to live in peace to the end of your life, do it.'

"Semyon became frightened. Of course, he had never thought of Israel, but maybe the purges of 1953 were coming again? Then whether he had thought about Israel or not, nothing would help.

" 'Look here,' the Minister continued, 'At the last plenum the old man (that means Brezhnev) gathered some of the Central Committee members together and talked for the whole of an hour on the Jewish problem. He said that the abortive hijacking took place on the 15th of June not by chance and the immediate press release was also specially planned. On the 17th of June, U Thant was arriving in Moscow and it was convenient to show the Jews as criminals.

" 'Brezhnev said also that the fact that collective letters by Jews go abroad and are published there compromises the Soviet Union in international bodies. He ordered the KGB to nip in the bud even attempts at gathering signatures for such letters and the initiators should be revealed and punished. Every Jew who had connections with Israel or was simply interested in the country must be relieved of his position, if it is a post in which he has the right to make decisions.' "

The end of the story was not important. The fact that the authorities were concerned about our letters delighted us. We understood we were on the right track and should keep on.

I remembered Marx's saying: "If your enemy praises you, look back and think what was wrong in your actions." We could take the saying in reverse. If our enemy was concerned, we were doing the right thing. So even Marxism-Leninism helped us in our struggle. And we really utilized it more than once.

For example, after I refused to give evidence, a KGB man later reproached me. I answered: "I acted according to Lenin. When the Czarist police interrogated him, he answered: 'I refuse to give evidence, as my evidence can compromise my friends.' " The KGB man asked me no more questions.

By the middle of February 1971, we were in despair. Everything that had been done led to no results. The OVIR gave only fifteen to twenty exit visas a month and only to those Jews who had made no noise. It was a self-evident warning: sit quiet and you will be let out. But we could not agree to this. Meanwhile the newspapers were filled with articles in which Jews who applied for exit visas were called the enemies of the Soviet people. Could we remain silent?

A rumor spread that Vilna Jews had gone together to the Central Committee. Was it really so or not? We had no time to check on it. But suppose we try this weapon now? Is it legal? Every citizen has the right to approach any official body, must be received, and can leave a letter. Does this concern only an individual? What about a collective visit? Well, we can judge by collective letters. There is no law forbidding collective letters, but there is nothing the Soviet officials fear more. Why? Well, if a group of neighbors complain of a leaky roof in their house, it is all right. But if they complain they want more freedom, what can it not lead to? God forbid, tomorrow a group of workers will come asking for higher wages—what then? The only organizing force in the country is the Party and no one except it can organize the citizens in their acts. This is the law. And if someone else tries to do something, then instigators should be revealed and punished. Thus the masses will become frightened and be silenced.

This is the official Soviet logic and we must understand it. But we have nothing of which to be afraid. We long ago passed that border of fear where we could be easily intimidated. I, personally, was ready for everything. Only two days before, Yossi was refused an exit visa. So they had fulfilled their threat.

Well, what office will be receiving tomorrow? Thursday, February 19—the Soviet of Ministers of the Latvian SSR has a reception day. It is not very convenient in the morning. People are working and not everyone can leave his work. But the next evening reception will not be until the 24th, in the Ministry of the Interior. No, we cannot wait. Even if not many people come, this will be the beginning. We shall all go together to the reception room and demand a collective reception. What an unheard of plan for a Soviet State! But we have thrown aside caution. Despair gives us courage. Isn't it also unheard of that people are not allowed to rejoin their families for five, ten, and fifteen years?

During the preceding evening, there was a chain telephone set-up: "Tomorrow at 11 A.M. in the reception room of the Soviet of Ministers."

Next morning I arrived at the place and saw about twenty people. A narrow corridor, a table, benches along the walls. There was already a collective letter on the table. "Come up and put down your signature." The boys were wonderful! They'd thought of everything. The letter demanded a meeting with the Chairman of the Soviet of Ministers on the subject of leaving for Israel. And this was also a new phase of action. Until now signatures had been collected in secret. And now it was being done quite openly among strangers, Latvians, Russians, and quite probably KGB workers.

We waited a long time until all the visitors left. The order could not be violated. At last our turn came. We were already forty Jews. Six people entered the reception room. I remained in the corridor and tried to calm the others. Everyone could not enter the room. There was not enough space and what might it not have turned into if all forty people talked at once. After a few minutes the voices in the room became louder as people began to argue. When they started to shout, I knew we could fail. I opened the door and entered the room with several other people. At that moment the official at the table was shouting at one of the six: "And you I just refuse to talk to." I addressed everyone: "Comrades, please, let me talk to the representative of the Soviet of Ministers. Please, leave the room for five minutes." Everyone left and the door was closed behind them. David and I remained in the room. We sat down. Now we had to be calm.

"We did not come to make a scandal. We just ask that the Chairman of the Soviet of Ministers receive our petition. The earlier you allow us to go, the better it will be for you and the international reputation of the Soviet Union. Try to understand this."

He interrupted: "To whom am I speaking, permit me to ask." Of course, he had to report the names of the instigators, the disturbers of the peace. We told him our names and addresses.

"Who taught you to write collective letters?" he continued. "Who taught you to come to reception rooms in a crowd?"

"Lenin," I blurted out. "He always said that strength lay in the masses. Where an individual can achieve nothing, the masses will succeed."

If the official had asked where and when Lenin said this, I would have been in difficulty. But fortunately he did not, and the reference to the classic theoretician helped. The man changed his tone and promised that the Chairman would get to our business after the forthcoming Party Congress.

In fact, I was following Jabotinsky's teaching, not Lenin's. I always remembered his speech in Warsaw in 1938 where he warned against adventures, against a loss of a sense of reality. And taking this warning into consideration in the difficult times of February–March 1971 I was certain that there was some limit of action, a border we should not cross. If we had forgotten about this border, the results would have been bad for us. The same would have happened if we had not seriously considered our steps and avoided provocations.

The Soviet authorities' point of view on the problem of Jewish emigration changed from time to time. Different periods indicated this. In Riga, from April until June 5, 1967, a significant number of visas was issued. But people had to leave without their Soviet passports, with a piece of paper with a photograph on it and a place for all the seals, which was called an "exit visa." Everyone leaving for Israel was obliged to denounce his Soviet citizenship.

On the 8th of June 1967, three days after the beginning of the Six-Day War, emigration was stopped. It recommenced only in September of 1968 and continued until March 1969. A great many active Jews left during this period. After March 1969, the doors were again closed and only a few individual cases of emigration took place.

It was clear that there were two competing points of view in the Government concerning the Jews. One group was eager to get rid of "those troublemakers"; the second was decisively against the emigration. Our task was to reenforce the first opinion and not to give the second group an opportunity or pretext to make us knuckle down.

The border of what can and cannot be done is not unchangeable. What was impossible yesterday can be possible and necessary tomorrow. The important thing is to understand this border. We cannot afford to make mistakes.

On February 22 in the evening, we went to the reception room of the Ministry of the Interior. By this time we were about sixty Jews. The Deputy Minister received us. He waited for a long time until all other "non-Zionist" visitors had left and then we all entered his room. After we put a letter, just composed and signed, on his table, everyone began to attack him. The Jews were all talking at once. But can they do it any other way? Can a Jew allow another man to talk? Everybody told his own story, how many years he had been waiting: one was not allowed to go to his mother, another to his sister, a third to his second cousin, a fourth to his beloved mother-in-law, and so on and so forth.

The Deputy Minister was trying to remain calm, but did not always succeed. Eva jumped at him like a tigress. She had just received a refusal.

"You say that my daughter is staying here. That is why you refuse me. But where were you when my husband was sent to a forced labor camp and my daughter was left without a father? You—or others like you—killed my husband. Who thought then of my daughter?"

It was the first time in his experience that the Deputy Minister had seen or heard such a thing. It was all right. It would be a good lesson for him. We left after having demanded that next time the Minister himself should receive us.

Two days later on the 24th of February, Yossi, among twenty-four other Jews, began a sit-in strike in the Presidium of the Supreme Soviet of the USSR in Moscow. It was a memorable day for me. The struggle was spreading all over the Soviet Union. We all felt shoulder to shoulder with our Moscow comrades and I felt my son was with me in our common struggle.

On the eve of March 1, we gathered to discuss our behavior at the Minister's reception the next day. We must be organized. We should not all push together into the room. Six persons would enter at a time and each would tell about himself and his close friends. No one would speak on behalf of everybody. If the authorities decided to strike at us, each would be arrested as an instigator. Of course, they could arrest all six. Well, at least they would be six and not alone. We discussed the possible reaction for a long time. This visit might have important consequences. About seventy people might come.

But we were mistaken. One hundred Jews came. The reception room was too small, the air was stuffy. There were five or six other visitors. The Minister knew what was awaiting him and did not hurry. We waited patiently from 4 P.M. to 7 P.M. At 7 P.M. the militia closed the door. Now anyone could leave the building, but no one could enter it. So the people remained in the reception room.

At last all the "non-Zionist" visitors had left and only our large group remained in the building. Our boys stood by the doors to keep order and not to allow everyone to rush together into the Minister's room. Six of us entered the room and the door closed behind us. We handed the Minister our collective letter just signed by everyone in the reception room and began to speak in order, one after another. But he interrupted and did not allow us to speak. He received people only on individual problems, he said; everyone's question of emigration was considered separately. He refused to accept our collective letter or to talk to all of us together.

For fifteen minutes we argued, but the Minister was implacable and at last showed us to the door. We went out embarrassed. What could be done? Had we failed? The Minister argued on principle, but at the same time in accordance with policy. An individual can be refused easier than a group. Suddenly we saw that the Minister was leaving his room with his secretary. He considered the reception over. But no, we had not come to be turned back. If he would deal with individuals, then we would go one by one.

We settled the order and a wearisome waiting began. The Minister talked to every visitor, for several minutes, but to each one differently. For example, Yehoshua entered his room and asked "Am I a human being or not?" meaning he wanted his human rights. The Minister roared, "Get out!" Others had a longer conversation, but still the same result—a refusal. In other words the Minister had the longest reception day in his experience, from 4 P.M. to 12:30 A.M. But let someone else pity him.

That evening was most memorable for me. At 10 P.M. Ilana ran into the Ministry building and cried out in joy, "Yossi has permission!" Of course, I didn't stay in the building, but ran out together with her. "How? When?"

"He just called from Moscow. You know, after that strike on the 26th they were told to come today to the OVIR for an answer. Can you imagine how this nasty boy told us about his permission? 'Ten people are allowed to leave.' 'And you?' we asked. 'And I among them.' "

I felt great joy overwhelming me. Yossi was leaving. Half of my life was not in vain. I went home and although I was dead tired I could not go to bed. Every ten or fifteen minutes people came to report on the course of the reception. At 1 A.M. we summed up. In principle, this reception was a failure. The Minister had refused to receive a delegation and had given the usual negative answer to each one individually. There were no practical results, but still I thought our visit would have a certain impact on their future decisions.

At the same time the failure had some positive sides. What should we do now? The idea of a collective trip to Moscow had been discussed long before, but there were great differences of opinion. How many people could go? Who could go on a working day? To leave your work on a working day without permission could result in losing your job. And not everyone could afford a trip to Moscow. It was difficult to get tickets and where could we all spend a night in Moscow?

But the Minister had helped us with his refusals. No one would have gone to Moscow and the famous "hunger strike" that shook the world would not have taken place if on the 1st of March the Latvian Minister had promised at least some of the Jews that he would reconsider their applications for exit visas to Israel. But now, under the present circumstances, everyone was unanimous in the desire to go to Moscow, to the Presidium of the Supreme Soviet. We set the date—March 10. A lot of preparatory work had to be done before the trip. Everything had to remain secret: finding those who wanted to go, getting tickets, deciding who would go by plane, who by train—and all by different trains—and who would go by car; helping those who needed money for the trip. All this had to be done out of the reach of the KGB. If they had found out something or had we all gone by one train, they could have taken us off the train.

But they were feeling some sense of a coming explosion and decided to use the old tactic of divide and rule. Some of us were promised, "Sit quiet, do not take part in all these actions and you will be let out." And to our credit it should be pointed out that all who were promised exit visas to "sit quiet" did not believe the promises and took part in the Moscow "outing." We could already feel that there was a certain embarrassment in the KGB ranks and that our new actions might break them completely. Still we were not confident of victory. We looked forward to the forthcoming struggle with mixed feelings of hope and fear.

I could not take part in the preparatory work of the strike. I left earlier for Moscow to spend a few days with Yossi before his departure. Who could tell how long it would be before we would see each other again? In spite of that, I think no father ever took leave of his son as calmly as I did. What would happen with us was of no importance if Yossi could leave for freedom, could be together with his wife, could be happy. That was what I dreamed of. Packing, running back and forth, suitcases, documents, and at last on the morning of March 10 we left for the International Airport.

A small group of Jews had gathered in the terminal. Many of the most well-known Moscow Zionists were leaving. They were all in a deep depression. What would happen to those who remained? What would be the result of today's demonstration? The authorities might decide to strike a final blow and arrest everyone. Strange people! They had run a bigger risk, had won their victory, and now they were concerned about us. They didn't even seem happy to be leaving for Israel, but would rather have stayed to continue the struggle. I really could not understand them, but maybe if I were in their place. . . .

At 11:30 the first messenger arrived from the Supreme Soviet and happily reported, "Our numbers have increased. Quite unexpectedly, a large group came from Vilna with their wives and children, several families from Lvov, some from Tallinn and other cities."

"How many all together?"

"Don't know, had no time to count everybody."

Not only had the KGB not managed to find out about the increase, we ourselves knew nothing about it.

Noon. The second messenger came. "We have decided that every half hour until the departure, messengers shall come to the airport and tell about the course of the strike. Those leaving will be in Vienna in three hours and release the information to the world." The messenger told us, "The first statement to the Chairman of the Supreme Soviet was handed in. The Jews demanded to be received by him. If there is no answer to this, in the evening we shall declare a hunger strike."

A hunger strike? It was unheard of in the Soviet Union. Frankly, I was very uneasy. Maybe they are overdoing things, losing their heads. But perhaps this time they, the younger generation, were right.

Half past twelve o'clock. The next messenger came: "The foreign correspondents have appeared. The corridors are filled with men in civilian clothes. One of them came up to the UPI correspondent and said: 'Jackson, we are sick and tired of you, get out.' The large hall of the Reception Room of the Presidium is filled. There are not enough places to sit down. We have counted about 150 people all together. The authorities have not given any reaction until now."

* * *

The last minutes. Yossi was calm, even businesslike. We had always called him *kalte bauch* (cool headed). He took his leave of his friends and then of mother and me. "Please, no tears. Everything will be O.K." We watched him go through the customs check and waited until he appeared on the glass gallery. Now we could only see each other and talk by signs. He is already on another side of the world. I tried to memorize his face. This is my son. Not bad, I thought.

My Moscow friends called me to go to the Presidium and I myself felt that I must go. I waved to Yossi for the last time, asked Roza to stay until the end, and left.

We arrived at the Presidium. Several boys were waiting at the entrance. "The statement of the hunger strike has already been handed in. People are excited. None of the officials had come out, so we decided not to wait until night."

It had been done. There was no way back. Now we would have to stand by until the end.

I went into the hall. Everyone was sitting in complete silence. I sat down together with our boys and listened to them: "When the statement was handed in, we all sat down and became silent. Can you imagine, Ezra, 150 Jews silent for a whole hour? Wonderful discipline. In the beginning some began to make noise, so we threw them out and it became silent. Fifteen minutes later, Jackson came in, looked at the silent Jews, and said, 'I'm going to the telegraph.' "

Little by little the Jews began to talk. What can you do with them? But no one left.

Five o'clock. The reception hours were over. The doors were closed. The Director of the reception room came in and told everyone to leave. But we had not come to leave. We began to express our demands and spoke for quite a long time. Our demands were: reconsideration of all applications; in case of refusal, a reason. No answer. We were again told to clear the building. We refused. The Director left and immediately darkness fell in the hall. They switched off the lights. Only thin rays of daylight came through the closed curtains. What would follow? The corridor was lighted and filled with people in civilian clothes and several militiamen.

The tension grew. People had to be distracted. Someone remembered: Today is Purim. But where can we get *Megilloth Esther*? Then someone said he has an *Haggadah shel Pesach* (the Passover Seder text) with him and he began to read it slowly and to translate it into Russian. I felt a holy fear. Maybe we were also on the way of exodus from Russia.

The *Haggadah* was not finished. They suddenly switched on the lights, but we saw that now the corridor was dark. Something was being prepared there. The dark corridor was full of militiamen.

At eight o'clock the doors were flung open and a militia detachment rushed into the hall. They stood along the walls and among us, dividing us into squares. We were locked in.

We were informed: "You will be addressed by a militia commissar." The Commissar of Militia was a general. He began his speech in a hard voice and unambiguously: "Enough. You've played these games enough. We are not going to endure them any longer. Those who do not leave the hall in two minutes will be detained as disturbers of the peace."

Two minutes. It was both a long time and a short time. It was a short time for a discussion, but quite long enough for making a decision. Several voices were heard: "Let's not leave. Let them carry us out. We'll raise our feet and let them drag us out."

But I was of another opinion. Fifteen days for disturbing the peace is nothing. But such behavior could also be called "resistance to militia" and this could have meant several years of imprisonment. But this also was unimportant if we considered what we had achieved so far. Nothing. And if we now gave them this opportunity to provoke us, tomorrow they would consider themselves winners. We exchanged a few words and the two minutes were over. Several of us took our coats and said to everyone, "Let's leave. Tomorrow at 11 A.M. here again."

Many people thought we were wrong, but the events of the second day showed that we were right. We left in small groups by different side streets all filled with militia. Neither we nor they had ever seen such a demonstration in the center of Moscow. In the reception room one of the militiamen asked a Jewish woman in a whisper: "Aren't you afraid to do this?" "We are afraid," she answered. "We are terribly afraid. That is why we are here." The man did not understand her.

On the 11th of March, we all came again. A delegation was received, but the answers were not definite. We were sent to the reception room of the Ministry of the Interior. Various high officials of the OVIR came out and talked to us there, but this was not what we had come for or what we had tried to achieve.

In the meantime the militia closed the doors. No one was allowed in; no one was allowed out. At four o'clock we suddenly felt that the ministry's staff was excited. In a minute a side door was flung open and the Minister of the Interior of the USSR, Schelokov, and several generals came in.

He talked to us for a long time. But the main thing he told us was that he had decided to send his representatives to all cities for reconsideration of all applications.

In that moment I felt that the hard work and struggle of all those years had not been in vain. We had won. I looked around and thought that I was proud of these people, the Soviet Jews. I was proud to belong to them.

26

In Freedom

Today I am in Flint, Michigan, somewhere in the North for a United Jewish Appeal dinner, a television interview. Tomorrow morning Harrisburg and then Pittsburgh, Pennsylvania. It is interesting how I've gotten used to all this flying. Tel Aviv, London, Amsterdam, and even that flight from Holland to New York. And now every day a flight and I feel at home. More than that, I even rest in planes, tired from all the speechmaking. I am no longer afraid to speak. I have learned. But I still feel very nervous meeting new people. I wonder whether they notice it. But when I begin to speak, I forget everything and feel very much at ease. In fact, I have come to like making speeches. When I see those interested faces in front of me, I feel very happy and want to tell them more and more. I try to explain to them what a Soviet Jew is, what his idealistic Zionism is, what his heroism is. I doubt that Americans can understand, but they listen attentively and this helps me.

Could I ever have imagined that I would be a speaker? In fact, I am not a speaker. I just like to talk to people who listen. I try to understand every new audience and talk to them accordingly—be it a UJA dinner or a meeting organized by the American Conference on Soviet Jewry, a university meeting, or a meeting of the clergy, be it an audience of fifty people or thousands of listeners.

My first speech in London, to a meeting of a thousand British Jews, was just terrible. I was so nervous and shy. I did not know what to say and spoke so slowly, so indecisively, that when I at last finished I wanted to hide under the table. But they did not give me the chance. They all suddenly stood up and applauded for several minutes. Then I wished the floor would open beneath my feet. But it was great. It gave me encouragement. I understood then what they wanted to hear. That's why the meetings in Holland afterward were so successful. And now I am flying to and fro in America, making speech after speech. A month and a half already, and it will go on until the end of March. And I came for only two weeks.

I don't feel bad here, I am just terribly tired. Especially when I am in New York. That strange stuffy air, even when you are outdoors, the constant piercing sounds of sirens, and the crackle of current whenever I touch something in the hotel rooms. It gets on my nerves terribly. When I am in New York, I feel ill. I can't eat anything. The food there seems as if from another planet. I dream constantly of hot boiled potatoes with herring and Russian brown bread with butter. Better not to think about it. In fact, New York is not to blame. It all began in London. It is just my nervousness. When I come back to New York and go into my room, I just fall on the bed and look steadily at the wall, unable to sleep or to think. Thank God, in the Barclay Hotel I can order food served in my room. In the Lexington I starved for days, nourishing myself only with that terrible crackle of current. Sometimes, looking out of the window at the city from my twenty-eighth floor room in the Hotel Lexington, I said to myself: "Well, you are in America. What do you think of it? You ought to think something." But I thought nothing. I just could not. All this is just too unbelievable to be able to comprehend it. I and America. America and I. Alla Milkina, a former young Pioneer-Leninist and a Komsomol member, comes to America. No, it sounds like a bad joke.

And yet people here are wonderful. Maybe it is typical for public relations or on the level where people really do not come to know each other well, but all the same I find delight in people. I have never seen so many smiles in all my life. They surround me everywhere, meet me in every city, caress me, and give me strength. Everyone is so easygoing that I do not really find it difficult to deal with strange people. They like to ask me whether or not I like America and I never know what to answer. On the one hand, I have no impressions at all; I am just afraid to have any. On the other hand, there are a lot of impressions which are all so different. And really this country is so big that it cannot leave one with only a single impression. It is all and it is everything. Sometimes it seems to me to be a world that had reached perfection in all its services and standard of living and has now started on the way back. But Americans on the contrary are very enthusiastic about great new challenges and think they have a lot to do. And in general they are very businesslike.

Even struggles here seem to be a matter of business. Every new struggle is immediately connected with an organization, an official hierarchy, money, fund-raising, competition, and so on. It seems to be a way of life. Civil rights, socialism, anti-smoking, Women's Lib (Oh, God!), Soviet Jewry, Jewish Defense League—everybody to his own liking. Those who don't like struggles struggle against struggles. Those who do not like to struggle through the establishment form their own establishment and think they are rebels.

It is good when good people are able to think something of themselves and it is good that people have that inner spiritual and physical activity to help others in need. I had never imagined that such readiness to help others was possible. American Jews are great. They deserve respect and gratitude from all of us. If it were not for them, we there would not be able to achieve anything. They are our second front. And whatever the psychological or political reasons for such activity, it helps us and we must be grateful.

I like to be here now with them—to travel, to speak. What is the use of going back? To whom? To what? This way time goes faster. And who knows how long I have to wait. It is nearly four months since I've seen Yossi. It is nothing. But I begin to forget his face. It is a terrible feeling. I close my eyes and try to imagine him. But his face does not come. Pictures don't say anything. They are not true. Only memory can bring his fullest image—his face, his mood, his body—all together. And it comes no more.

I know that it is because we have not had enough of each other. We did not have enough time to feel each other, to record each other on the tape of memory. These four months have felt like many years. I subconsciously add to them all the rest of the time which we have to wait and they grow into an eternity. But I am calm. Sometimes shamelessly calm. Why? All that has happened to us is too much like a tragedy, a plot for a film. And I am afraid to take part in a performance that is so banal. Even when I am alone, I cannot express my feelings with gestures or sounds—tearing the hair on my head, wringing my hands, groaning, wailing. My second self looks at me and mocks me. And in fear of it, I forbid myself to express the feelings. And after awhile, having been forbidden expression, the feelings themselves wear away. The other day I went to see *Love Story.* I cried. I resisted, but in the end I burst into tears. But about Yossi and myself, I do not cry. Yes, leukemia is terrible. You can't foresee it, you can't resist it. It is so cruel. And if it is not leukemia, but the Soviet Union? What do you do then? Isn't it also a tragedy?

Only once I collapsed, but it was only for a short time. On the 19th of February, in the morning, I learned that Yossi's application for an exit visa had been refused. Was it unexpected? I should have been ready for it, but I was not. The terrible news came by telephone. Miriam received the telegram and called our cousins in Brooklyn. It was a long time before they dared call me. Our dear cousins in Brooklyn, they hoped together with me, they cooked potatoes for me, on Saturdays they brought me half dead to their home and put me to bed, they dressed me "like a doll," they bought pots and pans for my new home, they read and gathered every piece in the newspapers about me. I love them so much and I am ashamed to be sad and suffer in their presence. Can anything compare with their untold stories of Bergen-Belsen, Maidanek, the stories of their neighbors and friends with blue numbers on their well-cared-for white hands; our dear cousins from Brooklyn, formerly of Poland.

And on February 19, they did not dare telephone me. But they called at last and told me with tense, fearful voices. And I put down the receiver. I was still in bed. The call had awakened me. How much I wished that it had turned out to be a nightmare, that nobody had called, or that I just hadn't understood. I sat in the bed, alone in the room, alone in the hotel, alone in the world. I wanted to move, but I was afraid. I wanted to cry, to shout, but it was only in my mind. I continued to sit motionless in bed. My mind was quite reasonable. It even persuaded me: "Nothing has happened. You had to be ready for this. It is only the beginning. You wanted to struggle for him. Then why do you collapse at the first failure? Now this unties your hands. Go on, speak, demand, beg, struggle for him! Didn't you come here for this?" But all my motionless self answered weakly: "No, I was not ready for this. I thought that I was at the end of my strength, but now I see how much more is demanded of me. And I am terrified. I know I should be ashamed to be so weak. He is there. How much he has lived through, how much is in store for him. And all this without me. I know how much I mean to him. And it is my responsibility. I must be stronger for his sake. Russia has declared war on me. Shall I be frightened when I have the whole world on my side? I must get up and go. I have a big meeting today, a very important one—a thousand women activists of the UJA. I must stand up. Why am I not moving? Maybe I am paralyzed?"

I had completely lost command of my body and sat that way until the telephone rang again and roused me from my shock. I had to go to the meeting.

And I continue to go to the meetings and shall go until the end of March, maybe longer. I have my itinerary. It is like a crutch for me. People decide, plan, arrange meetings for me with important people. And I ask them, I beg them, but I do not believe them. U Thant said that he was not strong enough to influence the Soviet Union. Who is strong enough then? Yossi?

Yes, only he has the strength and everyone else who is there. And for them I hope. They are already on strike. They go together to the Supreme Soviet, to the Central Committee building and demand. This struggle will be victorious. I feel it. The newspapers say that the Jews were eating sandwiches while on strike yesterday, the 1st of March, in the reception room of the Presidium of the Supreme Soviet. What did Yossi eat? Did he bring it from home? Oh God, what will they do to them all?

We are landing. Snow everywhere—like in Russia. It must be warm now in Israel. This was my first winter out of Russia and I've spent it all outside of Israel.

Detroit. "You will be met on your arrival in Detroit by our representative and driven to Flint. Hotel reservations are at the Holiday Inn." O.K., I am waiting to be met and driven.

Myra is pregnant. Hard to imagine my sister having a baby. It is interesting. All through our lives, we developed physically with a difference in time of only a few months, although the difference in age is a year and ten months. It was the same with our first appointments. Then in March of 1970 she married and in November of the same year my wedding took place. And now she is pregnant. Nonsense. A stupid analogy.

At last I am met and driven to my destination. Soft, big American cars which take me to comfortable American hotels. I shall never remember them all. The Holiday Inn is as good as the others. I would love to have breakfast now and lie down for awhile, but they will certainly drag me immediately to a television station or to a newspaper office and forget to offer me something nourishing. It is interesting that the farther you get from New York, people become more and more tired, forgetful, haughty, less attentive. Why is this so—hard work or provincial haughtiness? If they do forget this time, I shall give them a hint or just ask for a sandwich. Do they have anything besides those terrible roast beef sandwiches which I hate? Meanwhile I shall check in.

"A room for Mrs. Rusinek? Yes, I have it reserved. Mrs. Rusinek, there is a note for you here from New York."

The Israeli Consulate—"Call urgently." These words sound so familiar. Urgently? Something has happened. They want me back? But why? There was that second strike in Moscow yesterday. Something must have happened to him. Oh God, I don't want to know anything.

"Where is a telephone?"

"This way, please, on the wall."

"Thank you . . . Israeli Consulate? *Simcha, shalom.* This is Alla calling."

"Alla? *Mazel tov.*"

Do you know what joy is? Joy is when a grown-up person in a midi-skirt begins to skip like a monkey; when you laugh like mad, embrace everyone, then seize your coat from a chair, then put it back and don't understand why you find yourself at this end of the world at such a moment; when you lose all sense of duty and call the UJA and cancel all the meetings; when you rush insanely back to New York, lie on your Barclay bed, and refuse to move all that damned week until his leaving Russia passes; when you take a dozen suitcases with pots and pans, clothes, and presents from the whole of America, and with your hands full run to the plane. New York—Vienna. Kissing good-by the sweet cousins and those great kids from the Student Struggle for Soviet Jewry; when you roll yourself up into a ball like a kitten in your seat and close your eyes tightly to fall asleep as quickly as possible so that the last night will pass unnoticed.

On the way the plane landed first in Brussels and I had to lounge about the terminal for half an hour. I found nothing better to do than to buy Chanel and imagine that I was the most elegant lady. The last hour of flight and I arrived in Vienna. I was so overloaded with luggage that I didn't have the time or the strength to philosophize on my coming back to Vienna in quite a new capacity. I was sure I would lose or leave something behind, so I watched myself very attentively. But it was already late. On leaving the plane, I could not find my ticket to Tel Aviv. Since I was the last person still on the plane, I decided to get off and continue the search in the terminal.

In the terminal I stood among my eight suitcases, bags, and packages and looked through them several times. Nothing helped. There was no ticket. I spat on all that business, thought that here was a subject for our first family scandal, registered my luggage, and left for the hotel where I had reservations for two.

I had two hours to rest and to think about my appearance. I knew I had to be as well-dressed as possible. This would not offend Yossi. On the contrary he would be happy to see his wife so elegant. But what should I wear? My black pants suit? It had been good enough for the $10,000 minimum dinner in New York with the Baron de Rothschild. I remembered that someone had called me especially to warn me that it was a black-tie affair and that I had to be dressed accordingly. I could not understand what he meant. Did he think I would appear in hot pants or a Russian sarafan? No, I had better leave this for our arrival in Israel. I could imagine how Miriam would laugh to see what America had done to me. Now I shall put on the blue pants suit. That had been good enough for both Mr. U Thant and Mayor Lindsay. So, I think, Yossi will also be satisfied. And my big black hat would be the last blow for him. He would certainly say, "What an elegant wife I have."

In the afternoon I went back to the airport. The two curly-headed men were already there, excited. For how many years had they met hardly a couple of Jews a month—old, sick invalids. Some of these had not even reached Israel alive. And now twenty people in one plane. A real exodus. And what people! Young, strong. Engineers, doctors, scientists. And they were bringing their children to Israel. The first large group in all these long years. And in this group there were those who took part in the Moscow sit-in strikes on the 24th of February and the 1st of March. The first Jewish *aliyah* from Russia achieved in struggle.

Time passed. The plane was late. I sat in the terminal and suffered from waiting. At last the two men jumped from their seats and ran away. The plane had landed. A drum inside me began to thump violently. I paced back and forth in the terminal, trembling with nervousness. Then I sat down. Why should I be nervous? He is already here. I have been so self-composed for all this time and now I'm suddenly trembling like a school girl. I squeezed myself to stop the trembling and forced myself to sit motionless. But this was beyond my strength. I bounced to my feet and went to the glass wall behind which they would appear. Every minute was a new torture. I began to feel sick to my stomach and wanted to cry. That was a bit too much. I raised my head to make the tears go away. There was nothing to cry over now. I pressed my forehead against the cold glass wall and again compelled myself not to move.

The passengers were already arriving, light, quick Western businessmen with bright suitcases, hurrying to their homes or hotels or offices. Slender gentlemen with good color in their faces and smiles for everyone. I continued not to move, looking steadily at the end of the long corridor behind the wall.

Suddenly my heart missed a beat. I saw something dark growing slowly in the far end of the corridor. It looked like a frightful crowd slowly approaching. "Refugees," flashed across my mind. Women in terrible Soviet hats with big black bags, men in dark, long, thick cloth coats with gray flabby faces. Children holding their parents by the hands and no less frightened. They were walking indecisively as though they were afraid the floor would collapse under their feet. Little Russian Jews who raised their hands in a great struggle and were frightened at the victory they had achieved. Their first free steps were shy. They did not know how to feel happy and they all looked sad. The two men led them as carefully as a group of invalids or sick children.

I looked for Yossi in the crowd, but could not find him. At last when the crowd came nearer, I saw someone trying to walk more quickly but still afraid to pass ahead of the Jewish Agency officials. I felt that it was he. They came nearer and nearer. Now I could see him well. His appearance made me feel sick. Thin, pale, long arms hanging helplessly out of that awful old gray raincoat which was too tight for him. He had had his hair cut, probably just before leaving, and his head seemed too big and bony on his long neck. I felt ashamed of my own appearance.

He was looking for me with eyes like a helpless child, afraid he would not find me. Once his look passed over me, but he did not recognize me. I took off my stupid hat and then he saw me. A shy, somewhat guilty smile appeared on his face. I felt the corners of my lips trembling and forced a smile.

We stood on either side of the glass wall and our eyes did not know what to say. I showed him how to go to the door in the wall. He went, but stopped in hesitation. Still a Soviet man, afraid to violate discipline and order, to leave his group. I indicated to him that it was all right, but he did not know what to do. The door was closed. How could he know that he had only to step on that black rubber spot and it would open by itself? I beckoned him and he took the step. The door opened and I ran to him. The only thing I could do was put my head on his chest and hide from him and myself. He kissed me on my head. We were both afraid of each other. "It is all over," he said. "We shall have to begin everything from the very beginning." I remembered that I had written that in one of my letters from America. And it was so.

"Where are your suitcases?"

"Here they are." I saw three new small suitcases.

"What is there inside?"

"Your big pillow and a blanket from Aunt Musja in one, some plates and dishes in the second, and my clothes in the third."

"It is good that you brought a pillow. And I have eight pieces of luggage with me from America."

"Oho!"

"They are all presents from your cousins for us. They are so sweet. I'll tell you a lot about them. You know," I added happily, "I've lost my ticket to Tel Aviv."

"Really?" he answered no less happily. "You're still the same."

"Yes, I am quite the same."

The group was already leaving the terminal to board a bus to the Schoenau Transit Center of the Jewish Agency. "Let's go," I said. "I have a room for both of us in a hotel in the city, but first we'll go there to Schoenau to register you." I was explaining as I put on my hat and red midi-coat.

"What an elegant wife I have!"

We settled down in the bus. The Jews had already recovered and began to talk loudly, telling their usual jokes. The large, smoothly moving bus passed through the streets of Vienna, the clean small houses of the suburbs with their picturesque shops. All this—shop windows full of goods, signboards, clean streets, old people riding bicycles, the smells, colors, sounds—spoke of freedom and blessed capitalism.

Yossi leaned back with relief. "At last the Middle Ages are behind." He was very quiet. I didn't take my eyes off his face, watching his every reaction to that great event of exodus, expecting some unusual words from him.

"Why are you looking at me in such a manner?"

"I want to know what you feel, what you think. You must say something important."

"All right. I shall say—I love you."

* * *

Hemda-leh! Wake up, dear. My little sleepyhead. It's time for your milk. Nu, open your eyes. Yes, yes, stretch yorself. Fine! Now, did you sleep well? Aren't you hungry? I see you are, but let me change you first. Now, here is your milk. Oho! You are really hungry. Don't hurry, your bottle isn't going to run away.

Be a good girl today. Your grandfather Ezra is coming to visit you tonight. And he is a rare guest. There are so many Jews still in the Soviet Union, so he has a lot of work again. So let him see you as a good, quiet girl. And in two weeks we shall go to visit your great-grandmother. She will be ninety-one then, and you must give her a good wide smile. Please, try to. You are always so serious.

Myra writes that your little cousin Ilana was smiling in the hospital, and you are already three months old and smile so rarely. Papa will come soon. Will you give him a smile? He has his Hebrew classes now on Mt. Scopus, so he won't be very late. It is not far from here. He will come in and say: "Where is my Lapa?" He calls you La-pa, a paw, or Laponka, a little paw. I call you Boosja. What does that mean? Nothing. Just Boosja or Boosenka, little Boosja. Our neighbors say that in Arabic it means "a kiss." So in Arabic you are a kiss. I have nothing against that.

But when you grow and are asked, "What is your name?" you will say, "Hemda." You will know how to pronounce it. For us it is so difficult. So we call you many other names. But we shall learn: "Hem-dah, Hem-dah." It sounds very beautiful when sabras (those born in Israel) pronounce it. That's why we called you Hemda. It is wonderful that now we are three. Life seems wonderful. It probably has some great sense. Do you know what it is?

Hemda, what have you done? Shame on you! Why do you always do it when you eat? I shall have to change you again. Now you are smiling. You feel good now? All right, then I forgive you. Finish your milk. Don't want it? Well, you've had quite enough. And now your bubble, please. I shall pat you on the back. Fine! God bless you! Now back to your bed, Boosenka. No, no, please don't cry. Here's your beautiful rattle. I shall come back soon. I shall go and finish my book now, and then I shall come back and play with you. O.K.? In fact, I have only to put a full stop and write—

THE END.

Afterword: The Samizdat

BY

Ezra Rusinek

When does a Russian Jew learn for the first time that he is a Jew? Usually at school or even in kindergarten when he has been called by somebody with hatred or without it "Yid" or "Yidovka." Then he runs home crying, "Mama, I don't want to be a Jew!" And what does he hear from his parents? "Don't pay any attention." Can a small child understand? Never. But from that time on he does understand that his national origin is something shameful.

In 1955 we lived in deep Russia in the town of Taganrog after having escaped from exile. Sarah, our old friend from Riga, came to visit us.

"I have a book for you to read from Yasha. Read it quickly."

Yasha was a friend of my youth, a true Zionist, who had barely escaped prosecution but managed to live on in Riga under a constant threat.

To read quickly meant to read it in one night. The book was the articles and speeches of Jabotinsky, published in 1912. The first article was an address to Jewish teachers; in it Jabotinsky defines their task as bringing up Jewish youth in such a way that a downtrodden Srulik can become a proud Israel, that not a single Jewish boy or girl should be ashamed of his or her origin.

And this was said fifty years ago!

That made me remember a talk with a friend ten years previously in Siberia, when we were in exile. We were both fathers of children five or six years old. How should we bring them up?

He insisted, "When my son is sixteen, I shall tell him that he is a son of the Jewish people, that he has his motherland in Palestine. I'll explain to him who Herzl was, and Trumpeldor, Bar Kochba, and the Maccabees. But until then he should not be traumatized."

"You'll be too late," I answered him. "Your son won't understand you. We must begin now or we shall lose our children."

It seems to me that I was right.

That pamphlet of Jabotinsky was the beginning of *Samizdat* —self-publishing—in our family, though the Jewish spirit had always existed there. Quietly and cautiously we celebrated all Jewish holidays. Little silver stars of David were favorite precious things for our children. The words "shabbas," "bar-mitzvah," and "talis" were familiar to them. But Samizdat had to put into their minds and hearts something new and more important.

My daughter, Ilana, copied the text of the pamphlet and became interested. The manuscript was passed from one person to another among the few Jewish families in Taganrog. Some of them returned the pamphlet in an hour or two; others read and reread it several times and then came for a talk. And how long were those talks! There were a lot of things to discuss in those years: the Sinai campaign of 1956, the Youth Festival in Moscow in 1957 and the Israeli delegation which took part in it, and, of course, rare broadcasts in Russian and in Yiddish by "Kol Israel."

And again Yasha sent a book to read. This time it was *Exodus* by Leon Uris in German translation. And again—sleepless nights. What an explosive! But why don't they have this book in Russian? Why do they have it in English, German, Hebrew, French, and God knows what other languages, but no one has thought of publishing it in Russian for us here?

1963. We were able to move back at last to Riga. After settling down we immediately plunged into a Jewish atmosphere and became acquainted with the families that wanted to emigrate to Israel. Soon after that Yasha, my old dear friend, got permission to leave for Israel. Before this departure he begged that *Exodus* be translated into Russian and typed. "Do whatever you can," he said, and with these words he handed me the beginning of his translation.

But the book was so long. To abridge it would be to lose a great deal of the impact. What could be done? To whom could I speak? Who would translate? From what language? Where should we get a typewriter? Who would type?

One thing was clear: we must hurry. But equally clear was something else. If the KGB learned about it, prison awaited those who would be caught. Even if I could find someone among my acquaintances who could translate, he might become frightened or even report me to the KGB. And if someone did agree to do it, how could we pay for his work? My own salary was just enough to make ends meet. How could we buy a typewriter in a shop? The KGB registers all typewriters in shops as well as in offices and repair shops. There seemed no answers to all the questions. But we decided to try.

Cautiously, step by step, we looked for someone who might help. Finally we found a typewriter that had always been privately owned. The owner had left for Israel. I took the typewriter, changed the type a little, lubricated it, and headed for Sarah. "No one can do it but you. You also promised Yasha you'd do something. You can type, even if only with two fingers. Okay? Get on with it."

We asked Boris, one of our old Riga acquaintances, an expert in the history of Israel, a man with several languages at his fingertips, to translate the book. We didn't have to ask him twice.

And Sarah, after a long working day—living in one room with two daughters—typed evening after evening, two pages in two hours. The typewriter stood on a blanket to lessen the noise, so that neighbors passing her door would not hear her. Sarah chain-smoked and cursed indecently every time she heard a ring at her door. An acquaintance had dropped in for a chat and a cup of tea—these good-for-nothing people. Immediately the typewriter and the typed pages were covered with the blanket.

And what a typewriter it was! All my life I shall remember it. There was an "e" that would constantly stick, and after "n" the carriage would move twice. It was an ordeal, but what could we do? We didn't have our own typewriter repairman and taking it to a shop would be dangerous. There was nothing to do but bear it.

Every week the diligent Boris would call Sarah, "Come for a cup of tea, Sarochka," which meant that the next portion of the translation was ready.

Then there were problems with the paper. What kind should we use? If we used thin paper, we could make eight copies, if we used thick, only five copies. We decided "better fewer but better." These books would have to live and work among Soviet Jews for years, so the paper had to be good and thick. But good paper is not always in the stores and if we bought more than two packages at one time it would seem strange. So we waited for the paper to appear in the shops and then bought two packages in each of the shops, being careful that no acquaintances see us doing it.

The most difficult problem was with carbon paper. Soviet carbon paper is not good. The fifth copy is hardly readable. And good Polish carbon paper is on the market only once in an eternity. When it appeared, we declared a celebration, for the acquisition of a package of it meant that work could continue.

As each page was typed, the carbon paper was burned and the pages were taken to "the refrigerator," an incurious and true friend. And then I would be able to go home with a feeling of deep satisfaction at having done something useful that day.

Sometimes I committed the crime of stealing "state property" at my place of work. I took several sheets of carbon paper. But I did not feel guilty. The law that prohibits my people from learning their own language and history made this "crime" necessary. Nor were we concerned that we had violated Leon Uris's copyright by translating his work without his permission. We were sure he would not be bothered by it.

It took a whole exhausting year to translate and type the six hundred pages of the book. How many days of rest, movies, or theater performances were missed. Sarah sat at her work every evening and didn't leave the typewriter until two pages were ready. It was really the work of a "chalutz," a pioneer. Jabotinsky quotes Trumpeldor's explanation of the meaning of "chaltutz": "Ground must be dug? I dig. To shoot, to be a soldier? I go. Police? Doctors? Lawyers? Teachers? Water-carriers? Here you are, I do everything."

What a triumphant moment it was when on the last page Sarah could type "The End" in big letters. A great burden had been taken off our minds. The promise which we had given to Yasha and whose fulfillment had become our obligation toward the growing generation of proud Soviet Jews had been fulfilled.

But there were still problems. How should we bind our books? Giving them to a binding shop was out of the question. Again a friend helped. This time it was our pet crank; Tsipa. Few people knew his full name and it was hardly necessary. This middle-aged short man with the heart of a school-boy and the mind of a sage brought fun and laughter into every house. His asymmetrical eyes, like those of a kind Mephistopheles, twinkled with an always appropriate joke. But behind all this, his friends knew a devoted, selfless comrade who was to play an important role in the work.

This time Tsipa answered in his usual manner: "For a bottle of vodka? Okay." I promised to provide the bottle, and in a week the books were ready.

But the problems were not yet finished. Should the books remain in Riga or be sent to Russia? Who should read them first, young people or adults? How could we make certain that the KGB didn't find the books? And on and on.

After long discussions it was decided to keep two copies in Riga and to send the other three to true friends in Russia. The books should first of all be given to young people for reading. After each person read one, it had to be returned to the hands of the giver; there must be no passing from hand to hand. Every book must be kept under control.

A month passed. We were deluged by pleas from those who wanted to read the books. People came and begged: "For God's sake, put me on the list. My children must read it." Once in talking to a tourist from Israel I learned that many young tourists from the U.S.A. had begun to arrive in Israel and when they were asked why they chose to visit Israel rather than France, Italy, Spain, they answered that they had read *Exodus* by Uris.

But can this be compared with the book's effect on the Soviet Jews? The influence of *Exodus* on the national rebirth of Jewish youth in the Soviet Union can hardly be overestimated. May God give many years of happiness to Leon Uris!

The diligent Boris had received for his work a precious present—a book on the War of Liberation in 1948, and Sarah—a cigarette lighter which played incorrectly the melody of Hatikvah, the Israeli anthem. She was very proud of this little thing until the musical mechanism ceased to work.

The main thing was that nobody in the city knew who had made the books. The book began its life and successful work among hundreds of people, but the few who knew about its source never mentioned it, and it remained a secret for years.

One day suddenly Tsipa ran in very excited: "Congratulations! We are not alone! I have just seen an abridged *Exodus* in Russian—one hundred fifty pages." It had been made by another group. We were hiding from them and they from us. "Well," I said then, happy and proud. "Let them be fruitful and multiply."

* * *

One thing must be understood. This is a story of one little group in Riga, their rebirth and the beginning of their Samizdat. But there were scores of such small groups and individuals who were seeking their own ways, found them, and also began to be active. Some of them began earlier, some later. In different parts of the huge Soviet Empire Jewish eyes began to open, Jewish hearts began to beat. Only several years later were we to learn that in 1957, forgetting their fears, Jews in Moscow came in contact with the Israeli delegation to the Youth Festival.

The Sinai War and the Festival lit a tiny fire which was to flame into this big movement for liberation. The Festival brought to Moscow the children of those whom we had seen off to Palestine in the thirties. These youths came, and their Jewish brothers and sisters in Russia met them, youths whose parents could not leave for Palestine on time and had gone through Hitler's and Stalin's concentration camps. The Soviet Jews could not forget the young Israelis—their suntanned faces, their happy smiles, the songs and dances of a free people.

In 1958 small crowds of not more than two hundred people for the first time gathered in front of the Moscow synagogue to celebrate the holiday of Simhat Torah. In a few years this small crowd had turned into a sea of people, many thousands, a phenomenon that sends waves of emotion throughout the Jewish world now and rivets its attention to this small street in Moscow every year.

Who knows what has been going on in other cities: Vilna, Leningrad, Kiev, Odessa, Sverdlovsk. Their stories will also be told sometime. Gathered all together they will add one more page to the heroic history of our people. I am a bad teller of tales. This story deserves beautiful words, songs of praise and honor; it deserves its own Leon Uris.

Why is Jewish Samizdat necessary in Russia? Is it worth running such a risk? Aren't talks and "Kol Israel" broadcasts enough? Isn't the awkward Soviet anti-Israel and anti-Zionist propaganda enough in itself to arouse national self-consciousness in Russian Jews? What is the purpose of this Samizdat? Is it directed against the present social order in the country?

I think Jewish Samizdat is necessary so long as Soviet Jews are deprived of objective information about Israel and about their own past and present. The most important task of Samizdat until 1970 was to create a reserve of Jews interested in Israel and ready to come to it—in other words, the task of all Zionism.

One might ask the question: Weren't there in Riga and Vilna many people who were already potential emigrants? Yes, there were—several families—but the majority was completely ignorant about Jewish affairs. The younger generation was almost completely assimilated, dying in the national sense. Except for a narrow circle of intelligentsia in Moscow and Leningrad, the whole of Jewish Russia was sleeping. And in the Ukraine the Jews didn't even dare to dream about Israel. If asked about it, they waved their hands in fear and looked around to see who was watching.

No, talk alone couldn't help in this situation. Only written information could be decisive. Let's say a Jew read "Israel in Figures"; or Jabotinsky's 1910 pamphlet prophecying that the socialist revolution in Russia will not solve the Jewish problem; or the book about the Sinai campaign by Ben Gurion; or the book by Yaroslav Mniachko, *Aggressors**—and all this in Russian. The books would certainly inspire deep and long thinking, an inner struggle. Fifty years of Soviet power have played a role in the formation of the reader's mind. But the truth that falls like a seed into fertile soil wins out.

It was neither the fine words of talkers or tricks of adventurers that resulted in the explosion of 1970–71 but rather the systematic and tedious everyday labor of creating Samizdat. The notorious press conference of prominent Soviet Jews in the spring of 1970, aimed at intimidating Jews, opened the way to a huge force that had been hidden in Soviet Jewry and grew into a frightening and authoritative power. No tricks or blows of the KGB could stop it.

Jewish Samizdat is not directed against the existing social order. It is neither concerned with undermining Soviet power nor weakening it. Our interests are in Israel alone.

* * *

1966. Tireless Boris succeeded in getting issues of the Israeli communist newspaper *Kol Ha'Am* and translated several articles from them. Fine! The communist paper—anti-Zionist, pro-Soviet, denying the wishes of Soviet Jews to leave for Israel, but the only Israeli paper that is allowed to come by mail to the Soviet Union—proved very useful. They published many articles about the economy and the policy of Israel. You just had to read between the lines and look for the necessary information behind them. In that way every month we could make a very interesting press bulletin of ten or fifteen pages. At first this was passed from hand to hand in written form, but we soon managed to type two bulletins. Of course, the news was at least a month late, but that did not matter if we had so many real facts from Israel. A closed,

* A book about Israel by the Slovak Communist writer Yaroslav Mniachko, in which the author condemns the Soviet and Czechoslovak attitude toward the Israel-Arab conflict.

strictly defined and not very large circle of readers was created. The bulletin was passed among those readers in a fixed order. It was our first periodical.

And for this I would like to express my gratitude to the Communist Party of Israel.

* * *

Many times we got hints of other people who thought and probably already acted as we did. In 1962 Yasha had composed an anonymous "Letter to Brezhnev" in which he protested against the policy of forced assimilation of Jews in Latvia after World War II. "The Letter" was passed among friends in a manuscript of twelve pages. A year later it returned to Yasha as fifty pages. Some people had put in their notes on the same problem. These people were certainly going to meet each other one day.

May 1967. The atmosphere among Jews was growing tense; people were constantly talking about Nasser, the Canal, Eshkol, Dayan, Soviet policy, what the U.S. will say, what De Gaulle will do. Nervousness, fear—yet at the same time a deep confidence that Israel will stand. But who could even dream about the victory in six days? Jews lived next to their radios those days, dying for the news from Israel, the United States, Great Britain, Switzerland. Nothing was missed—neither the night discussions in the Security Council, nor the General Assembly news. There was no time to sleep.

But an exact systematic account of the events couldn't reach us. Israeli tourists stopped coming and with them we lost our only source of information. Then suddenly our Jewish luck helped us. A Jewish couple from Riga stayed in a hotel in Kiev in a room which had been previously occupied by tourists from France and on the table were two issues of *L'Express*, with a detailed description of the actions in the Middle East. The maid who had brought them up to the room became very confused. According to instructions she was supposed to take to the office every piece of printed information that foreigners left in their rooms. God forbid that Soviet citizens should read something from abroad! But a tip of ten roubles did its bit, and in a week the magazines were in Riga. Boris got to work immediately, and

Sarah, having opened her "monster," didn't get up until ten copies of the translation were ready.

But what were these ten copies for the whole of Riga, where everyone was now dying for a bit of information, where Jews who had not so long ago been indifferent to Israel now demanded news about it. This time Sarochka didn't have to overwork. Tens of former readers turned into typists or photographers, and scores of new copies spread through the city. So the Jews of Riga, and not only of Riga, learned the truth about the events before, during, and after the Six-Day War.

After that there was no stopping it. Translations from other foreign sources appeared like mushrooms after rain. People looked for them and found them. One day we even came into possession of a secret report of the Central Committee of the Communist Party which gave rather an objective account of the situation and a not very flattering characterization of Nasser. There was nothing mysterious in this. There just happened to be a good Jew in the information service of the Central Committee, and the Six-Day War meant something for him also.

It is difficult to describe how Jewish backs had straightened after the War. Exit visas had not yet been given, diplomatic relations with Israel had been broken off, but Jews were in high spirits. They began to hope. And the more anti-Israel articles appeared in the Soviet press, the surer we were that Israel and we were right.

There was no time for idleness. The work had to be continued. Young people had so many questions that had to be answered. And the main issue was—the War. And again we had luck. Someone brought from Moscow a picture book on the Six-Day War by General S. L. A. Marshall, which had been acquired from foreign tourists. Work began immediately. Photography is a typical Jewish profession in Russia, so we had only to look for a courageous photographer. Translation was not a problem. And soon a detailed description of the action with masses of illustrations passed from hand to hand. But this was still not enough. Time passed and the situation in the Middle East was still tense and eventful, but information still didn't come.

One day I was looking through a daily newspaper and came across an article condemning those young people who engaged in buying clothes from foreigners—socks, ties, shirts, and all such goods and chattels. There is a whole stratum of youth in the Soviet Union "seeking an easy life," according to the Soviet press. They buy goods from foreigners and then sell them to Soviet citizens for a great deal of money, making fortunes in this way. Well, God judge them, but for us it brought a new idea. We were not interested in all their trash, but perhaps they could buy for us foreign magazines in English, German, French?

One of our boys was sent to make contact and, certainly, they were ready to do anything for money. So after a time we received *Time*, *Life*, *Stern*, *Spiegel*, and the like. And there was always something about Israel in every issue—and every line was translated and typed.

September 1, 1968. The Jews in Riga are terribly excited. The Ministry of Interior has suddenly recommenced accepting documents and applications for exit visas. Hundreds of people rushed to post offices to send telegrams to Israeli relatives asking for immediate invitations. Not everyone knew how to compose these telegrams, but the post office girl—a Latvian—helped everyone: "Write such-and-such. I have already sent a hundred of them today."

But the joy was premature. After only a few months, the gates were closed again. But for all that the authorities had managed to create large gaps in the ranks. Most of the activists for Samizdat had left for Israel. At the same time the materials they had published had already become dated. Yet the interest of Jews, as well as the number of interested Jews, grew in geometric progression. The youth demanded information.

Therefore it became necessary that different groups existing in different cities should come together and unite their efforts in Samizdat work. The first meeting was held in Moscow, on the sixteenth of August. People from Moscow, Leningrad, Riga, Kiev, Tbilisi, Kharkov, Orel attended. There were hours of discussion in an apartment, a park, in the street, arguments and decisions, and the main principles of future activities were defined: unity, co-ordination, and co-operation in Samizdat work; exchange of all items both new and old; mutual help in the means of publishing. The idea of publishing a periodical collection of works was also discussed. This has been done under the name of "Iton."* There was also a discussion about exchanging information about emigration and the signing of collective letters.

The meeting proved very fruitful, and other meetings were later held in Riga and Leningrad. Delegates informed each other of activities in their cities and discussed their plans. At the Riga meeting it was decided to fix definite telephone numbers and addresses for contacts between different cities. For this purpose the names of the towns were put into codes: Riga became Roman, Moscow, Misha, Leningrad, Lyonia. The same meeting decided also on the creation of the editorial board for publishing "Iton."

We in Riga, in our turn, gathered and discussed local activities. Until that time every group had worked separately; now united activities began in full swing. Almost all of us agreed with the opinion expressed by the majority of the participants in the Moscow meeting that we should refrain from forming an organization. The Soviet Criminal Code has a special statute about participation in an anti-Soviet organization, and any kind of an organization can easily be labelled anti-Soviet. An organization would not have helped us in any way, but would have helped the KGB watch us. We could organize our work by just defining our main tasks. Those who took part in the activities were divided into two groups for the sake of more effective work. One group took part in an active open struggle, such as signing collective letters to the Government and to be sent abroad and demanding the right to leave for Israel. This group was usually called "Alef." The second group, "Beth," was engaged in preparing, duplicating, and distributing the materials of Samizdat.

The Moscow meeting had also discussed the problem of collective letters demanding the right to leave the country. We in Riga, in the summer of 1969, agreed that the time was not yet

* The Hebrew word for "newspaper."

ripe to come out with such petitions. Georgian Jews were the first to begin this heroic campaign in August 1969. With their "Letter of 18" addressed to the U.N. Committee for Human Rights.

A list of subjects about which information was needed was compiled and divided according to degree of importance. Then the information was typed, one subject after another. A number of old typewriters were acquired especially for Samizdat. But what monsters they were! Old-fashioned, terribly heavy. One of them weighed more than thirty kilograms and taking it from one house to another was an ordeal. Only one man was strong enough to do it. He walked with that monster on his back, sweating and stopping every twenty meters.

All the typewriters had to be coded. Could we say over the telephone "Bring me the Mercedes?" So this typewriter was christened "Crocodile." I wonder what the KGB thought listening to our telephone conversations about a crocodile. But the fact is that during the catastrophe of June 1970 and in later searches they didn't find the "Crocodile."

Every apartment where the materials were typed was thoroughly checked from the point of view of the neighbors: the noise of the typewriter could always betray us. The problem of typists was also a difficult one. Professional typists could work very quickly, but had little time for Samizdat. They had to earn their living. More than that they would never be willing to type on such typewriters as "Crocodile." But there were girls who could type with one or two fingers who agreed to work in any place and on any typewriter. Special attention was paid to secrecy. It was decided that each of us must know only his own typist and take the work to and from her only by himself.

In spite of numerous problems and obstacles, Samizdat materials came and went in a flood. Everyone had his own circle of readers among whom he worked. But it should be pointed out that we always thought it most important to send literature to Russia, to Jews who hadn't had it for fifty-two years, not just for twenty-five years like us Jews of Latvia. For this purpose young people would suddenly become very affectionate toward their relatives in other cities and would want to visit them. These trips were extremely dangerous and the boys and girls would spend sleepless nights on trains, keeping their eyes on their valises containing the literature. In return we received paper, carbon, tape, photo-paper, and so on.

While the means of copying and distributing material could be arranged and even planned, getting it still depended on luck. The appearance of that famous book by Mniachko, *Aggressors*, the typed translation of which is now so popular among the Jews, is a typical case of chance. A sick Jew went to a Latvian professor of medicine who had just returned from a business trip abroad. During the consultation the visitor noticed a book on a shelf with the name of Mniachko on it. He had already heard about this honest man and the book on the shelf remained in his mind after he left the professor's house. Two days later another sick Jew came to the professor for a consultation. This visitor was very strange. He couldn't really explain his illness, asked many stupid questions, and didn't leave until the professor finally left the room for something. When he returned, the visitor decided to go and did so in haste.

I don't know when the professor noticed the loss, but the same evening we middle-aged, reliable people, thieves by necessity, were standing bewitched around a table. The *Aggressors* itself had come into our hands.

Circles for studying Hebrew had existed in Riga for many years but had been of an individual character. In 1969 they began to be organized and by 1970 a whole network of these groups existed in the city. But the shortage of books prevented people from intensive studying. There were only a few copies of the primer *Elef Milim* (one thousand words) in the city, and teachers had to use old newspapers, calendars, and the Bible for lessons. Either new books had to be obtained or copies made. But then our inter-city ties helped. Our Moscow friends informed us that they had managed to make a large number of copies of *Elef Milim*, and we soon received two suitcases of wonderfully photographed copies of the book. I still remember the day those two suitcases arrived in Riga.

One of our young men, Moshe, a very quiet and effective worker, had gone to receive these books in Moscow and I was to meet him next day at the railway station to pick up the suitcases. They certainly were going to be heavy and I took along a friend, Tsvi, to help me. By the time the train was due to arrive, we were at the station. I decided to stay at the square in front of the terminal in order to be able to pick up a taxi the moment Moshe came out. The line for taxis was always terribly long and it was rather inexpedient to stand there for a long time. Tsvi went to meet Moshe at the train. A half hour passed, the train had arrived, and people came out of the terminal; then the crowd dispersed. But neither of them appeared. Ten minutes later Tsvi appeared in the door of the terminal, alone. "He didn't come by this train," he said. The next train from Moscow was due to arrive in an hour. We waited, but Moshe didn't arrive then either. There was nothing to be done and with sinking hearts we left. Had he been caught on the way, or earlier in Moscow? What else could have delayed him?

With these torturing thoughts in my head I went to a meeting that was being held in Rumbula in memory of thousands of Latvian Jews executed in this Riga suburb in 1941. I was standing in the crowd near the mass graves and heard neither the speeches nor the Kaddish. Suddenly something made me turn around and I looked into Moshe's eyes. He was standing behind me, staring at me quietly. Maybe his steady look had made me turn around.

"What happened?" I asked in a low voice, not looking at him.

"Nothing. Everything is all right." I heard his low voice behind me.

"Did you bring them?"

"Yes."

"Why didn't we meet you in the terminal?"

"I didn't see you."

"But Tsvi was there."

"Yes, I saw him. But you told me you would meet me, so I didn't go up to him. The suitcases are at my place."

I understood my mistake, and at the same time I could hardly contain the emotions I felt—joy and pride. So our young people taught us how to be exact in our dangerous activities and self-contained and cool in unexpected situations.

* * *

After we had acquired the textbooks, we began to seek among older Jews those who knew Hebrew and were ready to run the risk of teaching a group. The groups were formed of people of approximately the same age, knowledge, and activity. The places where the lessons were to be given were also thoroughly checked. It was necessary that the neighbors not be too curious. All these arrangements took much time and effort, but we had enough purpose and energy because we could see the results. Masses of new young people joined in the groups studying Hebrew. The interest in Israel grew and grew, and the youth began to get together in parties, learn Israeli songs, listen to records, show each other Israeli souvenirs; and they talked and talked.

* * *

And the tireless Boris was full of ideas. In 1969 he worked out and put into wide practice a wonderful thing. One of our strongest means of propaganda was Israeli picture post cards. Boris had a big collection of such postcards which was rapidly growing and which he arranged in geographical order. The post cards were photographed on slides and Boris began a series of public shows. Since he was an expert on Israeli geography and history he accompanied the shows by lectures on different themes: Jerusalem, Tel-Aviv, the Galilee, the kibbutzim, archeological excavations, agriculture in Israel, and so on.

The shows proved so successful that the idea was adopted by other cities also. Boris had to start a course for lecturers. And soon tens of shows were being held in Riga, Moscow, Leningrad. Silent, bewitched people sat in dark rooms, listening to the excited voice of their lecturer, not taking their eyes off the screen. Their hearts and minds were not in those dark rooms, but far away in the country of their dreams. Looking then at their faces

I saw that those young people were proud of belonging to their people. This meant that our task was fulfilled.

* * *

Of course, my story can be continued. It is certainly not finished. But let others continue it some day. Let them add to it their own stories.